American Women's History on Film

Recent Titles in Hollywood History

The Vietnam War on Film
David Luhrssen

The American West on Film
Johnny D. Boggs

The Civil War on Film
Peg A. Lamphier and Rosanne Welch

World War II on Film
David Luhrssen

The Cold War on Film
Paul Frazier

Sports on Film
Johnny D. Boggs

The 1960s on Film
Jim Willis and Mark Miller

The Great Depression on Film
David Luhrssen

American Women's History on Film

Rosanne Welch and
Peg A. Lamphier

Hollywood History

BLOOMSBURY ACADEMIC
NEW YORK · LONDON · OXFORD · NEW DELHI · SYDNEY

BLOOMSBURY ACADEMIC
Bloomsbury Publishing Inc
1385 Broadway, New York, NY 10018, USA
50 Bedford Square, London, WC1B 3DP, UK
29 Earlsfort Terrace, Dublin 2, Ireland

BLOOMSBURY, BLOOMSBURY ACADEMIC and the Diana logo
are trademarks of Bloomsbury Publishing Plc

First published in the United States of America by ABC-CLIO 2023
Paperback edition published by Bloomsbury Academic 2025

Copyright © Bloomsbury Publishing Inc, 2025

Cover Photo: Hidden Figures, 2016. (Pictorial Press Ltd/Alamy Stock Photo)

All rights reserved. No part of this publication may be reproduced or transmitted in any form or by any means, electronic or mechanical, including photocopying, recording, or any information storage or retrieval system, without prior permission in writing from the publishers.

Bloomsbury Publishing Inc does not have any control over, or responsibility for, any third-party websites referred to or in this book. All internet addresses given in this book were correct at the time of going to press. The author and publisher regret any inconvenience caused if addresses have changed or sites have ceased to exist, but can accept no responsibility for any such changes.

Library of Congress Cataloging-in-Publication Data
Names: Welch, Rosanne, author. | Lamphier, Peg A., author.
Title: American women's history on film / Rosanne Welch and
Peg A. Lamphier.
Description: Santa Barbara, California : ABC-CLIO, [2023] | Series:
Hollywood history | Includes bibliographical references and index.
Identifiers: LCCN 2022021253 | ISBN 9781440866609 (hardcover ; acid-free
paper) | ISBN 9781440866616 (ebook)
Subjects: LCSH: Women in motion pictures. | Women—United States—History.
| Motion pictures—United States—History—20th century. | Motion
pictures—United States—History—21st century. | Motion pictures and history.
| LCGFT: Film criticism.
Classification: LCC PN1995.9.W6 W46 2023 | DDC
791.43/6522—dc23/eng/20220517
LC record available at https://lccn.loc.gov/2022021253

ISBN: HB: 978-1-4408-6660-9
PB: 979-8-7651-6698-7
ePDF: 978-1-4408-6661-6
eBook: 979-8-2161-8291-7

Series: Hollywood History

To find out more about our authors and books visit www.bloomsbury.com
and sign up for our newsletters.

Contents

Series Foreword	vii
Preface	ix
Introduction	xiii
Chronology	xxiii
1. *Salt of the Earth* (1954)	1
2. *Norma Rae* (1979)	15
3. *Silkwood* (1983)	27
4. *The Joy Luck Club* (1993)	41
5. *G. I. Jane* (1997)	59
6. *Monster* (2003)	77
7. *Iron Jawed Angels* (2004)	93
8. *Confirmation* (2016)	111
9. *Hidden Figures* (2016)	129
10. *On the Basis of Sex* (2018)	143
Bibliography	155
Index	161

Series Foreword

Just exactly how accurate are Hollywood's film and television portrayals of American history? What do these portrayals of history tell us, not only about the events they depict but also the time in which they were made? Each volume in this unique reference series is devoted to a single topic or key theme in American history, examining 10–12 major motion pictures or television productions. Substantial essays summarize each film, provide historical background of the event or period it depicts, and explain how accurate the film's depiction is, while also analyzing the cultural context in which the film was made. A final resources section provides a comprehensive annotated bibliography of print and electronic sources to aid students and teachers in further research.

The subjects of these Hollywood History volumes were chosen based on both curriculum relevance and inherent interest. Readers will find a wide array of subject choices, including American Slavery on Film, the Civil War on Film, the American West on Film, Vietnam on Film, and the 1960s on Film. Ideal for school assignments and student research, the length, format, and subject areas are designed to meet educators' needs and students' interests.

Preface

There is a cynical saying that runs around Hollywood as the award seasons (Academy or Emmy) arrive that goes something like this: To win an award, an actress has to play a prostitute or a stripper—or a nun. It can also be explained as if wins only come from characters who require too much makeup or none at all. Since this book focuses on films—and females—who have influenced American history, the range of occupations that exists in these films is quite a bit larger. In these films, you will find miners' wives and (yes, a couple of non-makeup wearing) "monsters," soldiers, and scientists, activists and immigrants, and two (count 'em—two) lawyers—one who essentially ignited the MeToo Movement and one who is the reason we use the word "gender" and not "sex" in legal matters.

In chapter one, Rosanne Welch introduces readers to a film unique in that some film historians call it the only blacklisted American movie. *Salt of the Earth* (1954) dramatizes a real strike by Mexican American men of the International Union of Mine, Mill and Smelter Workers in New Mexico. They wanted equal pay to their white miner counterparts. Thwarted legally by their employer and forbidden to picket, their wives recognized a loophole in the contract and took their husbands' places on the picket line. That real-life decision forced the men to cook and care for their own children, which challenged gender roles and brought the message of the strike into their hearts.

Chapter two covers another union-focused film, *Norma Rae* (1979). Based lightly on the real life of North Carolina mill worker Crystal Lee Jordan, the Academy Award–winning *Norma Rae* tells the story of a female union organizer in the textile world. Best known for the visual of star Sally Field standing on a table defiantly holding up a sign with "Union" scrawled on it, the film focuses on the nonromantic relationship of Norma and Reuben Warshovsky. He has come to Norma's town to organize the millworkers and quickly recognizes that he needs Norma to draw this diverse set of employees—female and male, Black and white—to his pitch. Despite previous award-nominated films, the married screenwriting team of Harriet Frank Jr. and Irving Ravetch had a hard time convincing a studio that *Norma Rae* would be a female Rocky, another determined underdog, with more appeal to women.

Four years later, *Silkwood* (1983) explored a darker aspect of union-organizing. In chapter three, Rosanne Welch discusses this Nora Ephron/Alice Arlen scripted vehicle that starred Meryl Streep as Karen Silkwood. The Oklahoma nuclear factory worker became suspicious about safety measures—or the lack thereof—in her plant. Her covert investigations threatened her job, her family and friend relationships, and eventually her life. Both *Norma Rae* and *Silkwood* highlighted flawed women who still took on challenges to make life in their communities better for all.

In the volume's fourth chapter, Peg Lamphier examines *The Joy Luck Club* (1993). Based on Amy Tan's best-selling biographical novel of the same name, *The Joy Luck Club* follows the lives of four Chinese American women and their immigrant mothers. The film (and the novel upon which it is based) normalize the Chinese American experience by resisting stereotypes that hypersexualize or idealize women of Asian descent. The film, while not without its critics, also spawned a small wave of Asian American films, culminating most recently in *Crazy Rich Asians* and, in so doing, normalized the Asian, female immigrant experience in popular culture.

Lamphier next examines the position of women in the American military with *G. I. Jane* (1997). Hollywood makes a lot of war films, but very few of them acknowledge the reality that women have long served, first unofficially and later officially, in the United States military. The film appeared in movie houses at a time when the nation was in the midst of a hotly contested argument about women's fitness for military service of any kind, but particularly combat service. The film's plot follows one woman's journey to make it through Navy SEAL training, with the explicit goal of combat readiness. The controversy caused by the film's premise and its star, Demi Moore, cannot be overstated.

Chapter six takes on *Monster*, the 2003 film that takes on the serial killer Aileen Wuornos's extremely difficult story. Often billed as the first female serial killer, which she most certainly was not, Wuornos was sexually and physically abused as a child, and, after a lifetime of drug use, prostitution, and mental illness, she killed a customer who raped her. That first murder led to others, culminating in a nation-wide "manhunt" that led to Wuornos's arrest. The film portrays Wuornos as both a victim of the society that failed to protect her as a child and, later, as a sex worker (the most dangerous job in America) and as a psychologically damaged killer. Lamphier argues that Wuornos's story fundamentally suggests the cost of a nation unwilling to protect children and vulnerable women from violence, abuse, and oppression.

With chapter seven on *Iron Jawed Angels* (2004), Lamphier studies HBO Film's effort to tell the culminating events of the women's suffrage movement. Told from the perspective of the younger, more radical suffragists, the film's story of hunger strikes, forced feeding, and violent attacks by anti-suffrage mobs makes for compelling viewing. The film vigorously counteracts the traditional narrative where women are "given" the right to vote, instead highlighting the violence women faced in order to achieve the most American of rights: the right to vote. Though the film is made to appeal to twenty-first-century sensibilities, it nonetheless communicates the importance of voting, not just to women, but to all Americans.

Based on the book by Margot Lee Shetterly, *Hidden Figures* (2016) graces chapter eight. Welch highlights this film about three African American women—Katherine Johnson, Dorothy Vaughan, and Mary Jackson—who worked as female "computers," calculating high-end mathematical problems for the Langley Air Base when it was actively involved in the Space Race of the 1950s and 1960s. Though their work was crucial to the United States' success in space, the women were still exposed to discrimination in terms of educational opportunities and career advancement—until their talents are too prominent to ignore. Each woman achieved great things, culminating in Katherine Johnson receiving the Presidential Medal of Freedom at the age of ninety-seven from President Barack Obama.

In chapter nine, Lamphier examines *Confirmation* (2016), the story of the Clarence Thomas Supreme Court confirmation hearings and Anita Hill's testimony at those hearings. In 1991, Hill testified before a U.S. Senate Judicial Committee hearing that Thomas had sexually harassed her while she was working for him at two different Federal agencies. Thomas claimed Hill was lying and made much of his status as a victimized Black man. The film does a credible job of illustrating the way the hearings and the national discussion about sexual harassment divided the nation. While the Senate ultimately confirmed Thomas, the hearings forced Americans to face the realities of workplace harassment and do something about it. The Thomas hearings also presaged the Brett Kavanaugh hearings, where witnesses testified to the nominee's sexual impropriety and the nation divided in response to those allegations, making the film all the more relevant.

Fittingly, the volume ends with chapter ten and a film that tells the story of a young Ruth Bader Ginsburg, long before her time on the Supreme Court and her nickname as the "Notorious RBG." Welch finds that rather than doing what is known as a cradle-to-grave biopic, *On the Basis of Sex* (2018) highlights the first legal case that saw Ginsburg arguing a case in front of the Supreme Court alongside her husband. A clear case of discrimination based on sex, the couple argued against section 214 of the tax code, where the IRS denied a bachelor with a full-time job to write off the salary of a caregiver for his live-in elderly mother. At that time, only men whose wives were incapacitate or dead—or divorced—could take that deduction. While setting a precedent that no law could discriminate against a citizen based on gender, the story provides a glimpse into the Ginsburgs' feminist marriage and how their dedication to their partner's equality—and to the law—bound them together for life.

Even with this breadth of women's experience, we recognize we have not covered all facets of women's experience in the United States and that no collection can ever be complete. We understand that we have missed some historic events that occurred in underrepresented communities, in part because the movies that represent those women's experience do not exist in the mainstream. Still, we see great hope on the horizon as more and more female screenwriters from varied backgrounds begin to make progress in the industry telling their stories.

Introduction

The fight for suffrage in the United States hit its crescendo just as movies became the newest leisure-time occupation. Naturally, then, many silent films used suffragettes as characters, sometimes mocking them in comedies, sometimes criticizing them in dramas, and sometimes supporting their cause. None then—or yet—went backward in history to cover the beginnings of women's suffrage, which date to the ratification of the United States Constitution in 1789. That document granted states the power of setting voting requirement, and most only offered the elective franchise to property-owning or tax-paying white males, but New Jersey offered voting rights to unmarried or widowed women who held property, regardless of their color. That lasted until 1807, when due to political machinations and recognition that no other state had followed suit, New Jersey ended the right.

The largest early gathering to acknowledge a need for women to own the right to vote came in 1848, when five prominent female abolitionists thought it time to discuss giving women more political autonomy. Elizabeth Cady Stanton, Lucretia Mott, Mary M'Clintock, Martha Coffin Wright, and Jane Hunt put out a call and eventually three hundred women—and men, including famed abolitionist Frederick Douglass—met in the Wesleyan Chapel in Seneca Falls, New York. From July 19 to 20, 1848, they debated and then created a Declaration of Sentiments patterned after the Declaration of Independence. It opened with a similar phrase and one small, yet also large, word change: "We hold these truths to be self-evident; that all men **and women** are created equal."

The document included nineteen grievances and eleven resolutions, among them the right to vote, which remained so controversial in that era that many women left the movement before it officially began. Those who stayed deeded the goal to their daughters and granddaughters until finally, in 1920, with the passage of the Nineteenth Amendment, women gained the right to vote. That political struggle—and it was a struggle—took seventy years and included a few near misses. It required gaining voting rights state by state, the first state at this time being Wyoming, which allowed white women to vote in 1869. Other states joined in, which strengthened the argument for federal suffrage, but still there were obstacles in the way. Organizations formed and split, and the Civil War broke out and stalled the effort. The reconstruction amendments gave males the right to vote but left out females, despite much agitations and advocacy.

A federal amendment to grant women the right to vote was introduced by California Senator Aaron A. Sargent in 1878 but largely ignored in Congress, though his proposed language is what would eventually be used in writing the later amendment. Following the tactics of the abolitionist movement, Carrie Chapman Catt, president of the National American Woman Suffrage Association, began publishing the *National Suffrage Bulletin* in 1897. Then parades came into play, with Alice Paul, leader of the Congressional Union branch of the National American Woman Suffrage Association, organizing one in Washington, D.C., on the eve of Woodrow Wilson's inauguration in 1913. By 1916, as he prepared to run for a second term, Wilson added a plank to the Democratic Party Platform endorsing women's suffrage, though this upset the Southern politicians. Senator Pat Harrison of Mississippi suggested limiting the right to vote to white women in the writing of the amendment, but the women's rights activists stood firm that it must address all women, and the idea was voted down in Congress.

Finally, in the summer of 1920, the amendment had passed Congress and been ratified by thirty-five of the necessary thirty-six states, with Tennessee next to put it up for debate. When the vote in the house resulted in a tie, Representative Harry T. Burn changed his vote in favor of ratification, thanks to a letter from his mother in which she asked him to help "Mrs. [Carrie Chapman] Catt out if he could." He did.

While HBO produced *Iron Jawed Angels* in 2004, none of these very tense, very historical events— nor any of the women who organized them— have ever been the subject of a theatrical feature film.

In films that do cover the many other aspects of women's history and women's lives, the women are often depicted as individuals fighting for more than their own personal rights. This volume then focuses on a variety of other aspects of women in American history, which tend to be in the biopic genre. These films also tend to be social justice films where women are seen advocating and protesting for their own rights in tandem with demanding rights for others through union or political activism on behalf of immigrants and lower-income peoples. These social justice themes have been around since the beginning of film, often created by female activists and suffragettes who were also pioneers in this new medium, such as Lois Weber (*Where*

Are My Children?), Anita Loos (*The Women*), and Frances Marion (*The Big House*). Women have often turned to their varied artworks to showcase issues they hope to change, as did Dorothea Lange, whose *Migrant Mother* photograph illustrated the poverty of the Depression; or Kristen Visbal, whose *Fearless Girl* statue of a ten-year-old female facing down the Charging Bull of Wall Street advocates for workplace gender diversity; or any book by Pulitzer Prize-winning author Toni Morrison. Their mantles were taken up in later eras by many of the female screenwriters represented in this collection, including Harriet Frank, Jr., Nora Ephron, Susannah Grant, Alison Schroeder, and Patty Jenkins.

Stories of women achieving in history appear few and far between the many epic tales of men achieving, whether in print or on film. In many of those cases, the men achieved alongside women, but the female contribution never made it into the film. Examples include *Glory* (1989), which tells the story of the Union Army's first African American regiment in the Civil War. While it focuses on the admirable heroics of their commander, Colonel Robert Gould Shaw, the film forgets the fact that famed abolitionist Harriet Tubman served as a spy for that very regiment. Several films involving the Civil Rights Movement focus on the Rev. Dr. Martin Luther King, Jr. and forget that Jo Ann Robinson contributed to every step of the bus boycott that brought him to national attention.

Hollywood studio executives often greenlit films that dramatized male lives, which often involved war time heroics, but they did not find many of the moments of the women's rights movement as . . . moving. Rather than creating films with armies in physical battle, many of those moments that made it onto film were written from the point of individual women engaged in mental or intellectual battles for societal change. Rather than epics, women's history on film focuses on singular women when, in fact, much of what they accomplished involved their rallying troops toward their goals as much as war films required male characters to rally soldiers. This changed as more women entered the ranks of executives, but then the hurdle became the need to recruit female performers who wielded as much economic clout at the box office as their male counterparts. Also, films written by men about the female experience rendered those stories from a male gaze, which could hamper their authenticity—or the perception of authenticity.

The idea of a male gaze began in *Ways of Seeing: Based on the BBC Television Series* (1972), where English art critic John Berger analyzed the art world with a particular focus on the treatment of women as objects in everything from classic European painting to modern advertising. As mostly men purchased paintings of women (often the women they "owned" in their familial world) and mostly men painted such portraits, Berger described them as seeing women only through that male lens. In response, in 1975, British film critic Laura Mulvey fully coined the phrase "male gaze" when she discussed aspects of male voyeurism in her article, "Visual Pleasure and

Narrative Cinema." Though she didn't specifically use the phrase "female gaze," it was implied and became a theoretical term in feminist film criticism. It refers to the perspective a female filmmaker—whether that be a female screenwriter or a female director or producer or a female cinematographer—brings to a film. It anticipates that the female gaze would be less voyeuristic when it comes to viewing female bodies but can also be seen in the reverse as a way for heterosexual female viewers to view male performers through the lens of mere sex objects.

An example from one of the films discussed here is in a choice made between the shooting script (dated July 8, 1982) and the final cut version of *Silkwood*. Originally, the film began instead like the classic *Sunset Boulevard*, in medias res. It opens on the ending of a trucker pulling over on Highway Seventy-Four in Oklahoma and shining his flashlight on the wreck of a car. We hear the voice of Karen Silkwood's former lover, Drew, telling us that he had brought a *New York Times* journalist and their union rep to a local hotel for a clandestine meeting, but Silkwood was unusually late. He tells this reporter that after they received the call about her crashed car, they searched the area for documents she had planned to show the journalist, but there was no sign of them. The reporter asks the key question, "Did you think the name Karen Silkwood would become a rallying cry for so many causes?" Clearly, in the editing process, the director changed his mind and decided on a softer opening, lulling the viewer who might not know the ending into understanding the world these characters inhabited. This decision might also have come from realizing that beginning the story of a female whistle-blower with her male companion's voice gave the film a focus on the male gaze. Having been written by females (Nora Ephron and Alice Arlen but directed by a known feminist male, Mike Nichols) may have had a hand in this decision. Furthering the female-gaze concept, it should be noted that the actor who plays Drew, Kurt Russell, spends many scenes in *Silkwood* shirtless. Likewise, *Norma Rae* was written by a female/male married team of screenwriters (Harriet Frank Jr. and Irving Ravetch) and directed by a feminist male (Martin Ritt).

Another way of looking at how women have been (and still often are) portrayed in film comes from the Bechdel Test (or Bechdel-Wallace Test) for gender bias in films, named for cartoonist Alison Bechdel and her friend Liz Wallace from an installment of her strip *Dykes to Watch Out For*. In "The Rule," published in 1985, Bechdel illustrated a conversation she had had with Wallace using two female characters. In discussing three rules for the kinds of movies they are willing to pay to see in the theater, they included: (1) the movie has to have at least two women in it, (2) the have to talk to each other rather than only to the men in the film, (3) they have to talk about something besides a man. Bechdel attributed the idea to her friend Liz Wallace, who mentioned the standard to her as Bechdel was looking for ideas for her comic. The strip went viral and became fodder for film studies and women studies courses across the world. By 2014, the Film and TV School of the Academy of Performing Arts (FAMU) in Prague used the test to grade student screenplays. The idea bloomed, and many others added points and new names for similar tests. Emmy-winning writer Lena Waithe added that films need a Black female character in a position of power and a healthy relationship. The Mako Mori Test, which came from a post on Tumblr and was inspired by a character in *Pacific Rim* (2013), asks that films have one female character who does not exist merely to support a man's story but has her own narrative arc. Writer Kelly Sue DeConnick created the Sexy Lamp Test with the comment: "If you can remove a female character from your plot and replace her with a sexy lamp and your story still works, you're a hack" (Seth 2020).

Having a creative team that respects women means that the women in these films are active participants in their stories, with full arcs dedicated to their own decision-making moments. Also, no female lead plays what has been dubbed a Manic Pixie Dream Girl, a trope coined by film critic Nathan Rabin. He defined identified female characters in films like *Garden State* (2004) and *Elizabethtown* (2005), who "exist solely in the fevered imaginations of sensitive writer-directors to teach broodingly soulful young men to embrace life and its infinite mysteries and adventures." In other words, the females exist to service male character growth. Further, these women never seem to grow up or require anything more of the male characters, who then are enabled to say Peter Pan young forever. This style of character has no discernible inner life and usually exists only to provide the protagonist some important life lessons to the male (Rabin 2007).

Most of the films in this collection can pass the Bechdel Test, as well as many of these later ones that have since sprouted up online. Why? Because this collection focuses largely on films written by women and about women who tackled the humanist issues of their day and mostly won. The films cover several areas of women's experience from the laudable fights for voting rights or acceptance in the military or law or the space program to the PTSD caused by the combination of poverty and prostitution that lead to murder in the film *Monster*. Because many of the most beloved movie heroes are underdogs, labor union activists became solid fodder for three of the films discussed. Going against a giant, faceless corporation also satisfy all the steps of the hero's journey, as defined by Joseph Campbell and familiar in male-dominated films such as *Star Wars* and *Lord of the Rings*. Whereas those iconic male heroes are tasked with mastering a weapon and taking on their antagonist alone, heroines often work toward sharing power with a group so they can all rise together, as noted by Naomi Fry in a retrospective on *Norma Rae*: "On this viewing, what struck me even more strongly, however, was the movie's suggestion that no struggle can take place alone. Norma Rae is heroic, but she comes into her own, as a woman, because she is fighting for class solidarity—a struggle that, in turn, could not happen without a breaking down of long-standing ethnic and racial barriers" (Fry 2020).

Just as the male gaze had its opposite in the female gaze, the hero's journey of Joseph Campbell has its opposite in the heroine's journey of Maureen Murdock. Campbell traced ten stages of a male hero's journey:

Step 1: The Ordinary World
Step 2: The Call to Adventure
Step 3: Cross the First Threshold
Step 4: Trials, Friends, and Foes
Step 5: Magical Mentor (or the Mentor with Supernatural Aid)
Step 6: Dragon's Lair
Step 7: Moment of Despair
Step 8: Ultimate Treasure
Step 9: Homeward Bound
Step 10: Rebirth and the Champion's Return

While a female can certainly engage in the hero's journey, Murdock found more specific steps that suited women's journeys and created these stages of the heroine's journey for her book:

Step 1: Heroine Separates from the Feminine
Step 2: Identification with the Masculine and Gathering of Allies.
Step 3: Road/Trials and Meeting Ogres and Dragons
Step 4: Experiencing the Boon of Success
Step 5: Heroine Awakens to Feelings of Spiritual Aridity/Death
Step 6: Initiation and Descent to the Goddess
Step 7: Heroine Urgently Yearns to Reconnect with the Feminine
Step 8: Heroine Heals the Mother/Daughter Split
Step 9: Heroine Heals the Wounded Masculine Within
Step 10: Heroine Integrates the Masculine and Feminine

These steps can be found in all the films in this collection. Generally the women all learn that to succeed they must behave as men (Separating from the Feminine), that behavior leaves them empty or damaged (Spiritual Aridity/Death), and only once they embrace the strength found in their own femininity (Heals the Mother/Daughter Split) and combine it with some masculine qualities can they succeed. Those who do not complete these steps, fail.

Making women the underdog characters, especially in a film about unions, such as *Salt of the Earth*, *Norma Rae*, and *Silkwood*, tends to lend a more sympathetic view to unions, largely because the women work the system in a nonviolent way. The characters move the others to support unions through education and use of the ballot box, not through violent or subversive actions such as vandalizing businesses or threatening managers, as is the story in *On the Waterfront*. Similarly, such films tend to showcase the difficulties females face when balancing the needs of their families with their own desires to contribute to the larger world. The other recurring theme is best summarized by Esperanza in *Salt of the Earth* when she berates the husband she loves for allowing the same unequal treatment he derides in his work life to exist in their private life. Esperanza speaks for most of the women in most of these films when she asks, "Whose neck shall I stand on to make me feel superior? And what will I get out of it? I don't want anything lower than I am. I'm low enough already. I want to rise. And push everything up with me as I go." Thus, resistance appears as theme in all the films—resistance to patriarchy, systems of oppression, social inequities. In collecting films that showcased women's history, we found this pattern of focusing on underdogs challenging a system of oppression continued into the twentieth (and twenty-first century) with films such as *Iron-Jawed Angels*, *Confirmation*, and *On the Basis of Sex*. This makes perfect sense, as you can draw a line from the Seneca Falls conference to the legal decisions made by Supreme Court justice Ruth Bader Ginsburg.

While films were once the realm of strong female stories starring the likes of Bette Davis (*Dark Victory* and *The Little Foxes*), Joan Crawford (*Mildred Pierce* and *Johnny Guitar*), and Barbara Stanwyk (*Double Indemnity and The Lady Eve*), in the 1960s, 1970s, and 1980s, the "new cinema" turned movies into vehicles for antiheroes such as Al Pacino (*The Godfather*, *Dog Day Afternoon*, and *Scarface*), Robert DeNiro (*The Godfather II* and *Taxi Driver*), and Jack Nicholson (*Chinatown* and *One Flew over the Cuckoo's Nest*). The rise of television turned many female stories into television films or miniseries, so in order to cover the variety of films telling the history of women in the United States, this volume considers more made-for- television films than might be expected—though it must be understood that those films (and those women's stories) were often scrubbed clean to make them more presentable in a medium that entered the home. Hence, a television film like the biopic *Pancho Barnes* (1988) starred the scrubbed clean Valerie Bertinelli (famous as the straight-A younger daughter on the *One Day at a Time* television series of the 1970s), even though Barnes was a hard-drinking, cross-dressing woman of the 1930s.

Therefore, more TV films appear in this collection because male executives (recognized today as gatekeepers) relegated many films that dramatized women's history to the "small screen" (a phrase coined before the advent of big-screen TVs being sold at Costco or folks watching films on their phone screens). Such films are not often given as much academic study as films made for theatrical distribution. In fact, this may be the only volume in the

Hollywood History series to include films made directly for television. The small screen hosted many controversial topics surrounding women's lives before they appeared in films. *Sybil* (1976) explored the life of a woman suffering from multiple personality disorder and the female doctor who treated her. Casualties in Vietnam were the focus of *Friendly Fire* (1979), written by Fay Kanin (who won two Emmy Awards for her work writing and producing). Based on the book by C. D. B. Bryan, it told the story of a mother seeking the truth about her soldier son's death in Vietnam. Domestic violence formed the basis of *The Burning Bed* (1984). Written by Rose Leiman Goldemberg, the TV film told the story of a woman on trial for setting fire to the bed while her abusive husband slept.

The turn of the century gave rise to the limited series, which in turn gave more time (albeit still on the small screen), as it began to dramatize other achievements in women's history. HBO produced a biopic on *Temple Grandin* (2010), the autistic woman who rose to a highly respected scientist in the humane handling of livestock. *Good Girls Revolt* (2016) adapted Lynn Povich's book of the same name, fictionalized the lawsuit female employees brought against *Newsweek* where they were relegated to low-level positions. *Mrs. America* (2020) focused on the fight over the Equal Rights Amendment in the 1970s. Still, these have been produced and aired on television, not in theaters. The success of titles such as *Hidden Figures* may help change that trajectory and bring more female-focused stories back to the big screen. That film's critical, financial, and historical success showcases the value of films as vehicles for sharing stories, many of which never made it into history texts. It was the arrival of *Hidden Figures* that resulted in Katherine Johnson receiving the Presidential Medal of Freedom at the age of ninety-seven, almost fifty years after her major contributions to the space program. As both film and women's rights have crossed the hundred-year-old mark and this still relatively new century gets underway, there may be many more chances to render other lost stories of women's history on screens of all sizes.

FURTHER READING

Basinger, Jeanine. 1995. *A Woman's View: How Hollywood Spoke to Women, 1930–1960*. Middletown, CT: Wesleyan University Press.

Beauchamp, Cari. 1998. *Without Lying Down: Frances Marion and the Powerful Women of Early Hollywood*. Los Angeles: University of California Press.

Berger, John. 1972. *Ways of Seeing*. London: Penguin Random House.

Borda, Jennifer L. 2011. *Women Labor Activists in the Movies: Nine Depictions of Workplace Organizers, 1954–2005*. Jefferson, NC: McFarland.

Byrnes, Paul. 2017. "*Hidden Figures* Review: These Trailblazing Women Deserve Better." *The Sydney Morning Herald*. https://www.smh.com.au/entertainment

/movies/hidden-figures-review-these-trailblazing-women-deserve-better-20170214-gucbs5.html.

Cavell, Stanley. 1996. *Contesting Tears: The Hollywood Melodrama of the Unknown Woman*. Chicago: The University of Chicago Press.

Coontz, Stephanie. 1992. *The Way We Never Were: American Families and the Nostalgia Trap*. New York: BasicBooks.

Crist, Judith. 1967. *The Private Eye, the Cowboy and the Very Naked Girl: Movies from Cleo to Clyde*. New York: Holt, Rinehart and Winston.

Erickson, Glenn. 2017. *CineSavant*. https://trailersfromhell.com/silkwood/.

Fine, Richard. 1993. *West of Eden: Writers in Hollywood, 1928–1940*. Washington, DC: Smithsonian Institution Press.

Fry, Naomi. 2020. "The Ongoing Relevance of 'Norma Rae.'" *The New Yorker*. https://www.newyorker.com/recommends/watch/the-ongoing-relevance-of-norma-rae.

Hamilton, Ian. 1990. *Writers in Hollywood: 1915–1951*. New York: Harper and Row.

Horton, Andrew, and Julian Hoxter. 2014. *Screenwriting*. New Brunswick, NJ: Rutgers University Press.

Kamir, Orit. 2006. *Framed: Women in Law and Film*. Durham, NC: Duke University Press.

Murdock, Maureen. 1990. *The Heroine's Journey*. Boulder, CO: Shambhala.

New York Times. 1983. "The Chicanery on 'Silkwood.'" *New York Times*. Opinion, December 25, 1983, Section 4, Page 12. https://www.nytimes.com/1983/12/25/opinion/the-chicanery-of-silkwood.html.

Rabin, Nathan. 2007. "The Bataan Death March of Whimsy Case File 1: Elizabethtown." *The A.V. Club*. https://www.avclub.com/the-bataan-death-march-of-whimsy-case-file-1-elizabet-1798210595.

Seth, Radhika. 2020. "Why Are Films Failing the Bechdel Test When TV Has Progressed?" *Vogue*. https://www.vogue.co.uk/arts-and-lifestyle/article/the-bechdel-test.

Sklar, Robert. 1994. *Movie-Made America: A Cultural History of American Movies*. New York: Knopf Doubleday/Vintage.

Stempel, Tom. 1988. *Framework: A History of Screenwriting in the American Film*. New York: The Continuum Publishing Company.

Welch, Rosanne, ed. 2018. *When Women Wrote Hollywood: Essays on Female Screenwriters in the Early Film Industry*. Jefferson, NC: McFarland.

Chronology

1776	Abigail Adams admonishes her husband to "not forget the ladies" when creating the United States.
1777	All states pass laws that take away women's right to vote.
1792	*A Vindication of the Rights of Woman*, written by Mary Wollstonecraft, is published in the United Kingdom and appears in the United States shortly thereafter.
1839	Mississippi grants women the right to hold property in their own names if their husbands give permission.
1848	Seneca Falls Convention is held in New York.
1849	Harriet Tubman makes her first escape from slavery. She will eventually return to the South thirteen times, leading others to freedom.
1849	Elizabeth Blackwell becomes the first woman to graduate from medical school and become a doctor in the United States.
1851	Sojourner Truth delivers her famous "Ain't I a Woman?" speech in Ohio.
1855	In the case *Missouri v. Celia, a Slave*, a Black woman is not allowed to defend herself against a master's act of rape because she is his property.
1861	Clara Barton begins nursing Union soldiers fallen in battle in the Civil War. She will eventually found the Red Cross.

1861	After a career advocating for mental health care, Dorothea Dix is appointed superintendent of army nurses by the Union Army.
1869	The Wyoming territory becomes the first to grant women the right to vote and hold office.
1869	Susan B. Anthony and Elizabeth Cady Stanton found the National Woman Suffrage Association.
1873	Myra Colby Bradwell is excluded from practicing law when the U.S. Supreme Court rules that a state has the right to exclude married women in *Bradwell v. Illinois*.
1884	Teacher and journalist Ida B. Wells wins $500 award in her lawsuit against the railroad company that had her forcefully removed from the first-class car.
1916	Jeannette Rankin of Montana became the first woman elected to the House of Representatives.
1916	Margaret Sanger establishes a contraception clinic in Brooklyn that will grow to become Planned Parenthood.
1920	The Nineteenth Amendment to the U.S. Constitution is ratified.
1923	The National Woman's Party proposes the Equal Rights amendment. It has yet to pass receive ratification.
1932	Amelia Earhart becomes the first woman and second pilot ever to fly solo nonstop across the Atlantic.
1940	Hattie McDaniel becomes the first person of color (male or female) to win a major Academy Award when she wins the Oscar for Best Supporting Actress.
1947	The U.S. Supreme Court rules that women are equally qualified to serve on juries.
1954	The film *Salt of the Earth* is released. It tells the story of the Mexican American miners wives who helped their husbands win in the 1951 strike against the Empire Zinc Company in New Mexico.
1955	Rosa Parks refuses to give up her seat on a bus in Alabama, sparking the Montgomery Bus Boycott.
1960	The Food and Drug Administration (FDA) approves the birth control pill.
1961	Astronaut John Glenn refuses to fly his first Mercury mission until Katherine Johnson recalculates the computer launch numbers.

1963	The Equal Pay Act, prohibiting sex-based wage discrimination, is signed.
1963	Betty Friedan publishes *The Feminine Mystique*.
1963	The Equal Pay Act is passed by Congress. As of 2022, it has never received full ratification from enough state legislatures to become an amendment.
1965	The Supreme Court overturns one of the last state laws prohibiting the prescription or use of contraceptives by married couples.
1969	California adopts the nation's first "no fault" divorce law, allowing divorce by mutual consent.
1971	The U.S. Supreme Court outlaws the practice of private employers refusing to hire women with preschool-aged children.
1972	Title IX of the Education Amendments says that no one "shall, on the basis of sex, be excluded from participation in, be denied the benefits of, or be subjected to discrimination under any education program or activity receiving Federal financial assistance."
1973	The U.S. Supreme Court declares 7–2 for the *Roe v. Wade* decision, securing constitutional protection to woman's legal right to an abortion. In 2022, this right came up for renewed debate.
1979	Based on a true story of union organizing, *Norma Rae*, written by Harriet Frank Jr. and Irving Ravetch opens. It will earn Sally Field her first Oscar for Best Actress.
1981	Sandra Day O'Connor is sworn in as the first woman to serve on the U.S. Supreme Court.
1983	Ruth Bader Ginsburg begins her term as an Associate Justice of the Supreme Court. She is the first Jewish woman and the second woman to serve on the court.
1983	Sally Ride becomes the first American woman to fly in space (and the third woman overall).
1983	*Silkwood*, written by Nora Ephron and Alice Arlen and starring Meryl Streep, Kurt Russell, and Cher, opens in theaters across the country.
1984	U.S. Rep. Geraldine Ferraro (NY) becomes the first woman vice-president nominee by a major party when she joins the ticket with Democratic presidential nominee Walter Mondale.

1991	Lawyer Anita Hill accuses Supreme Court nominee Clarence Thomas, her supervisor, of sexual harassment.
1993	Janet Reno becomes the first female Attorney General of the United States.
1993	California became the first state in the nation to be represented in the Senate by two women senators, Dianne Feinstein and Barbara Boxer. This also became known as the Year of the Woman.
1993	*The Joy Luck Club*, adapted from the book by Amy Tan, opens nationwide.
1994	President Bill Clinton signs the Violence Against Women Act providing funding for gender-related violence.
1997	Madeleine Albright is sworn in as the first female United States secretary of state.
1997	*G.I. Jane*, starring Demi Moore and Anne Bancroft, opens.
1997	Based on Title IX, the Supreme Court rules that college athletics programs must actively involve near equal numbers of men and women to qualify for federal support.
2001	Hillary Clinton becomes the first former First Lady to win election to the United States Senate.
2004	*Iron Jawed Angels* premieres at the 2004 Sundance Film Festival.
2004	Charlize Theron wins the Academy Award for Best Actress for her role in *Monster* at the Seventy-Sixth Academy Awards.
2005	Condoleezza Rice becomes the first Black female secretary of state.
2007	U.S. Rep. Nancy Pelosi (D-CA) becomes the first female Speaker of the House of Representatives.
2009	Associate Justice Sonia Sotomayor is sworn in as the first woman of color and first Latina member of the United States Supreme Court.
2009	The Lily Ledbetter Fair Pay Restoration Act allows women who have been paid less than men in the same job category to file a complaint against their employer within 180 days of their last paycheck.

2009	Hillary Clinton becomes the third woman to serve as secretary of state.
2010	Associate Justice Elena Kagan becomes the fourth woman ever to serve on the U.S. Supreme Court.
2016	Hillary Clinton becomes the first woman to receive a presidential nomination from a major political party.
2016	*Hidden Figures* earns three Academy Award nominations, including for Best Film, but loses out to *Moonlight*.
2016	*Confirmation*, written by Susannah Grant, premieres on television, starring Kerry Washington as Anita Hill.
2018	Year of the Woman declared after ninety Democratic women and thirteen Republican women are elected to the U.S. House of Representatives.
2018	*On the Basis of Sex*, the story of the only case Ruth Bader Ginsburg and her husband, Martin Ginsburg, presented to the U.S. Supreme Court together, premieres.
2021	Kamala Harris is sworn in as the first woman and first woman of color vice-president of the United States.

Chapter 1

Salt of the Earth (1954)

Written by Michael Wilson; Directed by Herbert Biberman
Independent Productions & The International Union of Mine,
Mill and Smelter Workers, 1954, 1 hr., 34 min.

INTRODUCTION

According to screenwriter Michael Wilson, *Salt of the Earth* was the "first feature film ever made in [the United States] of labour, by labour, and for labour." More than that, it was "a film that does not tolerate minorities but celebrates their greatness." Mired in controversy from the start due to its many blacklisted participants, *Salt of the Earth* is one of the few films to have ended up in a court case for the right to be distributed in the United States. In fact, *Salt of the Earth* was so thoroughly suppressed on its release in 1954 that some film historians call it the only blacklisted American movie (Hockstader 2003). Many blacklisted writers worked under pseudonyms during the era, sometimes even hiring fronts to appear at studios pretending to be the actual writer. However, producers, directors, and actors could not work without being seen, as was the case with this film's producer, Paul Jarrico; writer Michael Wilson; director Herbert Biberman; and actors such as Will Geer (Sheriff) and David Wolfe (Barton).

Jarrico and Biberman soon realized the blacklist would keep them from being hired by studios. They formed their own film company, Independent Productions Corporation, "eager to tell stories drawn from the living experience of people long ignored in Hollywood—the working men and women of America" (Sandhu 2014). While vacationing in New Mexico, Jarrico learned of the strike by the International Union of Mine, Mill and Smelter Workers against the Empire Zinc Company. Mexican American miners wanted equal pay to white miners. The twist that made the story unique to the filmmakers and turned it into a chronicle of the experiences of one segment of Mexican American women came when Jarrico learned that after the male workers were banned from the picket lines, their wives recognized a loophole in the contract and volunteered to take their husbands' places.

That real-life decision forced the men to value women's work in the home, as they had to cook and care for their own children, which challenged gender roles and took the message of the strike into their hearts. The men demanded equality with their white male counterparts, and the women demanded equality with their husbands. In the same way women in the civil rights movement resented being asked to serve coffee to the men who made speeches, these Mexican American women were willing to risk retribution from the sheriff in order to show their worth to their husbands and to the world. While the cultural attitudes of the 1950s lacked appreciation for such a focus, by the 1970s, the film would be praised by feminist critic Ruth McCormick for its unrivaled attention to "the issue of women's liberation—from the politics of housework to the myth of male supremacy" (Sandhu 2014).

The film centers on the life of Ramon Quintero, played in the neorealist tradition by real-life miner, Juan Chacón. Chacón, a strike organizer, did not extend the search for equal treatment to his spouse, thirty-five-year-old Esperanza, played by Mexican actress Rosaura Revueltas. Pregnant with their third child, she becomes instrumental in encouraging the other miners' wives to join the picket line.

SUMMARY

Though it could have been a film from a male perspective, *Salt of the Earth* announces its female perspective when it opens on a montage of Esperanza chopping wood to start a fire to boil water to scrub clothing as her five-year-old daughter, Estrella, works by her side. Esperanza then begins to narrate her story of being a miner's wife. The theme of justice comes up immediately, as she explains that "the land where the mine stands—that was owned by my husband's own grandfather. Now it belongs to the company." We meet her thirteen-year-old son coming home after a fight with "those Anglo kids" who bully him. Then we leave the home setting to meet Juan and his colleagues, who are approaching the mine offices to complain about new rules that leave them yet more vulnerable when working underground.

When Ramon returns home, Esperanza reminds him that they are behind by one payment on her prize possession—a radio—which causes a fight over their individual personal expenses. Ramon's accusation illustrates how he sees her one simple luxury: "Can't you think of anything except yourself?" But Esperanza counters with her raw truth, "If I think of myself, it's because you never think of me. Never. Never." To her, the evidence of her claim is that in negotiating for better working conditions, the miners have dropped a request for indoor plumbing for their homes, an issue clearly of more impact on the women's lives than the miners'. Ramon brushes her concerns away with, "First we got to get equality on the job. Then we'll work on these other things. Leave it to the men" (Biberman 1965).

As the men debate a strike, some local women come to Esperanza to insist the men put their wives' demands for indoor bathrooms and hot running water back into the negotiations. These ladies have prepared signs reading, "We want sanitation, not discrimination" to hold outside the union offices where the men are negotiating. Will Esperanza join them? Not while she's pregnant. An accident in the mine interrupts their talk, and they race to see which of their men won't be coming home that night. This spurs the miners to meet and authorize the strike. The women attend the meeting to ask that sanitation be returned to the list and for the right to create a ladies' auxiliary. The men shut down the meeting rather than address those issues. Even Ruth, the Anglo wife of the Anglo union organizer, Frank Barnes (played by real-life union organizer Clinton Jencks) is disgusted with being ignored.

The men begin a strike that lasts eight months. Women bring food and make coffee for the strikers while the company men try to destroy morale among the strikers in several ways. They offer leaders like Ramon the chance to be foremen if they bring the others back to work. They smuggle in scabs who are also of Mexican descent, attempting to pit the men against each other. They even cut off credit at the company store to the family of any striker. The tension leads Ramon into a fight that allows the sheriff (Will Geer) to arrest him, just as Esperanza gives birth to their third child inside the squalid conditions of the coffee shack.

The minute Ramon is released from his thirty-day sentence, they hold the baby's christening, demonstrating the importance of family in the midst of this continuing trauma. Finally, the Empire Zinc Company gains a court injunction that prohibits union men from marching on company property. The solution comes from the women. They attend that evening's union meeting and offer to picket in the men's place, as the injunction says nothing about the rights of nonemployees to picket on company land. The union hall is alive with the debate. Some men refuse to "hide behind our women's skirts," while others think the idea is brilliant. But will the sheriff's men beat the women to stop them? Who will take care of the children at home? Who will make the family meals?

The women win their request and begin picketing, except Esperanza, whom Ramon forbids to take part. She watches from a nearby hillside, and, in her narration, she comments that the men came to watch the women on the picket line "afraid the women wouldn't stand fast—or maybe afraid they would." The sheriff's men arrive to scatter the women, but the women refuse to leave. Their husbands try to come to their aid, but the women wave them off, shouting, "It'll be worse if you get in it." This incites Esperanza to race over and help her friends. Flustered, the deputies leave the scene, and the women continue picketing, now with Esperanza in their ranks.

At home that night, Ramon again forbids her to return the next day. Esperanza berates him for allowing the same unequal treatment he derides in his work life to exist in their private life, saying, "Whose neck shall I stand on to make me feel superior? And what will I get out of it? I don't want anything lower than I am. I'm low enough already. I want to rise. And push everything up with me as I go." But it is too soon for Ramon to agree. He insists he will not stay with the children. "Then tomorrow, I take the kids with me to the picket line," Esperanza says with finality, and she does exactly that. The sheriff's final attempt to break the women's spirit is by arresting the ring leaders, including Esperanza, who brings her baby and her young daughter, Estrella, to jail with her. There, the baby refuses cow's milk, and the women locked up with her loudly demand that the deputies purchase formula, which the men have never heard of, as they do not care for their own children in their homes. Ramon arrives, and Esperanza lets him take his children home, but she stays in jail in solidarity with her female companions.

At home, Ramon finally learns how hard her daily work is after taking three hours to heat up enough water to do the washing. He realizes that the women's needs belonged on the strike's list of demands all along. The women are released from jail and continue picketing but it causes a deeper rift in the Quintero household, with Esperanza asking, "Why are you afraid to have me at your side? Do you think you can only have dignity if I have none?"

The company's final trick is presenting eviction orders for the Quintero home. Deputies begin to remove all the family's possessions and stack them in the yard, but this, too, backfires, as first, the local children throw dirt balls at the deputies. Then Ramon and the men arrive, followed by miners from other unions (local mill workers and bricklayers), who Frank Barnes has alerted to the situation. The women begin bringing items back into the house as fast as the deputies can drag them out. The sheriff and his men quit. The company bosses finally agree to settle the strike, and the family reenters their home stronger and prouder of each other than they had ever been.

Having been made outside of the studio system and rumored to be a film about communist propaganda, *Salt of the Earth* did not receive the normal premiere experience. To be considered for Academy Award nominations, a film had to be shown in a theater. Yet, projectionists belonged to the powerful International Alliance of Theatrical Stage Employees (IATSE) union and were ordered not to run the film. Jarrico and Biberman found themselves making deals with nonunion theaters in order to secure a few nights of showings, in hopes of creating enough buzz to be offered a slot at a better theater. On March 14, 1954, the film premiered at the Grand Theatre in New York, far off the beaten path. Advertisements drew a solid crowd and, most importantly, a review from Bosley Crowther of the *New York Times*, who highlighted the importance of the female focus and approved of the way "Michael Wilson's tautly muscled script develops considerable personal drama, raw emotion, and power. For this conflict of human personalities, torn by egos and traditions, is shown in terms of sharp clashes at union meetings, melees on dusty picket lines, tussles with 'scabs' and deputy sheriffs and face-to-face encounters between the husband and wife in their meager home. It is a conflict that broadly embraces the love of struggling parents for their young, the dignity of some of these poor people and their longings to see their children's lot improved" (Crowther 1954).

At *Variety*, they assigned the review to the unnamed staff, and it ran only a short couple of paragraphs, with the overriding opinion stated in its subhead, "Salt of the Earth is a good, highly dramatic and emotion-charged piece of work that tells its story straight. It is, however, a propaganda picture which belongs in union halls rather than theatres" (*Variety* 1953). Despite all this, *Salt of the Earth* won the International Grand Prize from the Academie du Cinema de Paris in 1955. In 1992, the Library of Congress selected it for preservation in the United States National Film Registry for being "culturally, historically, or aesthetically significant" (Brief Descriptions). But, in 1982, a representative of the copyright office gave Jarrico the wrong information about the copyright renewal date, so the office rejected his application, and the film fell into public domain (Ceplair 2007). That gave it a new life in Chicano Studies and Film Studies courses, helping introduce *Salt of the Earth* to new generations of cinephiles.

HISTORICAL BACKGROUND

According to Apache history, mining existed in the area that became Grant County, New Mexico, for centuries. When the Spanish arrived, they fought to extinguish the local tribes and took over the copper mining in the late 1700s. Mexico ceded the area to the United States after the U.S.-Mexican War in 1848, and then the Industrial Revolution mechanized production of raw metals, making them even more valuable. The New Jersey Zinc Company developed a flotation process that separated zinc from lead, which made western areas ripe for profitable mining. By 1902, a decade before the territory officially became a state, the Empire Zinc Company, a subsidiary of New Jersey Zinc, began developing mines in Grant County. They largely employed Mexican Americans for the dangerous work and segregated the communities the company provided for workers to live. This included segregated schools (except the local Catholic one), segregated bathrooms, and segregated water fountains (Baker 2007).

While the Industrial Revolution birthed new ways of doing business, it also planted the seeds of the union movements that would wage economic war on companies to extract fair labor practices. This fight took half a century and a couple of world wars to achieve major concessions from corporate America, including the five-day work week and eight-hour day. The International Union of Mine, Mill and Smelter Workers (also known as Mine-Mill) began organizing in earnest in the western United States in 1916. By 1941, the union was pushing what were then considered communist ideas involving organizing interracial and interethnic groups. The union hoped to use their anti-racist policy to organize Mexican American workers and take advantage of the federal government's wartime labor shortage to raise wages and living conditions. This plan worked until the war ended and the Cold War led to anti-Communist sentiment against unions. Countering that, Mexican American soldiers returning from World War II pushed for more civil rights as payment for their wartime service. Mexican American women, especially in company towns, also came to recognize how labor action effected their ability to make purchases at company grocery stores and provide for their families (Baker 2006).

Still, the fact that many local mines had individual unions and had not yet joined forces held them back until Clinton Jencks, himself a miner but more importantly now a representative of Mine-Mill, arrived after a stint in the Air Force during World War II. He and his wife, Virginia Derr Jencks, had been such union supporters when he worked at Asarco's globe smelter in Colorado that the union sent them to Grant County. Having a wife who believed in the union become decisive in the success of the strike that inspired *Salt of the Earth* because she helped encourage the other wives to participate in union affairs. In short order, the couple helped organize five smaller union groups into the Local 890, and, in 1948, the union purchased a hall in Deming (Caballero 2019). In 1950, contracts came up for renewal. Miners demanded a 15-cent raise, two extra paid holidays per year, and a payment system that wouldn't favor white miners. Empire Zinc refused, and the men decided to strike.

On October 17, 1950, around 140 of them formed picket lines covering both entrances to the mine, guarding them to keep scabs from arriving to relieve the company. Empire Zinc tried to outlast the strikers for five months. In March, they even tried a back-to-work movement, which failed. On June 12, 1951, the Zinc Company lawyers found a loophole that convinced New Mexico's Sixth District Court that the strikers were blocking the road illegally. The judge found for the company and issued an injunction for all officers, agents, and members of Local 890 to stop picketing so that those who wanted to work could pass (Baker 2006).

Normally, unions could take such a finding to federal court, but not the Local 890 because of an Act passed by Congress in 1947. Among many things, the Taft-Hartley Act required all union officers to sign affidavits swearing they weren't communists. If not, they lost the right to have their disputes heard by federal government. Local 890 had refused to sign, so the union couldn't ask for federal support. Now if the men stayed on strike, they would be arrested, which would allow scabs to enter the mines and help the company get back into production. If they quit the picket lines, the scabs could enter. Either option would clearly end the strike without forcing the company to agree to any of the union's demands.

Only thinking outside the box could keep the strike going, which was exactly what Aurora Chavez, Virginia Chacón, and Virginia Jencks had brainstormed at an earlier meeting. The wives and mothers of the union's ladies' auxiliary proposed taking the injunction on the face value of its language and recognized an important loophole in the court order. It only prohibited striking miners from picketing. While some women had worked in the mines during World War II, none of them now were miners. If no "officers, agents, or members" could picket, why couldn't their wives, who had an equal need for the strike to succeed, since the workers' demands stood to benefit their lives as well? The demands included that the company end the segregated housing system and add indoor plumbing and hot water to the homes of Mexican American workers, as they already existed in the homes of the Anglos.

Being a new idea and one the men did not create and one that challenged the traditional gender roles of their society, the men balked at first at having women replace them on the picket lines, even though it was for their own benefit. Some feared the sheriffs would have no qualms about wounding women who dared to stand up to them. The majority of the others, though, refused to care for children while women took over the marching. Debates ensued for several hours with women like Anita Torrez, who said, they could "do [their] own problem-solving [if] the men didn't want to share in solving the problem" of childcare. Finally, Jencks offered women the chance to vote on the suggestion, since they would be the ones carrying it out. Because there were more women—more sisters, wives, and mothers—than men, the vote came out 183–85 in favor of the idea. The evening meeting lasted until two in the morning, but, by then, the women began to plan their shifts (Baker 2006).

The women's picket line began on June 12, 1951. Some of the men watched from the nearby hillsides, with their children beside them. Some refused to watch children, so the children joined their mothers on or near the line. After their first day of picketing proved successful, defined by the fact that the sheriff didn't choose to arrest women and the scabs who came to take their husbands' place in the mine refused to cross a female line, the women knew they needed reinforcements. Calls were made to women across the county with an interest in achieving the demands of the strikers, and many heeded the call. The women were fighting the double battle for their husbands and for their own dignity.

Local police, working for the company, even arrested the women, who brought their children to jail with them, as they had nowhere else to go. The newspapers brought unwanted attention to the police department for such behavior, and, when the company secured another injunction, this time for the women to stop picketing, the police refused to enforce it. The women persisted for the next six months, until January 1952, when the Empire Zinc Company finally agreed to negotiate. The women's picket line broke them. On January 21, the company ended negotiations, giving miners wage increases, vacation benefits, a health plan, and a pension plan. For the women, perhaps the most important concession brought the promise of hot water to their family homes.

Shortly afterward, the making of the film became a part of the history of the strike due to the participation of the miners and their wives in the production, which documented their involvement as a visual form of oral history. Then the anti-union sentiment drew vigilantes to the union hall (which did double-duty as the production offices) to tell the filmmaker that if they didn't leave town in twelve hours, they would "go out in little black boxes" (Borda 2011). Then, before she could finish filming, the Immigration and Naturalization Services arrested Rosaura Revueltas for not having had her passport stamped when she entered the United States. The officials deported her when her appeals were denied, hoping her absence would cripple the film. The director strategically filmed a few final scenes over the shoulder of a Revueltas double. For her voice-overs, Revueltas recorded in an unused Mexican sound studio, and, for the final frontal shots, a mini-crew visited her in Mexico and smuggled the film back over the border (Boisson 2002).

Life became equally complicated for Jencks, who faced criminal prosecution lasting several years. In January 1954, a federal court, using the testimony of a paid informant, convicted Jencks of falsifying a noncommunist affidavit he had signed in 1950. Jencks's appeals case reached the U.S. Supreme Court in 1957 and resulted in a landmark decision, with that high court overturning his conviction. Later, a new law passed in the U.S. Congress—the Jencks Act—requiring federal courts to provide defense attorneys any documents used by government employees and agents testifying in federal criminal trials (Caballero 2019).

Despite all that, according to Lee Hockstader of the *Washington Post*:

> The film had a strong second act. The story of its suppression, as much as the movie itself, inspired a cult following of leftists, feminists, Latinos, historians and film buffs. They rediscovered it in the '60s and resurrected it gradually in film schools, union halls and women's centers. Having sustained it for 50 years, hundreds of "Salt" fans converged here for a conference sponsored by the College of Santa Fe that was part tribute to the film and part political protest rally. As the theater lights dimmed for a showing of "Salt," Dolores Huerta,

the renowned labor leader who, with Cesar Chavez, founded the United Farm Workers, cried, "Viva la justicia!" (Hockstader 2003).

DEPICTION AND CULTURAL CONTEXT

Reviewers from *The Guardian* acknowledged that *Salt of the Earth* "treated, uniquely for the time it was made, questions of race and class as inseparable from those of gender. This annoyed some union leaders, such as the Longshoremen's Harry Bridges: 'Why did you have to bring in the woman question? Why couldn't you have made a straight film?'" (Sandhu 2014).

While the film did indeed address issues of race and class, so did many other strikes that occurred around the country at the time. What stands out for *Salt* is how it respected the unwaged labor of women in the home as equally as the paid labor of men in the mines.

In the context of the rising of second wave feminism, *Salt* depicts the life of the women in close to a documentary style. Opening the film on the hard work of Esperanza chopping wood (to start a fire to boil water to scrub clothing) illustrates the importance of the women's unwaged labor to the success of the corporations employing their husbands. The Women's Bureau of the Department of Labor studied this concept as early as 1925 and reported, "The miner's wife occupies a position of peculiar industrial and economic importance" because "only the presence of his family can keep the mine worker in the mining region." The report concludes the male worker—and, therefore, the corporation for which he labors—"is more continuously dependent upon his home for the essentials of health and working efficiency" (U.S. Department of Labor 1925). In essence, the presence of a family kept a workforce more willing to live in the isolated places where mines exist. And the women kept those families going by virtue of their unpaid labor. Hence, the film "connected women's domestic labor with men's 'productive' labor in a way that presaged later feminist analyses of class and gender" (Baker 2007). Having her five-year-old daughter work by her side further illustrates that this is a cycle of life all lived for the benefit of the owners of the corporation.

The newly formed Independent Productions Corporation, comprised of blacklisted writers, directors, and producers, were eager to tell "stories drawn from the living experience of people long ignored in Hollywood—the working men and women of America" (Sandhu 2014). They began by sending award-winning screenwriter Michael Wilson to the area. He wrote the script after weeks of interviews with the women on the picket lines, as well as the striking men. Then, in an unprecedented move, he discussed it with them at union meetings. The real-life participants vetted the material for any stereotypes of Mexicans as alcoholics, and they even checked that the local authorities be portrayed "not so much as persons but as a force" (Sandhu 2014). While they still lived in segregated communities, many men and women from both sides of the strike attended the same Catholic churches and engaged in other community events. The miners and their families did not want to offend many who had been on their side.

Long before the advent of #OscarsSoWhite or the promise to begin casting performers to play characters from their own ethnic backgrounds, *Salt* confronted the idea. Most of the male filmmakers were blacklisted, and banks calculate the profit on their investments based on bankability of the creatives involved in a film. That made Biberman's original idea, to have Gale Sondergaard, his Academy Award-winning wife, play Esperanza a smart one initially. She, too, relished the idea of playing such a nuanced character as well as the idea of helping the film succeed with whatever contribution she could make. However, soon Biberman realized his mistake. "We were preparing a film of the Mexican American people. But we had selected two 'Anglos' to play the leads! We had planned to use Mexican Americans in all the small parts. But we couldn't entrust Mexican Americans with the *important* Mexican American roles. The Hollywood tradition! And we were carriers. The first humiliating recognition of our discriminatory inheritance was sufficient. We knew what we had to do. Perhaps the hardest task was breaking it to Gale. For months she had been growing slowly, happily, into the role. Her immediate reply was, 'Of course. How unfeeling we have all been!'" (Biberman 1965).

As the aforementioned Hollywood tradition had kept many Mexican American actors from gaining the stature and experience needed to helm a movie, the filmmakers asked friends in Mexican cinema, who immediately recommended Mexican actress, Rosaura Revueltas. Famous for *Los Islas Marias* (1951) and *Soledad's Shawl* (1952), Revueltas spoke five languages (English among them) and had been a dancer. She had the grace of movement that helped her stand out from a crowd. Once the U.S. Embassy agreed to offer Revueltas a visa to work on the film, Sondergaard stepped aside (Klawans 2002). After recommending several Mexican actors, Revueltas instead suggested a nonactor, Juan Chacón, the soft-spoken, newly elected leader of the local union, for the part of Ramon. Biberman initially rejected the idea, but when no other Mexican American actors would take the role for fear of being blacklisted, he tested Chacón and agreed. Casting was also hampered by a new edict set down by Ronald Reagan, Screen Actors Guild president (and friendly witness to the HUAC hearings). Reagan warned any actors who worked with people on the blacklist that they likely would not work again while he ran their union (Jarrico and Biberman 1992).

In the mid-1950s, the United States was in the throes of the anti-Communist craze that had included the Hollywood blacklist, the conviction and execution of Julius and Ethel Rosenberg in Sing Sing Correctional Facility in 1953 for spying, and the Army-McCarthy hearings before Congress. The fact that the filmmakers had all been blacklisted when they moved to distribute the film created a problem.

In the context of film history, for its casting and many other reasons, *Salt of the Earth* can be considered an example of the influence of Italian neorealism on American cinema of the 1950s. The genre prizes using more real people than actors while telling stories of the masses, set among the poor and the working class, filmed on location. Born of the necessity to make films in the midst of war-torn Italy, with scant resources and little funds, neorealism came to the United States with the premiere of *Rome, Open City*. Written by Sergio Amidei, Federico Fellini, and Roberto Rossellini. the film covered the German occupation of Rome while it was still taking place. *Open City* came to the attention of filmmakers in the United States when it won the prestigious Cannes Grand Prix and earned a nomination for the Best Adapted Screenplay Oscar at the nineteenth Academy Awards in 1947. Quickly, the style took form in such films as *Body and Soul* (1947) before *Salt*, which qualifies for the genre by having used only five professional actors and makes poetic use of the landscape of New Mexico. The film announces that genre with the words that fill the screen in the opening scene while Esperanza is seen washing clothes: "Our scene is New Mexico, land of the free Americans who inspires this film, home of the brave Americans who played most of its roles" (Borda 2011).

In the context of the history of Mexican American civil rights activism, the story of the Empire Zinc strike was rarely covered in favor of the later, more famous strikes created by Cesar Chavez and Dolores Huerta in order to form the United Farm Workers (UFW) in the 1960s and 1970s. Though he, too, was considered a communist subversive by farm owners, Chavez had the added punch of celebrity support from people such as former attorney general Robert Kennedy, California governor Jerry Brown, and Coretta Scott King. When *Salt of the Earth* fell into public domain, that began to change, and the film gained a following in Chicano and Women's Studies programs, particularly in the western states.

In terms of popular culture, though it had been squelched from distribution, *Salt* was well known enough among cinephiles for a screenwriter like John Sayles to include mention of it among the reuniting political protestors of his *Return of the Seacaucus 7* (1981). The following year, Barbara Moss and Stephen Mack codirected *A Crime to Fit the Punishment*, a documentary about the making of the film. Finally, the making of the film also became its own narrative film in 2000, when Welsh screenwriter Karl Francis made *One of the Hollywood Ten* with joint Spanish-British financing. The film stars Jeff Goldblum as Biberman, Greta Scacchi as Sondergaard, and Geraint Wyn Davies as Wilson.

HUAC, *ONE OF THE HOLLYWOOD TEN*, AND *SALT OF THE EARTH*

When the House Un-American Activities Committee (HUAC) convened a hearing in Washington, D.C., to investigate subversive (suspected Communist) activities in the entertainment industry, they subpoenaed forty-one screenwriters, directors, and producers. If a person confessed to membership in a Communist group, they were then asked to name others they had seen at meetings, which would cement their standing with the committee, and the studios could then continue to hire them on their films. Among this first group, ten refused to answer, using their First Amendment rights to freedom of speech, freedom of association, and the right of assembly. *Salt of the Earth* director Herbert Biberman was one of them. HUAC found them all to be in contempt of Congress and fined each $1,000 and up to a year in federal prison. The studios then canceled any outstanding contracts (seven were writers, and three were directors) and began to blacklist anyone whose name was given to the committee. Once out of prison, some of the writers moved to Mexico or Europe and sold scripts under pseudonyms. Dalton Trumbo won two Oscars under other names. But the directors had to be seen on set to do their work. One of them, Edward Dmytryk, returned to HUAC and gave names of others in order to go back to work (Gevinson 1997).

Though not *One of the Hollywood Ten*, screenwriter Michael Wilson found himself on the longer list of names the studios refused to hire. Though he served as a tactical communications officer in World War II and had withdrawn from the American Communist Party in response to the Soviet invasion of Hungary, Wilson was called to testify before the HUAC. A director for whom he had worked, Frank Capra, had given Wilson's name to the committee. Wilson did not name names. Instead, he said, "I am not surprised to be hauled before a Committee that is trying to make peace a dirty subversive word. . . . Had I remained silent before this onslaught on reason, I would not have been summoned here today. But my life has no purpose without the prospect of peace. This Committee has no purpose without the prospect of war" (McBride 2002). The career damage did not set in immediately, so that, in 1952, he won both the Academy Award and Screen Writers Guild (SWG) award for cowriting *A Place in the Sun* (1951). After that, things became more difficult. Though he was asked to write both *The Bridge on the River Kwai* (1957) and *Lawrence of Arabia* (1962), Wilson did so from France, where he moved with his family for eight years. Their passports were revoked by the U.S. government while they were abroad, making it impossible for them to return to the United States until 1964. In later years, Wilson often referred to the HUAC hearings as "the Great Witch Hunt." His scripts for both of those films earned Academy Award nominations, and the *River Kwai* screenplay won, though it had been credited to Pierre Boulle, the author of the 1952 French novel on which the film is based, even though Boulle did not speak or write English.

Biberman spent six months in prison. Around the time of his release, his wife, Academy Award-winning actress Gale Sondergaard, received her summons to the committee. The couple feared she would be sentenced, but she chose to plead the Fifth Amendment. In the speech explaining her choice, Sondergaard said she had been criticized for being "a Jew-loving, Negro-loving, Red-loving, culture loving, peace-loving, un-American woman," and she added that it felt "incredible to be hated for loving so much and so many and so well" (Sondergaard 1951).

In 1960, in return for agreeing to star in *Spartacus*, actor Kirk Douglas demanded that Dalton Trumbo be given public billing for writing the film. This effectively rendered the blacklist null and void (Smith 1999).

FURTHER READING

Baker, Ellen. 2006. "'I Hate to Be Calling Her a Wife Now': Women and Men in the *Salt of the Earth* Strike, 1950–1952." In *Mining Women*, edited by J. J. Gier and L. Mercier. New York: Palgrave Macmillan. https://link.springer.com/chapter/10.1007%2F978-1-349-73399-6_12.

Baker, Ellen R. 2007. *On Strike and on Film: Mexican American Families and Blacklisted Filmmakers in Cold War America*. Chapel Hill: University of North Carolina Press.

Biberman, Howard. 1965. *Salt of the Earth: The Story of a Film*. Boston: Beacon Press.

Boisson, Steve. 2002. "*Salt of the Earth*: The Movie Hollywood Could Not Stop." HistoryNet. https://www.historynet.com/salt-of-the-earth-the-movie-hollywood-could-not-stop.htm.

Borda, Jennifer L. 2011. *Women Labor Activists in the Movies: Nine Depictions of Workplace Organizers, 1954–2005*. Jefferson, NC: McFarland.

Caballero, Raymond. 2019. *McCarthyism vs. Clinton Jencks*. Norman: University of Oklahoma Press.

Ceplair, Larry. 2007. *The Marxist and the Movies: A Biography of Paul Jarrico*. Lexington: University Press of Kentucky.

Crowther, Bosley. 1954. "The Screen in Review; 'Salt of the Earth' Opens at the Grande—Filming Marked by Violence." *New York Times*, March 15, 1954. https://www.nytimes.com/1954/03/15/archives/the-screen-in-review-salt-of-the-earth-opens-at-the-grande-filming.html.

Gevinson, Alan, ed. 1997. *American Film Institute Catalog—Within Our Gates: Ethnicity in American Feature Films, 1911–1960*. Berkeley: University of California Press.

Hockstader, Lee. 2003. "*Salt of the Earth* Is Back from the Blacklist." *Washington Post*, March 4, 2003. https://www.latimes.com/archives/la-xpm-2003-mar-04-et-hock4-story.html.

Jarrico, Paul, and Herbert Biberman. 1992. "Breaking Ground: The Making of *Salt of the Earth*." In *Celluloid Power: Social Film Criticism from Birth of a Nation to Judgment at Nuremberg*, edited by David Platt, 478–484. Metuchen, NJ: The Scarecrow Press.

Klawans, Stuart. 2002. "The Hollywood Three." *The Nation*. https://www.thenation.com/article/archive/hollywood-three/.

Library of Congress. "Brief Descriptions and Expanded Essays of National Film Registry Titles." Accessed October 22, 2020. https://www.loc.gov/programs/national-film-preservation-board/film-registry/descriptions-and-essays/.

Lorence, James J. 1999. *The Suppression of* Salt of the Earth: *How Hollywood, Big Labor, and Politicians Blacklisted a Movie in Cold War America*. Albuquerque: University of New Mexico Press.

McBride, Joseph. 2002. "'A Very Good American': The Undaunted Artistry of Blacklisted Screenwriter Michael Wilson" (PDF). February.

Nikolaidis, Aristotelis. 2011. "Rethinking the Representation of Gender and Activism in Film." *Feminist Media Studies* 11 (4): 501–505. https://doi.org/10.1080/14680777.2011.615586.

Quevedo, Sayre. 2019. "And They Will Inherit It." *Studio 360*, June 13, 2019. https://www.pri.org/stories/2019-06-13/and-they-will-inherit-it.

Salt of the Earth Recovery Project: Digital Archive. Accessed May 30, 2022. https://saltoftheearthrecoveryproject.wordpress.com/.

Sandhu, Sukhdev. 2014. "*Salt of the Earth*: Made of Labour, by Labour, for Labour." *Guardian*, March 10, 2014. https://www.theguardian.com/film/2014/mar/10/salt-of-the-earth-labour-workers-blacklisted-filmmakers.

Smith, Jeff. 1999. "'A Good Business Proposition': Dalton Trumbo, Spartacus, and the End of the Blacklist." In *Controlling Hollywood: Censorship/Regulation in the Studio Era*, edited by Matthew Bernstein. New Brunswick, NJ: Rutgers University Press.

Sondergaard, Gale. 1951. "We Speak of Peace." *Jewish Life* (August): 7–8.

Starfield, Peggy. 2016. "Striking Women: *Salt of the Earth*, *Norma Rae* and *Bread and Roses*." In *Social Class on British and American Screens: Essays on Cinema and Television*, edited by Nicole Cloarec, David Haigron, and Delphine Letort. Jefferson City, NC: McFarland.

U.S. Department of Labor, Women's Bureau. 1925. *Home Improvement and Employment Opportunities of Women in Coal Mine Workers' Families*. Washington, DC: U.S. Government Printing Office.

Variety Staff. 1953. "Salt of the Earth." *Variety*, December 31, 1953. https://variety.com/1953/film/reviews/salt-of-the-earth-1200417641/.

Chapter 2

Norma Rae (1979)

Written by Harriet Frank Jr. and Irving Ravetch;
Directed by Martin Ritt
Twentieth Century Fox, 1979, 1 hr., 54 min.

INTRODUCTION

Based lightly on the real life of North Carolina mill worker Crystal Lee Jordan, the Academy Award–winning *Norma Rae* tells the story of a female union organizer in the textile world. Best known for the visual of star Sally Field standing on a table, defiantly holding up a sign with "Union" scrawled on it, the film focuses on the nonromantic relationship of Norma and Reuben Warshovsky. Reuben has come to Norma's town to organize the mill workers. He quickly recognizes Norma as the magnet he needs to draw this diverse set of employees—female and male, Black and white—to his pitch. More importantly, he sees her as the glue he needs to make the union idea stick.

Two female film producers, Tamara Asseyeu and Alex Rose, purchased the rights to Jordan's memoir and brought the project to director Martin Ritt, who agreed on the condition that he could choose his own screenwriters for the adaptation. Ritt had previously worked with the husband-and-wife writing team of Irving Ravetch and Harriet Frank Jr., earning awards, which should have smoothed their approach to studios. Yet "Columbia Pictures, Warner Brothers and United Artists all rejected the idea because of proposed films pro-union subject matter," an unexpected turn in a strongly union town. The creative team then approached 20th Century Fox, which had recently enjoyed unprecedented financial success with *Star Wars* and both critical and popular success with the low-budget working-class hero, *Rocky*. The team convinced the studio that *Norma Rae* would be a female Rocky, another determined underdog, but this one would have more appeal to women (Borda 2011).

Landing a studio should have been the end of the production's issues. Next, they had to deal with Jordan, who refused to sign rights to her likeness unless the contract granted script approval to her real-life organizer Eli Zivkovich and his wife—a rarity in film adaptations. So names were changed, and the production team moved forward.

Oddly, the lead character did not attract then current box office big names, as Faye Dunaway, Diane Keaton, Meryl Streep, and Jane Fonda, all turned down the part. The creative team turned to Field, better known for light comedy on television's *Gidget* (1965) and on film in *Smokey and the Bandit* (1977). They knew she had also won an Emmy for her dramatic role in *Sybil* (1976). Their choice proved prescient, as her performance in *Norma Rae* earned her the first of two Academy Awards and still ranks number fifteen on the American Film Institute's heroes list, compiling one hundred years of The Greatest Screen Heroes and Villains.

The next production issue became where to film factory scenes. Because the J.P. Stevens's company had such influence, the filmmakers could not initially find a Southern town in which to film, and building their own textile mill proved far too costly. Finally, the management at a unionized mill in Opelika, Alabama, agreed to let them use their location. Local union mill workers then became extras in the film (Nathan and Mort 2007).

In the end, the film proved worth the effort. *Norma Rae* earned four Academy Award nominations including Best Picture (which it lost to *Kramer vs. Kramer*). It won for Best Actress, bringing Field into the top tier of American actresses, and Best Original Song, *It Goes Like It Goes*, written by David Shire and Norman Gimbel. Meanwhile, Ravetch and Frank, Jr. (who had been nominated previously for *Hud* in 1964) again lost out in favor of Robert Benton and *Kramer vs. Kramer*.

The film stands as a testament to a kind of union-creating event that dwindled soon after. "Indeed, soon after its release, with the 1980 election of Ronald Reagan, it seems the door mostly closed on explicitly leftist feature films for many years. The list of pro-union films ever since is far too short" (Dirnbach 2019). In 2011, the Library of Congress selected *Norma Rae* for the National Film Registry for being "culturally, historically or aesthetically" significant.

SUMMARY

As with *Salt of the Earth*, the opening montage of *Norma Rae* is of women at work, but these women are working for wages. As the title song begins, the mostly female textile factory workers run huge thread-winding machines, carding machines, and looms, while tufts of raw cotton waft through the air like falling snow. The montage blends into a series of photos of Norma's childhood from cradle to current day, underlined by the lyric, "Bless the child of a working man; she knows too soon what she is." When the song ends, the gentle quietness is broken with the loud, incessant sounds of all that machinery.

In the lunchroom scene, we learn that Norma was seen downtown at a local hotel over the weekend by gossipy coworker Bonnie. It's an insinuation Norma does not duck. When she turns her attention to her coworker and mother, Leona (Barbara Baxley), Norma realizes her mother's gone deaf. Norma drags the older woman back through the loud factory floor to the office of the staff doctor. He tries to placate her with, "It'll pass. It happens," but Norma snaps back, "Well, not to my momma." That night at home, we see she and her two middle-school-aged children live in a bedroom of her parent's home. Norma changes clothing and tells her father, Vernon, that she's heading out for an evening "in town," when she finds someone on their doorstep.

The outsider is looking to rent a room with a local mill family, as he has been sent to town by the Textile Workers Union of America (TWUA) to help unionize the very mill in which they work. He identifies himself as Reuben Warshovsky. Vernon asks, "What kind of name is that?" Warshovsky answers, "It's the kind you have to spell for telephone operators and headwaiters." This simple reference to headwaiters immediately illustrates the class differences they will have to overcome, on top of the intellectual differences, the ethnic differences, and the geographic differences.

Later that night, Norma and Reuben reconnect at the local hotel. Reuben has gone to rent a room and Norma has gone to meet another one-night stand. But that night is different. She tells the man who meets her that she's done being his on-again, off-again mistress. He slaps her hard, sealing her conviction against the life she's been leading, just in time to run into Reuben in the hallway. He offers her ice for the black eye. During this encounter, Norma (and the audience) learns his mission at the mill, that he's an educated Jewish man, and that he's married.

When her supervisors see Norma becoming interested in Reuben's efforts, they make her a supervisor. Unfortunately, this only turns her into a snitch and alienates her from her friends and coworkers, so she takes a demotion. Almost as soon as Norma starts helping Reuben with suggestions to make his pro-union flyers more readable, she starts dating another divorced mill worker, Sonny Webster (Beau Bridges), who has a daughter. Sonny soon proposes, "I got me and Alice, and I'm alone. You got your two kids, and you're alone. If you could help me, maybe I could help you."

Tellingly, friend Bonnie joins Norma at one of Reuben's meetings, showcasing how women are more willing to risk union involvement, as they see it means a better life for their children. Once she's assured that she can't lose her job for talking about the union during her breaks, Norma fully joins the effort, still not understanding how tough this will be. She asks her minister to let her use the church for a union meeting and knows she has to tell him up-front, as it means "Blacks and whites sitting together." He turns her down. She says if she can't use the church for a good cause, then what's the point of attending? He counters with, "We're going to miss your voice in the choir, Norma." She replies, "You're going to hear it raised up somewhere else." The racial tensions particularly bother Sonny as well. Without a meeting place, Norma invites several African American male employees to a meeting in her home, and Sonny fears they might make trouble. "I never had any trouble with Black men. Only trouble I ever had in my life was with white men," Norma says knowingly.

This begins further tensions at home when Sonny complains, "We're eating them frozen TV dinners, the kids are going around in dirty jeans, and I'm going *without* altogether!" Here *Norma Rae* echoes *Salt of the Earth* in this iconic scene where Norma begins doing three things at once, even crassly inviting him to stand behind her while she irons so they can make love. It's telling that in the script, the action line reads, "Sonny stands looking at her, half-admiring, certainly defeated" (Frank 1988). That scene allows Norma to show her dedication to the union. Reuben is given his chance to show his dedication to Norma when his superiors come to town and question having her as his number-one supporter, considering her . . . reputation. Reuben sends them away. Further showing her dedication to the cause, Norma offers to quit, but Reuben refuses.

The final showdown between Norma and her superiors at the mill comes when she is arrested for copying a letter from the supervisors warning white employees that the Black employees will run the union, thereby rising in status above the whites. Reuben knows that's illegal, but he needs the copy. The owners don't want that fuel handed to him, so they call the police. While she waits to be arrested, she writes the word "Union" in lipstick on a piece of cardboard and climbs on a table to hold the sign aloft. Slowly, her friends and coworkers turn off their machines, and the room falls silent. It is significant that the first person to turn off her machine is a female, Norma's friend Bonnie, and the second person is a Black female.

Following union rules, Norma demands that the sheriff promise to drive her home, which he does, but the minute she exits the mill, she sees the police car waiting to take her to jail. She bolts back into the factory, and it takes four men to carry her into the cruiser and lock her in. At the police station, she uses her one phone call to call Reuben, not her husband, knowing it will be seen as an insult to his masculinity. Reuben bails her out, and, upon returning home, she takes all three children aside and tells them what they may hear about her in school the next day but that they must hear it from her first. When they are alone, Sonny only wants to know if she's ever slept with Reuben. She promises she has not, "But he's in my head." In a testament to the equality of their marriage, Sonny responds, "I'll see you through anything that comes up. 'Cause there's nobody else in my head. Just you."

The film ends with the employees voting to start a union in their plant and Norma watching Reuben drive off to his next assignment. In their goodbye scene, Reuben offers to send Norma a copy of a Dylan Thomas book she found in his room and considered reading. In a nod to her continued independence, Norma says, "I already bought one for myself." They shake hands, and he drives off.

Though box office numbers did not reach the blockbuster status of *Rocky*, with only $12 million gross profit, the film garnered the aforementioned Academy Awards and placed it in competition for the Palme d'Or at the 1979 Cannes Film Festival.

HISTORICAL CONTEXT

Though not commonly known, workers from industries such as fishing and carpentry attempted small labor unrests even before the American Revolution. By 1842, other groups had attempted to band together for higher wages and improved working conditions, but those who tried could be convicted of criminal conspiracy until the advent of *Commonwealth v. Hunt*, a case where the Massachusetts Supreme Judicial Court ruled that workers could combine to demand improvements if they used legal means to achieve their goals (Tomlins 2013).

The revolution that brought on more frequent and more organized labor movements was the industrial one. The rise of railroad workers coupled with the dangers of the job brought short-lived groups such as the Brotherhood of Locomotive Engineers and Trainmen, the Brotherhood of Locomotive Firemen, and the Brotherhood of Railroad Trainmen. By the early 1900s, other occupations saw the success of collective bargaining and wanted the same powers. The American Federation of Labor (AFL) focused on supporting unions specific to certain crafts, which allowed them to include African Americans but not women, who they thought would take jobs from men (Kessler-Harris 2007).

Women laborers became involved through the Women's Trade Union League, dedicated to supporting the AFL but also encouraging more women to join labor unions. In terms of female textile workers, the 1911 Triangle Shirtwaist Factory fire in New York City proved to be the most galvanizing event, bringing more women into the International Ladies Garment Workers Union (ILGWU). In that fire, 146 immigrant workers died, making it one of the deadliest industrial disasters in U.S. history, a fact that influenced future politicians, including the first female cabinet member, Secretary of Labor Frances Perkins. She often called the Triangle fire the birth of the

New Deal (von Drehle 2006). The ILGWU formed in New York City when several smaller trade unions banded together. Attention came to them during through early strikes that attracted thousands of workers. First came the fourteen-week Uprising of the 20,000 in New York City in 1909. They used the phrase "We'd rather starve quick than starve slow" to succinctly explain their demands (Leupp 1909).

The International Workers of the World (formed in 1905) supported the largely female- and immigrant-filled textile industry in their next major strike, the Bread and Roses Strike in Lawrence, Kansas, in 1912. There, twenty thousand workers went on strike for two full months against a pay cut, with a leadership consisting largely of immigrant Italian immigrants. Union leaders had the innovative idea of publicizing the profound hunger suffered by the children of the strikers. They shipped them to families in other states, an act covered by many major newspapers, and which led to congressional hearings that, in turn, led to investigations of the terrible conditions in the mills. To avoid further negative publicity, the mill owners settled the strike (Watson 2006).

The greater union movements appear across history to move in parallel ways with the various waves of feminism, dipping and then regaining momentum together. This can be seen in the way the combination of the first wave of suffragists and the U.S. involvement in World War I brought even more women into factory work—and into unions. After the war, employers urged women to return to their first duties in the home so that fighting soldiers could return to work. Those same employers began to blacken the cause of unions by connecting them to the new flood of immigrants, some from communist countries, who took many of the vacated jobs. The Great Depression of the 1930s brought unions back into focus after a series of high-profile strikes where businesses hired strike busters, who often resorted to violence. Finally, the New Deal brought government onto the side of workers (and unions) when President Franklin Roosevelt allowed for collective bargaining and required businesses to bargain in good faith using the National Industrial Recovery Act and National Labor Relations Act. Much of this president's interest came from the combined influence of the aforementioned Secretary of Labor Frances Perkins and First Lady Eleanor Roosevelt. To their entreaties, FDR could add the overall fear that socialism would overtake capitalism in the United States, and, so, the New Deal was born.

Once again, a world war brought more workers into unions, helping to make the materials needed to prosecute the war. This time that included men and women of color, thanks largely to the efforts of A. Philip Randolph, who had created and ran the Brotherhood of Sleeping Car Porters, the largest African American labor union in the country. Knowing the economic power of union membership and wanting that for men of color, Randolph was one of three civil rights leaders in 1941 who began to plan a March on Washington to insist on more access to defense-plant employment. Rather than risk the public relations backlash of thousands of African American men marching on the capitol, President Roosevelt issued Executive Order 8802, which banned discrimination in the defense industries during the war. Because the order utilized the phrase "all persons," as in "Reaffirming Policy of Full Participation in the Defense Program by All Persons, Regardless of Race, Creed, Color, or National Origin, and Directing Certain Action in Furtherance of Said Policy," it brought many more women—as well as men—of color into unions and led to furthering the country's postwar prosperity (Pfeffer 1990).

The communist witch hunts lead by Joseph McCarthy followed this era and whittled away at the public's belief and trust in unions, as did a move toward deregulation and free competition, so that, by 1976, when *Norma Rae* was being written, union membership had peaked at 40 percent and began a steady descent. In 1981, then-president Ronald Reagan broke the Professional Air Traffic Controllers Organization (PATCO) strike (Derthick and Quirk 1985). According to the U.S. Bureau of Labor Statistics, union membership became 20.1 percent of workers in 1983, and the percentage of American workers in unions continued to drop from a high of 35 percent in the 1950s to less than 11 percent in 2011 (Greenhouse 2021).

Though never named in the film, the union represented in *Norma Rae*, the Textile Workers Union of America (TWUA), merged with the Amalgamated Clothing Workers of America in 1976. Therefore, the union that negotiated the contract with the J.P. Stevens Company was the Amalgamated Clothing and Textile Workers Union (ACTWU). They, in turn merged with the International Ladies' Garment Workers' Union in 1995, using the new acronym UNITE. The film tells the story of the unionization of the plant but does not detail what happened next or how long it took until the employees used their union membership to force a new contract with J.P. Stevens (Dirnbach 2019).

It required a full sixteen years after a successful union election at the Roanoke Rapids mill for union members to bring J.P. Stevens to the bargaining table. The film became a part of that real history during a nationwide boycott against Stevens. In turn, that boycott became a model for other pro-union parties across the country. Reverend David Dyson, who helped spearhead the Stevens boycott when he was on the union's staff, recalled: "The movie came along at the two-year point in the boycott, which hadn't picked up any steam. We found Crystal Lee Jordan [now Crystal Lee Sutton, the worker who inspired the Norma Rae character]. . . . We put on a tour, including a great event in Los Angeles with Sally Field and Crystal Lee. The lights would come up and there would be the real Norma Rae and people would leap to their feet" (Nathan and Mort 2007). The situation has not improved much since. In 2006, the only remaining Stevens factory in the United States (owned by its successor company, Westpoint Home) is a unionized blanket mill in Maine. That same year, "According to the labor advocacy group American Rights at Work more than 23,000 Americans were fired or penalized for legal union activity" (Nathan and Mort 2007). As of this 2021 writing, employees at Amazon warehouses began the ambitious effort to unionize its fifty-eight hundred workers. It became "not only the first effort to organize an entire Amazon warehouse in the United States, but also the biggest private-sector union drive in the south in years." Thirty percent of the warehouse's workers signed cards calling for a unionization election and the right to join the Retail, Wholesale and Department Store Union (RWDSU) (Greenhouse 2021).

As to skewing close to the real life of Crystal Lee Jordan, this film assignment allowed the Ravetch/Frank Jr. team to play to one of their core strengths as writers—the art of adaptation. Borda calls the film a docudrama—it involves dramatized reenactments of actual events. Therefore, *Norma Rae* is an adaptation, as divergent from the original story as the film of *Breakfast at Tiffany's* diverges from Truman Capote's original novel, but it is still an adaptation. The screenwriters chose to concentrate on creating a relationship between two main characters to find the film's "emotional resonance" (Frank 1988). They kept some of the facts of Jordan's life—the fact that she had been the third generation to work in the local mills, the fact that she had been widowed young, and the fact that she had children by different men and eventually remarried more for economic stability than love. The screenwriters also kept the fact that the activist who came to town to unionize Jordan's mill, Eli Zivkovich, was Jewish, and that Jordan became one of his lead operatives. Jordan offered Zivkovich a voice inside the mill and outside in a Southern town not yet open or comfortable with his big city, Jewish persona. This real-life pairing made for the right balance of tension and conflict expected of a character drama.

Then the Ravetch/Frank Jr. team utilized a few key moments in Jordan's life; the scene where she is arrested after writing down the boss's letter, which attempted to create racial division among the workers and the union; the iconic scene where she stands on the table waving her union sign; and the more nuanced scene where she confesses her haphazard history with her children (Frank 1988). Ravetch and Frank Jr. also employed a frequent element from their other films by choosing to keep the unconsummated romantic relationship in the film against Hollywood's tendency to create a couple out of any male/female pair. A romantic tryst wasn't true of Jordan and Zivkovich in real life, and the screenwriters made sure it wasn't true in the film.

DEPICTION AND CULTURAL CONTEXT

Overall, *Norma Rae* has retained its power over time. Historians, activists, and film critics who check in on the film once a decade or so across its forty years of existence still find it an honest and compelling film about union activism. In *Stayin' Alive*, Jefferson Cowie's book chronicling U.S. labor in the 1970s, Cowie considers *Norma Rae* a pro-labor standout among the films of the decade: "*Norma Rae* was thus a distinct oddity in seventies popular culture: an optimistic message about the capacity of working people and one of the very few unabashedly pro-labor movies of the decade" (Dirnbach 2019).

In a 2007 article in *The Nation* celebrating the film's thirtieth anniversary, journalists Robert Nathan and Jo-Ann Mort saw:

> It is virtually the only American movie of the modern era to deal substantially with any of these subjects. Even today it remains iconic—a major studio movie about the lives of working people with a profound and, for its time, disturbing political message: The little guy may have a prayer of getting social justice, but he'll have to fight desperately to get it. As everyone knew at the time, the mill and the town were unambiguous stand-ins for J.P. Stevens and its sixteen-year war against union organizers in Roanoke Rapids, North Carolina, and the movie accurately depicted the state of American labor in 1979. (Nathan and Mort 2007)

From a feminist standpoint, Naomi Fry wrote in 2020 that "what struck me even more strongly, however, was the movie's suggestion that no struggle can take place alone. Norma Rae is heroic, but she comes into her own, as a woman, because she is fighting for class solidarity—a struggle that, in turn, could not happen without a breaking down of long-standing ethnic and racial barriers" (Fry 2020). In the course of the film, Norma Rae learns that Jewish people don't have horns (from a line of dialogue that might have come directly from Ravetch's life, as he was of Jewish descent). She also learns to stand up for herself as a working woman.

Further, *Norma Rae* offers an early depiction of women struggling with double duties—caring for the union activities and caring for their children and aging parents. Though, in truth, that's a triple-duty because they must also maintain their day jobs for the wages that keep their families running. Unlike the focus in *Salt of the Earth*, where wives challenge their husbands to work for the same equality at home as they expect at work, this movie allows the male character in Norma Rae's life to become angry rather than pick up the slack at home. This is odd, since Drew is a working laborer who stands to be aided by the establishment of safety at work that will come through the union efforts of his female partner. Where some see this coverage of women's triple-duty lives as an example of how they fail, I see it as proof of their nobility, for they are sacrificing the personal relationships that are meant to span their lives to create better conditions in their (and their fellow workers) shorter-term work lives. Heroes sacrifice, and there is no bigger sacrifice for a mother than losing time with—or losing the respect of—their children.

In her book *Women Labor Activists in the Movies*, Jennifer Borda feels the film shows how a working-class woman needed the intervention of an educated outsider to realize her own potential. Others argue that these women knew their potential but also recognized how their place in society had been proscribed to them based on the economic world in which they were born. The outsider male union operator did not teach them so much as open up a bridge to the opportunity to use their higher organizational and leadership skills to provide better economic opportunities to their fellow laborers and the generations that would come after them. That is more the heroine's journey than the more famous hero's journey advocated by Joseph Campbell. In many ways, Norma Rae ushers in the beginning of a trend of female antiheroes (though some would argue the iconic Scarlett O'Hara is an antihero), showing women as tainted heroes in need of a cause to divert them from their socially unacceptable lifestyles.

Union organizer Eric Dirnbach reviewed the film for the *Organizing Work* website and found the depiction of how Reuben does his job particularly unreal, perhaps in pursuit of conflict and drama. "He starts the campaign by handing out flyers at the plant gate, which was enough to make me cringe. Way too soon, dude! This alerted the boss and exposed workers to risk right away before there was any chance to help them build confidence and trust in the campaign. We would ideally want to see individual worker organizing and the formation of a strong rank-and-file committee before 'going public' with the campaign." Later, Dirnbach finds another rookie mistake when plant managers let Reuben walk through the plant to see that his union flyers are visible to the workers, he stops to ask a worker if he liked his job. Doing so in front of management "is not how you build a good relationship with workers," according to Dirnbach, who also finds Reuben spends too much time lecturing the workers about how much they need him rather than showing them he's on their side.

The most misleading moment Dirnbach found came when Norma Rae asks if she could lose her job for supporting the union. Reuben says that can't happen, when, in truth, it happens very often around the country. Lying to workers who support your movement is not a way to form the bonds needed to keep the group together as they fight. "I analyze NLRB election data as a hobby (really), and in the mid-1970s, unions ran over eight thousand elections per year but only won about half of them. If Reuben's organizing strategy was at all typical, we can see why" (Dirnbach 2019).

Jordan herself said, "I wanted it to be about more than two people because it took more than two people to win a campaign involving over three thousand workers" (Borda 2011). In that way, the film fed into the trope of a male union organizer arriving in town, "who is Jewish and from New York, which sets up an inevitable 'fish out of water' framework in that small, southern town. Indeed, later in the film, Norma Rae literally calls him that when they go swimming in a river" (Dirnbach 2019). The film neglects to cover the largess of the movement and all the many people involved, but that is typical because such a large number of humans is difficult to portray, similar to how so many civil rights movies distill the players into Rosa Parks and Dr. Martin Luther King.

Left on the proverbial cutting room floor, according to Aimee Loiselle in her dissertation, "The Erasure of Puerto Rican Needleworkers and Southern Labor Activists in a Neoliberal Icon," is the more global story of the international textile and garment industry as an example of contested cultural production. "In recycling the narrative of white working-class individuals in isolated circumstances, *Norma Rae* elided a history of collective southern activism and contributed to the erasure of Puerto Rican women" in favor of making "the Norma Rae icon, a representation of a white woman standing alone, with its individualist narrative and affect of inspirational defiance." Loiselle's detailed study of *Norma Rae* raises questions about how popular culture rearticulates familiar meanings and obscures disconcerting complexities due to its own reliance on gendered, racialized, and colonial narratives and about who shapes the visibility and meanings for "working class," "worker," and "American" (Loiselle 2019).

Finally, in her book, Borda writes that "the social conflicts (read labor issues) of the films are, for the most part, subordinate to the two primary plot devices: the heroine's coming of age and the romantic storylines." However, no one who speaks of either of these films defines them as either coming of age or romance; they call them female heroine stories or films about union history. Few even remember Norma Rae's low-key marriage as being part of the movie. Director Martin Ritt proudly called the film "probably the most pro-union film in the history of Hollywood" (Borda 2011), though it would seem he's missing *Salt of the Earth*, whose short distribution life means he likely never saw the other "most pro-union film in the history of Hollywood."

FURTHER READING

Allan, Angela. 2019. "40 Years Ago, Norma Rae Understood How Corporations Weaponized Race." *The Atlantic*. https://www.theatlantic.com/entertainment/archive/2019/03/norma-rae-40th-anniversary-racial-solidarity-unions-labor-movement/583924/.

Arnold, Gary. 1979. "'Norma Rae': Haymaker for the Heartstrings." *Washington Post*, March 7, 1979.

Borda, Jennifer L. 2011. *Women Labor Activists in the Movies: Nine Depictions of Workplace Organizers, 1954–2005*. Jefferson City, NC: McFarland.

Derthick, Martha, and Paul J. Quirk. 1985. *The Politics of Deregulation*. Washington, DC: Brookings Institution Press.

Dirnbach, Eric. 2019. "Movie Review: *Norma Rae* (1979)." *Organizing Work*. https://organizing.work/2019/01/movie-review-norma-rae-1979/.

Dunn, Megan, and James Walker. 2016. "Union Membership in the United States." U.S. Bureau of Labor Statistics. https://www.bls.gov/spotlight/2016/union-membership-in-the-united-states/pdf/union-membership-in-the-united-states.pdf.

Frank, Michael R. 1988. *Hud, Norma Rae, The Long, Hot Summer: Three Screenplays by Irving Ravetch and Harriet Frank, Jr.* New York: Penguin.

Fry, Naomi. 2020. "The Ongoing Relevance of 'Norma Rae.'" *The New Yorker*. https://www.newyorker.com/recommends/watch/the-ongoing-relevance-of-norma-rae.

Greenhouse, Steven. 2021. "'We Deserve More': An Amazon Warehouse's High-Stakes Union Drive." *The Guardian*, February 23, 2021. https://www.theguardian.com/technology/2021/feb/23/amazon-bessemer-alabama-union.

Kessler-Harris, Alice. 2007. *Gendering Labor History*. Champaign: University of Illinois Press.

Leupp, Constance. 1909 (1998). "The Shirtwaist Makers' Strike. The Survey." In *How Did the Perceived Threat of Socialism Shape the Relationship between Workers and Their Allies in the New York City Shirtwaist Strike, 1909–1910*, edited by Thomas Dublin, Kathryn Kish Sklar, and Deirdre Doherty. Binghamton: State University of New York at Binghamton.

Loiselle, Aimee. 2019. "Creating Norma Rae: The Erasure of Puerto Rican Needleworkers and Southern Labor Activists in a Neoliberal Icon." (Doctoral Dissertations, 2128). https://opencommons.uconn.edu/dissertations/2128.

Murray, Susan. 2007. "The Female Social Activist in American Cinema—A New Genre: Norma Rae, Silkwood, Erin Brockovich, and North Country." (Thesis, Masters of Arts, University of Miami).

Nathan, Robert, and Jo-Ann Mort. 2007. "Remembering *Norma Rae*." *The Nation*. https://www.thenation.com/article/archive/remembering-norma-rae/.

Nikolaidis, Aristotelis. 2011. "Rethinking the Representation of Gender and Activism in Film." *Feminist Media Studies* 11 (4). https://www.tandfonline.com/doi/abs/10.1080/14680777.2011.615586?journalCode=rfms20.

Pfeffer, Paula R. 1990. *A. Philip Randolph*. Baton Rouge, LA: LSU Press.

Starfield, Peggy. 2016. "Striking Women: *Salt of the Earth, Norma Rae* and *Bread and Roses*." In *Social Class on British and American Screens: Essays on Cinema and Television*, edited by Nicole Cloarec, David Haigron, and Delphine Letort. Jefferson City, NC: McFarland.

Tomlins, Christopher. 2013. "The State, the Unions, and the Critical Synthesis in Labor Law History: A 25-Year Retrospect." *Labor History* 54 (2): 208–221.

Toplin, Robert. 1995. "Norma Rae: Unionism in an Age of Feminism." *Labor History* 36 (2). https://www.tandfonline.com/author/Toplin%2C+Robert.

von Drehle, David. 2006. "Uncovering the History of the Triangle Shirtwaist Fire." *Smithsonian Magazine*. https://www.smithsonianmag.com/history/uncovering-the-history-of-the-triangle-shirtwaist-fire-124701842/.

Watson, Bruce. 2006. *Bread and Roses: Mills, Migrants, and the Struggle for the American Dream*. Westminster, UK: Penguin Books.

Chapter 3

Silkwood (1983)

Written by Nora Ephron and Alice Arlen; Directed by Mike Nichols
ABC Motion Pictures, 1983, 2 hr., 11 min.

INTRODUCTION

Often paired with *Norma Rae, Silkwood* offers up the case of another female factory worker, but where both real-life women were union activists, Karen Silkwood also became a whistle-blower. The film then opened up the discussion of whether movies create myths when they mean to memorialize history, because Silkwood, who worked for a Kerr-McGee nuclear fuel-rod producing facility in Oklahoma, found irregularities in production and issues with safety. As a union representative, she collected evidence to present to a reporter for *The New York Times*. Then, in the early evening of November 13, 1974, the twenty-eight-year-old died when her car veered off the road and smashed into a concrete culvert. Thus began a mystery that will likely never be solved. Movies love mysteries. They love antiheroes. They love underdogs. The story of Karen Silkwood had all three—and more—so it was no surprise when Hollywood took over the story.

Formed in 1981, ABC Motion Pictures only lasted four years, making six films, *Silkwood* among the more profitable of the batch. As with most films, a writer was hired first to bring narrative form to the true story. Company president Brandon Stoddard hired Nora Ephron to write the script. The daughter of screenwriters Phoebe and Henry Ephron, Nora had worked first in journalist in New York. Being newly divorced with two young children she couldn't do the location research needed in Oklahoma, so she invited another female journalist, Alice Arlen (who also worked as a film editor), to collaborate. Of their teaming, Ephron said, "Alice and I disagree on almost everything . . . But what's great about working with her is that she comes at things in a way that is so original and interesting" (Blades 1990). Both women were awarded when they were later nominated for the Academy Award for Best Screenplay.

After the writers' draft achieved studio approval, the director, Mike Nichols (*The Graduate*) came on board. Then Meryl Streep signed on to play the lead, followed by former Disney child star turned action star Kurt Russell as her boyfriend and Cher in her second dramatic role. She had made her Broadway debut in the play *Come Back to the Five and Dime, Jimmy Dean, Jimmy Dean* and starred in its film adaptation the year earlier. They filmed on location in various cities in Texas and in Washington, D.C. The film cost about $10 million to produce. It eventually earned $35,615,609 worldwide.

The opening credits unroll over gentle banjo music, as a car drives across the natural beauty of the state of Oklahoma. Karen Silkwood (Meryl Streep) drives her boyfriend Drew Stephens (Kurt Russell) and their roommate, Dolly Pelliker (Cher) to the work. The music picks up as they rush into the nuclear processing facility, dress in their safety equipment, and man their stations. A tour of the plant allows Karen to show off her knowledge of the process they are a part of when someone asks about the effects of radiation. The supervisor quickly compares it to a bad sunburn. Casual conversation among her colleagues clues the audience in to issues with relatives dying of cancer and contamination of vehicles used to transport the product. Karen then asks her colleagues if one will work the weekend so she can visit her three children, living with their dad in Texas.

The next morning Karen, Drew, and Dolly drive to Texas, but her ex-husband has made other plans for the weekend, and he is moving their children yet farther away from her. On the drive home, she explains that her husband has more legal rights because the casualness of their relationship meant they had only been common-law, married and now that he's legally married, the courts granted him full custody. This further accents her underdog status and the issues women have with being treated fairly by authorities.

Returning to work Karen, learns the plant was shut down over a contamination issue, and someone blames her for doing it as a way to ensure the weekend off. Drew suggests she talk to the head of the union, but they are interrupted when they learn an older, female colleague, Thelma, has been "cooked," which, in their casual parlance, means contaminated. Karen (and the audience) watches the decontamination process, which involves Thelma being scrubbed raw in a shower by other employees. At home that night, the three roommates are shaken by the reality of working with such dangerous material. Karen and Dolly also share a moment, with Dolly admitting that she loves Karen, and Karen admitting she knows it's in a deeper way than she can reciprocate.

At work the next day, Karen has to stay after to clean up. On leaving the plant, she sets off the radiation detector and undergoes the same raw scrubbing shower she witnessed earlier. At home, she's still disturbed by the experience and talks to Drew about her fears. The next morning Karen reads union materials that state there are no acceptable levels of radiation exposure. When Drew comes home, he tells her she's been transferred to metallurgy, which means she'll need to work three solid months to earn overtime again. Also, she'll have to work with Winston (Craig T. Anderson), who has already been shown to be a sexual harasser.

Karen attends a union meeting and learns that they are facing a decertification election, which means the union can be voted out of the plant. Karen volunteers for the union negotiating committee. After a boisterous night of sex, she and Drew meet Angela, a beautician friend of Dolly's who spent the night boisterously as well. Drew and Karen express no problems with a lesbian roommate, who moves into Dolly's room the next morning. As Karen gets more involved with the union, Angela reminds her, "There are two streets in this town. One's named Kerr and one's named McGee. They own the state, and they own practically everybody in the state." Drew insults her work as a beautician and learns she works at a funeral home, where many of her clients are former Kerr-McGee employees. "I can always tell when a dead person I beautify worked for Kerr-McGee because they all look like they died before they died."

Similar to *Norma Rae*, Drew complains about Karen being on the phone all day, clearly not available to him as she once was. She takes her first airplane flight to Washington, D.C., to meet with the national union and the Atomic Energy Commission. Her naïveté shows, as she asks the flight attendant how much the meal costs. She and her local union leader worry if their bosses will learn about their testimony and fear there will be retaliation. There, she secretly tells union leader Paul Stone (Ron Silver) about how the metallurgy department touches up negatives, which hides flaws in the nuclear rods they ship to plants. They ask her to collect negatives as proof, and she agrees.

When she returns home, Drew is bothered by her deeper union involvement and how it will cost jobs at the plant. He'd like her to quit the union and the job and go away with him, but she declines. Karen learns that Drew quit his job that day, and he's moving out on her and Dolly, saying, "Sweetheart, it's like you're two people. I'm in love with one of them."

At another union meeting, Karen sits at the front table with Paul and other union leaders, as the leader lectures her colleagues about the truth of how plutonium—even a pollen-sized amount—causes cancer. Afterward, Winston challenges Paul to prove these things, since the company disagrees. We learn that Paul and Karen have become involved, against his better judgement. Karen's helps promote a pro-union vote, but, unlike *Norma Rae*, her union connection, Paul, is not nearly as supportive, leaving her talking to answering machines more than to him.

Soon Angela leaves Dolly, and Karen misses Drew, and that starts a fight between the roommates, culminating in Dolly accusing Karen, "You took about as good care of Drew as you took of your kids." Dolly quickly apologizes. In their ensuing conversation, the women discuss quitting the plant and moving somewhere "clean."

Paul pushes too hard, seemingly uninterested in employee health issues as much as the doctored negatives. Soon colleagues stop talking to her in fear of losing their jobs. Then Karen is contaminated a second time, scrubbed raw a second time, and is told she's had only an "acceptable dose" a second time. On her drive home, she swerves to miss a deer and has the tow-truck driver to call Drew to drive her home, which restarts their relationship. But on her way into work the next day, she sets off the contamination warning and is scrubbed raw again. Then plant investigators come to their home, checking for radiation, which they find everywhere, including in the toothpaste. They strip mattresses, picture frames, curtains, and food from the refrigerator. It turns out Drew and Dolly are clean, which makes the supervisors suspect Karen contaminated her own home to take down the company. She has readings of forty-five thousand disintegrations per minute (dpm) readings on the nasal swab, meaning she's internally contaminated. Karen realizes she spilled her urine sample in the bathroom that morning, and it must have been spiked with plutonium. The company rep offers to help her with money and security if she signs a statement "in her own words" blaming herself for the contamination.

The investigators take Dolly away for tests. Drew returns to the empty house. Luckily, he had not yet moved all his things back. He finds the extra key on the doorframe and pockets it in memory. Winston has stopped by as well, and Drew takes the opportunity to punch him as he leaves, leaving the impression that perhaps Winston spiked Karen's urine. Drew finds Karen at his new apartment, and the three friends fly to Los Alamos for a full body scan. On the plane, Karen is worried about what Dolly might have told the company when they interviewed her. Dolly insists, "They know everything about us," but Karen isn't sure, leaving the impression her friend might have ratted her out.

The three undergo full tests, and Drew and Dolly are told they have minimum exposure, but Karen has an internal exposure of 6 nanocuries of plutonium (spe) which is far under 40, the amount permissible. Then the doctor admits the accuracy rate of the tests can be off by plus or minus 300 percent. Karen makes the appointment with the *New York Times* reporter while Drew dreams of moving to New Mexico and building a home for them and their future children. Karen leaves to go to work, "get some things," and go to a union meeting. She waves good-bye to Drew, who is sitting on the steps outside his place without a shirt, showing the audience what she is sacrificing for her cause, though she doesn't yet know she'll lose.

Under the strains of *Amazing Grace*, sung by Meryl Streep, the ending montage includes headlights forcing her off the road, her car in the ditch with Karen slumped over the dashboard, and her car towed through town as Dolly sits in the café crying. The final cut returns to Karen smiling at Drew as he watches her leave that morning. The classic lyrics, "I once was lost but now I'm found, was bound but now I'm free" end as her car fades down the street. The screen fills with, "The precise circumstances of Karen's death are unknown. It is also not known whether she had any documents with her. None were found. An autopsy revealed a high level of the tranquilizer Methaqualone and some alcohol in her bloodstream. Oklahoma police ruled her death a single car accident. A year later, the plant shut down."

Reviews were generally positive, thanks to the pedigree of the actors, writers, and director. The *Hollywood Reporter* wrote, "Screenwriters Nora Ephron and Alice Arlen have etched with their earthy down-home scenes the story of a company town: Kerr-McGee has a large contract to deliver; its managers have a deadline to meet; its workers must supply the product. But here the product is nuclear fuel rods, and faulty fuel rods can cause a nuclear breeder reactor to explode, which could wipe out a few million people in the surrounding area" (The Hollywood Reporter 1983).

The audience found the story of Karen Silkwood worth seeing, as the film stayed in the top ten for eighteen solid weeks; grossed $37 million; and garnered five Academy Award nominations, including Streep for Best Actress, Cher for Best Supporting Actress, and Nichols for Best Director. Outside of success in the history of film, *Silkwood* did what few other films have ever accomplished. The film led to a landmark court decision giving filmmakers the same first amendment protection afforded print journalists. Subpoenaed by Kerr-McGee (the nuclear company where Silkwood had worked), producer Buzz Hirsch refused to give testimony in a suit against the company. The U.S. Court of Appeals ruled in Hirsch's favor.

HISTORICAL CONTEXT

Women have exposed wrongdoing in some of the largest corporations and organizations in the country. Among them are Sherron Watkins, vice president of corporate development at Enron, who warned about the company's improper methods of accounting; Alayne Fleischmann, who gave federal prosecutors evidence of mortgage-securities wrongdoing at JP Morgan Chase; and legendary PG&E whistle-blower Erin Brockovich (herself the subject of a film in 2000). Karen Silkwood joined that list posthumously when she died at the age of twenty-eight on her way to an interview with David Burnham, a reporter for the *New York Times*, and Steve Wodka, a health and safety expert for the Oil, Chemical and Atomic Workers International (OCAW) union.

What is known, based on court documents and testimony, is that Karen Silkwood was hired at the plant in 1972 to work in the laboratory, not in any of the production departments. She heard other workers talk about the chronic contaminations and grew outraged. She started agitating to have the plant cleaned up or shut down. The Oil, Chemical and Atomic Workers International Union eventually called a ten-week strike at the plant over demands for higher wages and improved safety and training conditions. Silkwood walked the picket line with her colleagues, but the strikers lost. Conditions at the plant were such that the turnover rate was high; during a ten-month period in 1974, 99 of 287 employees (essentially one-third of the workforce) had to be replaced because they quit or were fired (Kohn 1977). In September 1974, she joined other union leaders on a trip to Washington, D.C., to testify in front of the Atomic Energy Commission about the facility's "unsafe working conditions" (Latson 2014). Afterward, top officials of the Oil, Chemical and Atomic Workers International (OCAW) asked her to "return to the plant and gather evidence that could be used in a formal grievance against Kerr-McGee" (Kohn 1977).

In court, lawyers for the Silkwood family claimed she had been contaminated with radiation from plutonium while working the late shift July 31, 1974. On November 5 and 6, they say, she discovered that she had been contaminated again at work and underwent decontamination showers, having her skin scrubbed raw on both days before going home. When she arrived at work on November 7, six days before her death, monitors showed high levels of plutonium in her body, indicating she had been contaminated outside the plant. According to a 1979 *TIME* report, evidence of radiation was found in her kitchen, her bathroom, and in a bologna-and-cheese sandwich in her refrigerator.

Investigators for the Atomic Energy Commission (AEC) were called in the next day and were told that Kerr-McGee, which had become increasingly aware of and concerned about Silkwood's union activities, suspected she had contaminated herself to dramatize her beliefs about negligence in the handling of plutonium. The agency arranged for Miss Silkwood to travel to New Mexico for special diagnostic examinations. On November 12, she was barred by Kerr-McGee from the plutonium-processing areas of the Cimarron plant.

On November 13, 1974, Silkwood headed out to meet with a union representative and a *New York Times* reporter when her car hit a concrete culvert. She had claimed to have paperwork showing the company's safety negligence, but no such paperwork could be found in the vicinity after the accident. Investigators found she had taken a large dose of quaaludes before driving. But they also found skid marks and an unexplained dent in her rear bumper, which her family believed showed she was driven off the road by another car. After she was killed, an autopsy showed she had mysteriously ingested plutonium (UAW.org 2017). While the Oklahoma Highway Patrol called it an accident, the Oil, Chemical and Atomic Workers investigation concluded that another car deliberately forced her off the road. "The AEC subsequently produced a twenty-page report about conditions at the plant which conceded Kerr-McGee was guilty of some safety violations but dismissed them as technicalities and aberrations" (Kohn 1977).

Shortly before her death, Silkwood charged that the plant posed a danger to its employees and the public, having strayed so far from federal nuclear code. Allegedly, she had been collecting proof. Some investigators later speculated that Silkwood had also inadvertently exposed a smuggling ring at the plant and that her evidence also held information about missing plutonium.

The plant owner, Kerr-McGee Corporation, denied both accusations. The AEC investigated a total of thirty-nine allegations of safety violations that Silkwood had presented to them two months earlier. "Gerald Phillip, a special investigator for the A.E.C., interviewed Miss Silkwood and others extensively, in an attempt to determine how she had become contaminated. He was conducting his investigation when she was killed. The A.E.C. took no official position on how Miss Silkwood became contaminated, but Mr. Phillip told reporters outside the courtroom that he believed that Miss Silkwood had stolen plutonium from the plant after finding that she was unable to produce sufficient evidence to document her case, and apparently had inadvertently contaminated herself" ("Trial Nears End" 1979).

In response to the idea that ends the film, that "It is also not known whether she had any documents with her. None were found," a *New York Times* article about how "Fact and Legend Clash" in the film by William Broad reported that "At the movie's close, Miss Silkwood goes off to meet a *New York Times* reporter. We see her with a fat folder, apparently thick with incriminating papers. The myth, repeated in a written statement at the end of the movie, is that documents were never found. This is wrong. Lots of documents were found—but they in no way substantiated Miss Silkwood's charges that the company was doctoring evidence of faulty fuel rods" (Broad 1983).

Eventually, male department heads Jim Smith and Jerry Cooper, two former members of the Kerr-McGee plant management, validated most of Silkwood's allegations about the company's neglect and disregard for safety. Smith challenged Kerr-McGee's rationalization of what happened to substantial amounts of plutonium that went missing from its inventory. Arguing that the plant operation was dangerously mismanaged and in conflict with AEC guidelines, Smith and Cooper also asserted that leaking pipes and defective equipment had contaminated workers with plutonium. Instead of stopping production, the men said that upper management ordered employees to keep working and only authorized repair to any leaks to take place during slow production days.

The two former managers also claimed that Kerr-McGee regularly shipped plutonium waste in leaking containers that sometimes spilled on the plant grounds and may have been responsible for contaminating an area in Kentucky where the waste was buried. "An even more alarming problem is the possibility that plutonium was diverted from the plant. On two occasions, Smith says, Kerr-McGee did not recover plutonium that the company had originally reported missing to the AEC. As many as fifty pounds, enough for four nuclear bombs, could be lost if Smith is correct" (Kohn 1977).

Soon after Silkwood's death and without explanation, Kerr-McGee switched from an acid-mix process to a more expensive system to eliminate the problem with leaking containers that Jim Smith and Jerry Cooper had alleged. That switch, along with Jerry Cooper's transfer into the plutonium plant, was part of a reform effort that followed humiliating national publicity concerning Silkwood's death. "I was sent in to be part of the solution," Cooper says. "But nothing would ever have been done at that point if the Silkwood case hadn't called attention to the plant" (Kohn 1977).

In August 1975, the National Organization for Women asked for another Justice Department investigation of the case. Kerr-McGee closed the Oklahoma City plant in 1976, fourteen months after Silkwood's death, when Westinghouse, which had been buying its fuel rods, complained of their poor quality and refused to renew its contract. "Three months later the last fuel rods were assembled and the front gates of the plant were locked. The Energy Research and Development Administration (ERDA), which inherited partial jurisdiction over the nuclear industry when the AEC was abolished in January 1975, had decided not to renew Kerr-McGee's contract. Some feel this was due to lingering doubts about the Silkwood controversy" (Kohn 1977). Others felt it was connected to the company's report that it had found ninety pounds of plutonium missing from its stocks.

Karen Silkwood's father won a $1.3 million lawsuit against Kerr-McGee in a nine-week trial over seen by Judge Frank G. Theis of Wichita, Kansas (UAW.org 2017). "Eleanor Smeal, the national president of NOW, said in a statement yesterday that the decision in favor of Miss Silkwood's estate was 'particularly gratifying' to the organization, which had viewed the Silkwood case as 'a symbol of feminist concerns about health and safety in the workplace'" ("Activist to Protest Symbol" 1979).

"Nine years after his girlfriend's death, Stephens still believes the car wreck that killed Karen Silkwood may have been 'caused.' He recalls that Silkwood's allegations of safety violations and her union 'spying' didn't make her the most popular employee at Kerr-McGee's Cimarron plutonium plant back in 1974" (Triplett 1984).

DEPICTION AND CULTURAL CONTEXT

Like *Norma Rae, Silkwood* is often seen as a response to the second wave of feminism of the early 1970s. The fact that *Silkwood* came out four years after both *The China Syndrome* and *Norma Rae* caused critic Roger Ebert to write, "I pictured it as an angry political expose, maybe *The China Syndrome, Part 2* . . . That could have been a good movie, but predictable. Mike Nichols' 'Silkwood' is not predictable. That's because he's not telling the story of a conspiracy, he's telling the story of a human life. There are villains in his story, but none with motives we can't understand. After Karen is dead and the movie is over, we realize this is a lot more movie than perhaps we were expecting." Ebert also recognized the similarity to *Norma Rae* and saw the film as "the story of some American workers. They happen to work in a Kerr-McGee nuclear plant in Oklahoma, making plutonium fuel rods for nuclear reactors. But they could just as easily be working in a Southern textile mill (there are echoes of 'Norma Rae'), or on an assembly line, or for the Chicago public schools. The movie isn't about plutonium, it's about the American working class. Its villains aren't monsters; they're organization men, labor union hotshots and people afraid of losing their jobs" (Ebert 1983).

The story of Karen Silkwood captured so much attention it became the basis of many articles, a few books, and an episode of the television newspaper drama *Lou Grant* before becoming the film by Nora Ephron and Alice Arlen. In his review of the Howard Kohn book, Pete Hamill notes that one of the issues regarding the Silkwood case is that "the same process that creates instant myths also robs their subjects of genuine life while transforming them into bits of slogans or posters waved at rallies." He also cites the effect of Howard Kohn's book as it is not a work of nonfiction but rather, like *In Cold Blood*, a nonfiction novel.

In many ways, what happened to Karen Silkwood's reputation in court was similar to what happens to rape victims who come forward or to the reputations of young Black men who are killed by police. In the trial her family instigated to pursue damages, "Defense Attorney William Paul argued that she was emotionally unstable and possibly had been affected by the use of tranquilizers. Paul said she had become deeply involved in a bitter fight between her union and the company and charged that she had set out to prove that the plant was dangerous by making herself seriously ill. She was, he suggested, kinky." Words such as *kinky* and *unstable* are not synonymous. They are negative, and the defense attorney chose them specifically. Lawyers for Kerr-McGee even went so far as to suggest that the plutonium in her system did not come from the most obvious reason—her daily work with dangerous chemicals—but "hypothesized that Silkwood had intentionally taken plutonium home to contaminate herself" (Latson 2014).

A *New York Times* article on *Silkwood*, written by William Broad, ended with, "In short, the evidence in the case suggests that Miss Silkwood was not a nuclear Joan of Arc but an activist outraged by terrible working conditions who mistook a technician's shortcut for corporate cover-up and eventually became a victim of her own infatuation with drugs. That tale, while not very seductive, at least sticks to the facts" (Broad 1983). Broad writes as if he had been privy to some special evidence of his own that allowed him to make that accusation. The audacity is about as hard to swallow as the idea that the bottle of Snapple in Trayvon Martin's hands looked like a gun to the vigilante who killed him.

Kerr-McGee's official reaction was that the movie was a work of fiction. Company spokesperson Ann Adams labelled the film "a highly fictionalized Hollywood dramatization," which portrays Kerr-McGee in a "false and defamatory manner." She declined to name specific scenes or dialogue in the film, which Kerr-McGee found objectionable. James Ikard, Silkwood estate attorney (who appears as an extra in the film), said, "I think the film in many ways portrays Kerr-McGee in a better light than they're really entitled to . . . I don't think they came across well (in the film), but I do think they're not treated as badly as they're entitled to be treated" (Triplett 1984).

The company tried to paint Silkwood as a lunatic out to destroy its reputation with lies. Here, the female writers let their subject down in that they dramatize that Silkwood *volunteered* for the union negotiating committee. It's important to remember that, in reality, her colleagues saw her as responsible, illustrated by the fact that she was elected to the bargaining committee for the plant's union and testified for them. The film further contributes to this misconception when it insinuates that Silkwood's own instinct for survival pushed her into union activity when, in fact, she had joined a union strike only a few months after taking the job at the plant in 1972 and managed to keep her job when the strike failed and most other employees who took part were fired.

In her book *Women Labor Activists in the Movies: Nine Depictions of Workplace Organizers*, Jennifer Borda claims that showing Silkwood as a flawed female makes her motivation for activism uncertain, using this quote from the screenwriter to back up her claim: "Nora Ephron attributes this effect to the filmmaker's efforts to get, 'closer to the truth' about [Karen] than a great deal of what had been written . . . A lot of which either sanctified her or attempted to blacken her entirely" (Borda 2011). In another interview, Ephron defined Silkwood as "an extremely complicated, occasionally self-destructive woman who was, incidentally, a hero" (Bonavoglia 1984).

Some of the verifiable truths brought up in the film include the fact that Silkwood had been a national honor student, won a scholarship to Lamar College from the Business and Professional Women's Association, and had aspirations of becoming a scientist. Also, the film never explains why her children live with their father. His wealthy father hired divorce lawyers that she couldn't afford. Her family and her boyfriend said had taken the Kerr-McGee job, despite its distance from them, to earn more money faster and, therefore, win her children back faster.

Outside of the murkiness of who Silkwood was as a woman, watching the film gave audiences information about the reality of working with plutonium. Silkwood had been exposed to so much radiation poisoning that cancer was essentially guaranteed, according to a doctor who testified in the case. Also, "During a Congressional investigation, Dr. Karl Morgan, a former health physicist at the Oak Ridge National Laboratory, said he had never seen a facility so poorly run" (Broad 1983). "Kerr-McGee had gone out of its way to downplay the dangers, its health manual saying in capital letters: RADIATION IS SAFE. That is a terrible half-truth. Although radiation from plutonium is easily stopped by a piece of tissue paper or, in humans, by dead cells that make up the outer layer of skin, once the metal enters the body through the nose or mouth it fires a continuous barrage of subatomic 'bullets' into soft tissues, wreaking havoc with cellular machinery. Caught in a lung, a dust-size speck of plutonium is widely thought to be able to cause cancer" (Broad 1983).

As to its place in the history of labor unions as fodder for screenplays, after World War II, a new interest in social justice films arose. These included films such as *Best Years of Our Lives* (1946), which dealt with a disabled American veteran returning home, and *Gentleman's Agreement* (1947), based on Laura Z. Hobson's novel about a journalist posing as a Jewish man to expose widespread anti-Semitism earned accolades. Then anti-Communist fear spread through Hollywood via the House Un-American Activities Committee (HUAC), changing the playing field once again. As a subject of films, labor unions were out, even though the existence of the International Alliance of Theatrical Stage Employees (IATSE) angered other film industry creatives, who were forced to take pay cuts during the Depression, though those union members had not. This effectively supported the rise of the Screen Actors Guild (SAG) and the Writers Guild of America (WGA) in 1933, followed by the Director's Guild (DGA) in 1936. Even in *Silkwood*, "Big Unions aren't exactly lauded either. The Washington reps eagerly entreat the guileless Karen to stick her neck out for their aims. What conclusions can we make when Karen sleeps with another Union rep—is it evidence of more Silkwood flakiness, or more exploitation by the Union?" (Erickson 2017).

From a writing standpoint, the film was credited with making all the side characters distinctive, but that can lead to stereotyping as well, since each has so few moments on screen to set themselves in the mind of the viewer. Stereotypes are a form of shorthand writers fall back on when working with ensembles. For instance, Silkwood's union leader Paul Stone (Ron Silver) pushes too hard, seemingly much more interested in the doctored negatives than the health issues. This makes him too much of a stereotypical Jewish male from New York. Meanwhile, as the film took place in Oklahoma, the filmmakers made sure to include an indigenous character, Morgan (played by Fred Ward), but he's stereotypically stealthy and protective of Silkwood, as in this example from the script:

> Karen is digging through a filing cabinet, trying to find the film negatives and records from the plant. When she turns around, she sees Morgan next to her and nearly screams.

Karen Silkwood : [gasps] Morgan! . . . Jesus you scared me!
Morgan : Had to.
Karen Silkwood : . . . I'm doin' somethin' good.
Morgan : I know what you're doing, and you're the wrong person to be doing it. It's dangerous . . . that's all I'm going to say.

While that exchange shows him to be on her side, Glenn Erickson of *CineSavant* found him to be "a deadpan Indian who likes to tell demeaning Indian jokes" (2017).

Likewise, the film is often lauded for its early and progressive depiction of a lesbian, played by Cher. When we meet Angela, a friend of Dolly's who spent the night, Drew and Karen express no problems with a lesbian roommate, quite modern for a mainstream film in 1983. Karen and Dolly share a scene where Karen says, "The only thing everybody says I'm crazy about is to live with you," and Dolly answers, "You mean, with a dyke?" But the portrayal keeps one stereotypical aspect when Dolly admits that she loves Karen. Karen defers, saying it's in a deeper way than she can reciprocate.

A smaller issue with depictions and the changing meaning of symbols comes from the fact that Karen and Drew share a bed with a giant Confederate flag hanging on the wall behind them. In 1983, this was still seen as a code for rebellious and independent Southern characters. In 2020, it became synonymous with its original intent, as a standard for white supremacy, sedition, and traitors. Likewise, the massive amount of smoking in the film is also a remnant of earlier films, which used smoking as another sign of independence and rebellion in a character, rather than the risk of early death from lung cancer. In 2020, it becomes almost satirical to see people worry about unexplained exposure to radiation while drawing deadly toxins into their own bodies of their own accord. Finally, the film includes a rape joke, no longer accepted in 2020. Karen says to Dolly, "Leave the key under the mat. I don't want to get raped 'cause you lost your key again." Dolly retorts, "Who's gonna rape you that you haven't already f—?"

In terms of its popular culture collateral, the decontamination sound and scene are re-created in homage in *Monsters Inc*. The term "Silkwood shower" has likewise been referenced in shows including *Seinfeld*, *Mystery Science Theatre 3000*, *Sabrina the Teenage Witch*, *Will and Grace*, *Everybody Hates Chris*, and *iZombie*.

FURTHER READING

Blades, John. 1990. "When Nora Met Alice: Pals Ephron and Arlen Muse on Their Script for Success in High-Stakes Hollywood." *Chicago Tribune*, C1. ProQuest Historical Newspapers, Chicago Tribune.
Bonavoglia, Angela. 1984. "Review of *Silkwood*." *Cineaste* 13: 38–40.

Borda, Jennifer L. 2011. *Women Labor Activists in the Movies: Nine Depictions of Workplace Organizers, 1954–2005*. Jefferson City, NC: McFarland.
Broad, William J. 1983. "Fact and Legend Clash in *Silkwood*." *New York Times*. https://www.nytimes.com/1983/12/11/arts/fact-and-legend-clash-in-silkwood.html.
Ebert, Roger. 1983. "Silkwood." Roger Ebert. https://www.rogerebert.com/reviews/silkwood-1983.
Erickson, Glenn. 2017. "Silkwood." https://trailersfromhell.com/silkwood/.
Hamill, Pete. 1981. "The Life and Death of an Idealist." December 13, 1981, Section 7. https://www.nytimes.com/1981/12/13/books/the-life-and-death-of-an-idealist.html.
The Hollywood Reporter. 1983. "*Silkwood*: THR's 1983 Review." https://www.hollywoodreporter.com/news/silkwood-review-1983-movie-751496.
Howe Enterprise. 2017. "35 Years Ago This Week, 'Silkwood' Was Filmed in Howe." https://howeenterprise.com/35-years-ago-week-howe-became-movie-set/.
Kohn, Howard. 1977. "Karen Silkwood Was Right in Plutonium Scandal: Plant Managers Add Fuel to the Fire." *Rolling Stone*. https://www.rollingstone.com/culture/culture-news/karen-silkwood-was-right-in-plutonium-scandal-47908/.
Kohn, Howard. 1981. *Who Killed Karen Silkwood?* New York: Summit Books.
Latson, Jennifer. 2014. "The Nuclear-Safety Activist Whose Mysterious Death Inspired a Movie." *Time*. https://time.com/3574931/karen-silkwood/.
Mulvey, Laura. 1975. "Visual Pleasure and Narrative Cinema." *Screen* 16 (3): 6–18.
New York Times. 1979. "Karen Silkwood: From Activist to Protest Symbol." May 19, 1979. https://www.nytimes.com/1979/05/19/archives/karen-silkwood-from-activist-to-protest-symbol-apartment.html.
New York Times. 1979. "Trial Nears End in Silkwood Death." May 6, 1979, 49. https://www.nytimes.com/1979/05/06/archives/trial-nears-an-end-in-silkwood-death-source-of-exposure-to.html.
Rashke, Richard. 2000. *The Killing of Karen Silkwood: The Story Behind the Kerr-McGee Plutonium Case*. 2nd ed. Ithaca, NY: ILR Press.
Sterritt, David. 1984. "*Silkwood*: Good Intentions Are Fogged in by Ambiguity." *The Christian Science Monitor*. https://www.csmonitor.com/1984/0105/010506.html.
Triplett, Gene. 1984. "Silkwood's Boyfriend Likes Film." *The Oklahoman*. https://www.oklahoman.com/article/2050536/silkwoods-boyfriend-likes-film.
UAW.org. 2018. "Karen Silkwood." https://uaw.org/karen-silkwood/?

Chapter 4

The Joy Luck Club (1993)

Written by Amy Tan and Ronald Bass; Directed by Wayne Wang
Hollywood Pictures, 1 hr., 19 min.

INTRODUCTION

In 1989, Amy Tan published her first novel, *The Joy Luck Club*. Part autobiography, part biography, the book sold two hundred and seventy-five thousand copies in hardback, making it the first best-selling novel by an Asian American writer since Maxine Hong Kingston's *The Woman Warrior* (1976). In a back-handed compliment, a reviewer from *The Paris Review* said, "If Oprah Winfrey had had a book club in 1989, she surely would have selected it" (Fickle 2014). The book's ubiquity created a demand for books by and about Asian Americans, as well as revitalized the mother-daughter or generational novel.

Wayne Wang approached Tan to see if she'd like to collaborate on adapting her novel into a movie. Considered the first Asian American director to have significant power in Hollywood, Wang had already had some minor success with *Dim Sum: A Little Bit of Heart* (1985) and *Eat a Bowl of Tea* (1989). Wang said he wanted to do the film because, as the child of Hong-King immigrants, he identified with the daughters' stories. "I despised my parents because they were from the Old World, not knowing what they'd gone through to give us the life we had" (Johnston 1994).

Tan and Wang worried that neither production companies nor American moviegoers were ready for an all-Asian cast movie, particularly one written and directed by Asian Americans. In 1990, Tan and Wang met with Ronald

Bass, a mainstream Hollywood screenwriter with a proven track record. Two years previous, Bass had won a best original screenplay Oscar for *Rainman*. Bass would cowrite the screenplay with Tan, helping her figure out how to take a sweeping, multigenerational story and distill it to a marketable two-hour film.

Intent on keeping control of the project, Tan also went shopping for producers who would cooperate with her vision. She found them in writer and director Oliver Stone and Disney Studios head, Jeffrey Katzenberg. Stone was a particularly odd choice because, at the time, he was underfire for anti-Asian xenophobia for *The Year of the Dragon* (1985). Characters in the film used terms like *chink*, *yellow nigger*, and *slant-eyes*. Wang weighed in on the controversy, calling Stone's characters "violent" and "evil." Stone responded by calling Wang's films "boring" (Johnston 1994). The film's director defended the script by pointing out the film's anti-Asian characters were roundly condemned for their racism. Nonetheless, the script won Stone a Razzie nomination for Worst Screenplay.

Tan brought Wang and Stone together, and Stone joined the project as an executive producer. The group then took the project to Katzenberg, though Disney Studios had a record of overinterfering with film productions. Tan argued that the film, like the book, would have appeal to a diverse audience. "Many [Americans] didn't go through wars and severe economic depression. Yet we are faced with a lot of choices in our lives. . . . choices that weren't allowable to the previous generation" (Johnston 1994). Disney agreed to the project, granting it a minuscule $10.5 million budget. The small budget let Disney gamble on Tan and Wang by not meddling with the story.

The budget left no room for name stars, though, to be fair, there were very few big-name Asian American stars in Hollywood at the time anyway. Many of the actors cast in the film would go on to great success in both films and television. Ming-Na Wen, for example, voiced Mulan in the Disney films of that name and starred in *E.R.*, *Agents of S.H.I.E.L.D.*, and much more, while Rosalind Chao would star in both *Star Trek: The Next Generation* and *Star Trek: Deep Space Nine*, as well as dozens of movies.

SUMMARY

The film begins with a voice-over parable about a duck that grew into a swan. A woman and the swan sailed across the ocean to America. The woman tells the swan that her daughter will have a perfect life in America, but the immigration officials take the swan, leaving her with one feather. She says she will give the feather to her daughter and say, "This feather may look worthless, but it comes from afar and carries with it my good intentions."

The film visually opens on a mix-race family party. June (Ming-Na Wen), a young Chinese American woman, joins three older women in a game of mahjong. There is an empty seat where her mother Suyuan (Kieu Chinh) used to sit. Suyuan has died. This is the Joy Luck Club and also the "aunties." The women talk and remember their pasts.

In the first paired remembrance, as a young girl, June plays the piano. Her mother wants her to be a piano prodigy, but June is not interested. She performs badly at a recital and wants to quit the piano. June's mom makes her continue playing. "I wish I were dead. Like them. The babies you killed in China." June's mother Suyaun was a young mother with two babies in a cart. With many other people, she was fleeing some unknown horror in World War II China. Suyuan became progressively sicker and left her babies on the roadside. Back to the present, one of the aunties tells June that the two babies have been found, alive. They want June to go to China and tell them about their mother.

In the second pairing, Aunty Lindo (Tsai Chin) remembers when she was four and her mother promised her to Mrs. Huang. When Lindo is fifteen, her family moves away, except for Lindo, who is turned over to the Huangs and married to their prepubescent son. He never touches her, though he tells his mother it is Lindo's fault she is not pregnant. Lindo tells the Huangs she had a dream that their ancestors want the son to marry a servant girl, who is already pregnant. Lindo leaves the Huangs and moves to Shanghai to start a new life.

Lindo's daughter Waverly (Tamlyn Tomita) is a chess champion and so good that she appears on the cover of *LIFE* magazine. Waverly doesn't like that her mother uses her to show off and swears she will never play chess again. Her family ignores her. Waverly announces she will play chess again, but Lindo is unimpressed. Her self-confidence gone, Waverly cannot win at chess anymore. Years later, she brings her white boyfriend Rich (Christopher Rich) to dinner. He makes several mistakes, demonstrating his ignorance of Chinese manners. At a beauty parlor, adult Waverly tells Lindo that nothing she does can please her. Lindo assures Waverly that she loves her and likes Rich.

In the third pairing, Aunty Ying-Ying (Frances Nuyen) meets and marries an attractive, well-to-do man in China, and they have a son. He brings a prostitute home, hands the son to the woman, pushes his wife to the floor, and takes his lady friend to their bedroom. Grieving, Ying-Ying lets their baby son drown in the bath. In America, she remarries and has a daughter, but she cannot escape the depression that followed her from China. She says her daughter Lena (Lauren Tom) has no spirit because she had none to give her. Lena eventually marries a controlling man who makes her unhappy. Ying-Ying tells Lena to stand up for herself or leave the husband. Lena says she can't, but her mother says she can. When we next see Lena (at the party), she is with a new man.

The fourth aunty, An-mei (Lisa Lu), remembers when she was four years old and her mother was kicked out of the house. We find out that An-mei's father died, and while her mother was visiting his shrine, she met a woman who invited her home. The woman was Second Wife, and she helped her husband rape An-mei's mother. Pregnant and rejected by her husband's family, the mother must return to the rapist's house, where she becomes Fourth Wife, and Second Wife takes the baby for her own. An-mei's mother killed herself. An-mei threatens the husband and Second Wife with her mother's ghost, and they swear to treat her like the daughter of an honored first wife.

Back in the present, An-mei's daughter Rose Hsu Jordan (Rosalind Chao) remembers how she met and married Ted, a rich, white guy. She gives up her life to take care of Ted (Andrew McCarthy). They grow apart and agree to divorce. An-mei tells Rose that she must know her worth, so Rose tells Ted she will not sell the house, and that this distance is her fault because she acted like she had no worth. Later at the party, we see they Ted and Rose are still together, reconciled and happy.

The film returns to June's point of view and how she spent much of her life thinking she disappointed her mother. She remembers when her mother told her she has "best-quality heart." As the party ends, Aunty Lindo tells June the twins in China do not know their mother is dead. June travels to China to meet them. She takes with her the white swan feather, given to her by her father before her trip. She tells the twins she has come to bring them her mother's hopes.

The film first premiered to the Asian American Journalists Association and later at the Telluride and Toronto Film Festivals. It opened nationwide in October 1993 and earned a respectable $33 million at the box office. *Jurassic Park*, which was also released in 1993, earned over a billion dollars worldwide, while *Schindler's List* made $320 million and, along with *Philadelphia*, pretty much owned that year's film awards. *The Joy Luck Club* garnered a few nominations and awards, including a Top Ten Films of the Year from the National Board of Review.

HISTORICAL CONTEXT

The first wave of Chinese immigration to the United States began in earnest between 1850 and 1853, though small numbers of Chinese had immigrated in the first decades of the century. Chinese persons were so rare that the Carne brothers exhibited Afong Moy, the first female Chinese immigrant, in 1834. Moy's stage appearances made much of her high status, diminutive size, and four-inch feet, the result of childhood foot binding. Moy's popularity led to a rash of Chinese women offered up to Americans as curiosities by showmen like P. T. Barnum. Conjoined twins Chang and Eng Bunker made their fame even earlier than Moy, though technically they were ethnically Chinese from Thailand (then called Siam, thus siamese twins). The twins retired from show business in 1839 and purchased a North Carolina plantation, where they owned thirty-nine slaves (Chang 2003).

The discovery of gold in California Territory, coupled with the hardships caused by the Taiping Rebellion (1850–1864), a deadly Chinese war, caused Chinese immigrants to flood into California. By 1952, there were twenty-five thousand more Chinese in the United States than there had been in 1848, most of them traveling to San Francisco. Unlucky Chinese men fell into the hands of "coolie traders" in Canton and other port cities and were bought and sold for transport to Peru, Hawaii, Cuba, or the United States. The Pacific crossing took four to eight weeks, depending on the time of year and weather, and ships were notoriously overcrowded, filthy, and underprovisioned. Those who made it to San Francisco got off the ships half-starved, sick from scurvy and dysentery, to find themselves in a city that didn't really want them.

The Gold Rush transformed San Francisco into one of the largest cities in America. More than half the city's population was foreign-born, though few more "foreign" than the Chinese. Reviled for their difference in appearance, religion, cultural habits, and food, Chinese immigrants were relegated to the most dangerous, low-paying jobs. At the same time, their reputation for hard work and sobriety made them valuable workers. While a few Chinese men (there were essentially no female immigrants in these early years) got lucky and found enough gold to become rich, most ended up working for other miners or mining companies for extremely low wages. In 1852, the California state legislature declared Chinese Americans "a great moral and social evil" and enacted two new taxes aimed at discouraging further immigration (Chang 2003). Legalized persecution and oppression of Asian Americans had officially begun.

Reviled and oppressed, Chinese Americans banded together in "China Towns," where they created facsimiles of life in China. Most immigrants came to America with the idea that their sojourn was temporary and that they would, someday, return to their families in China. This is one of the reasons there were so few female Chinese immigrants—they stayed behind to care for elders and children, while men went to America and sent home money for the family's support.

Railroad building projects also employed a large number of Chinese immigrants. The Central Pacific Railroad won the contract to lay track from Sacramento, east through the California desert, and over Sierra Nevada Mountains. The job was tailor-made for Chinese immigrants, whose reputation for hard work and a willingness to work for less than other immigrant groups made them popular with railroad company owners, if not with white workers. By 1868, the Central Pacific Railroad began recruiting workers in China. The Burlingame Treaty (1868) gave China "most-favored nation" trading status and allowed for free migration of Chinese citizens. Chinese American railroad workers proved more disease-resistant than workers of

European descent because they boiled their drinking water for tea. One team of Chinese railroad workers laid ten miles of track in one day, a record that has never been beaten (Ong 1985).

By the late 1870s, both gold mining and railroad building had run their course, and the United States government, fueled by anti-Chinese sinophobia, decided to effectively end Chinese immigration. In the 1870s, a white labor organization calling itself the Workingmen's Party flooded California with anti-Chinese propaganda, saying the Chinese could never be real Americans and constituted a threat to white workers. The American Federation of Labor (AFL), a labor union, followed suit and became a national force for anti-Chinese sentiment. In the Chinese Massacre of 1870 in Los Angeles, racists invaded Chinatown and killed at least seventeen Chinese Americans.

Sinophobia peaked with the passage of the Chinese Exclusion Act (1882). The law was the first in United States history to entirely ban a specific racial group. The act also made it impossible for Chinese immigrants to become American citizens and denied them property-ownership rights. Americans followed up the act with a wave of anti-Chinese violence called the "Driving-Out" period, which included the Rock Springs Massacre (1882) and the Hells Canyon Massacre (1887). A bubonic plague outbreak (1900–1904) in San Francisco's Chinatown only exacerbated anti-Chinese sentiment across the nation (Chang 2003).

By the turn of the century, the United States had firmly embraced the notion of "yellow peril." This ideology held that American democracy was in danger from hoards of invading Asians, none of whom could ever be Americanized because they were subhuman (a common refrain in racists ideologies of all stripes). The Chinese and other Asian immigrant groups were often portrayed in the press as human-monkey hybrids. Yellow peril (or yellow terror) proponents believed that Asian men were engaged in sex-trafficking schemes by kidnapping white women and selling them for sexual purposes. The hysteria reached such heights that Congress passed the White Slave Act of 1910 (also known as the Mann Act), which made it illegal to transport women across state lines for purposes of prostitution or debauchery (Frayling 2014).

The United States remained anti-Chinese immigrants until Japan's hostility to both the United States and China made the latter two countries allies. The Second Sino-Japanese War began in 1931 when Japan invaded Manchuria in northern China. After setting up a puppet state with Chinese emperor Puyi at its nominal head, Japan began plans for taking control of the entirety of China. In the summer of 1937, Japan launched a full-scale invasion of China and laid siege to Shanghai. The conflict became notorious for war atrocities when the Japanese took Nanjing. The Nanjing Massacre or Rape of Nanjing (1937) resulted in the deaths of upward of two hundred thousand Chinese civilians and disarmed combatants.

Japan continued its assault on Chinese cities in 1938 and 1939, capturing several regional capitals and decimating the Chinese Army and Air Force. China had some hard-won victories in 1939 and 1940, but ongoing Japanese atrocities in northeastern China made life exceedingly difficult for the Chinese peasantry. Tensions between Chinese Communists and the existing Chinese government only exacerbated the Chinese people's problems. Before the conflict was over, twenty-five million Chinese civilians were killed in the hostilities (Hsiung 1992).

In 1940, President Franklin D. Roosevelt allowed China to buy war supplies from the United States and instituted an embargo on Japan, thus declaring China an ally of the United States. Soon after, the United States began sending military supplies to China (Chang 2003). After the Japanese bombed Pearl Harbor in December 1941, the United States declared war on Japan, and the Sino-Japanese war was essentially folded into World War II.

Prominent Chinese Americans lobbied for increased immigration given the very real humanitarian crisis in China. They also educated Americans about the difference between the Chinese and Japanese in the hopes of staving off racial violence aimed at any Asian American mistaken for Japanese. Soong Mei-ling, the wife of the president of China, Chiang Kai-shek, visited the United States in 1942. Her tour was nothing less than a triumph, in great part because Americans approved of her Western ways. She addressed the U.S. Congress to a standing ovation. Soong's visit and speech paved the way for the Magnuson Act (1943), repealing the Chinese Exclusionary Act (Leong 2005). The repeal made it possible for Chinese Americans to become citizens, but limited Chinese immigration to 105 visas a year and continued the property-ownership ban.

When the war ended in 1945, China regained all the territory formerly claimed by Japan, including Manchuria. The decade's long conflict left China in shambles. The economy crumbled, inflation spiked, and the government did little but make things worse. Millions of displaced Chinese roamed the countryside, homeless and starving. Civil war between the Communists (under Mao Zedong) and Nationalists (under Chiang Kai-shek) created further displacement and misery for the Chinese people. The United States declared itself neutral in the conflict. That war concluded in 1949, and the Communists' victory transformed the Republic of China into the People's Republic of China, while anti-Communist Nationalists made Taiwan their home (Hsiung 1992).

The "aunties" in *The Joy Luck Club* were part of the post-World War II immigration wave, refugees from a war-torn country that slopped from one war to the next in the 1940s. The women meet in San Francisco in 1949, a date that suggests the women fled the Chinese Civil War that began after World War II, though the film never specifies each woman's immigration story (the novel is clearer). Suyuan, for example, survived the Japanese invasion of Guiling, which took place in 1944. That invasion killed more than two hundred thousand Chinese civilians and wounded another 430,000 more. In the novel, Suyuan is found sick on the roadside after abandoning her babies, nursed back to health, remarries, and immigrates to the United States soon after.

In reality, few Chinese immigrants came to the United States in the twentieth century until 1965, when the U.S. Congress abolished quotas on Asian-Pacific immigrants. Chinese immigrants made up only a small portion of the overall Asian immigration, but nonetheless, Chinese-American populations swelled from two hundred and seventeen thousand to eight hundred and five thousand between 1960 and 1980.

Late twentieth-century Chinese immigrants faced many of the same challenges as their nineteenth-century counterparts. Sinophobia or anti-Asian ideologies continue to plague the nation, as did a more general anti-immigrant sentiment, at least among some segments of the American population. Unlike more recent Asian immigrant groups, Chinese Americans have long-established enclaves or "Chinatowns," as well as decades-old social and political institutions. Also, China's status as an ally in the 1940s made many Americans view Chinese immigrants with less negativity than in the decades before World War II.

The twenty-first century has brought a renewal of anti-Chinese sentiment to the United States. In early 2020, President Trump referred to the deadly COVID-19 virus as "the Chinese virus," on several occasions to blame the global pandemic on the Chinese. Months later, he called COVID-19 "the Kung flu," at a Tulsa, Oklahoma, rally. He was not alone in his racist ideologies. From San Diego to New York City, news outlets and social justice groups report a rise in racially motivated violence against Americans of Asian descent in 2020.

The problem became so pervasive that the Asian Pacific Policy & Planning Council launched a website where people can report anti-Asian hate crimes. By June 2020, the site had collected more than 2,000 incident reports, 502 of which specifically mentioned China or Chinese Americans. The report divides hate incidents into five categories: virulent animosity against anyone perceived of as Chinese, scapegoating of China, anti-immigrant nationalism (as in "go back to your own country"), parroting of the term "Chinese virus," and orientalist and racist depictions of Chinese people as dirty and/or diseased people from a backward nation (Borja et al. 2020). Excepting the "Chinese virus," none of these categories of racist expression are new. Chinese immigrants in the 1850s would have been all too familiar with each racist category.

DEPICTION AND CULTURAL CONTEXT

Movies like *The Joy Luck Club* or, more recently, *Crazy Rich Asians*, go a long way to "normalizing" Asian Americans. It would not be inaccurate to say there were no movies like *The Joy Luck Club* in 1993, which might be one of the reasons it generated controversy from the moment of its release. The non-Asian public loved it, as its box office returns can attest, but some literary critics took umbrage at the cultural phenomenon created by both the film and the book. One scholar referred to the book as a "powerful arbiter of middle-brow taste," of the sort found in Oprah Book Club selections (Fickle 2014). The very fact that the book was made into a movie was damning to serious literature critics, who seem to equate popularity with bad literature. Another reviewer said the book was too "relentlessly therapeutic" and "consciously self-improving" to qualify as serious literature. Others pointed to the way Tan's gentle approach to race and immigration issues soothed and reassured anxious middle-class white readers. Indeed, both the novel and the movie became a favorite target for Asian American critics and scholars. Tan's work has been called neo-Orientalist, neoconservative, and even neo-racist (Adams 2006). This polarized response, between adoration and disdain, suggests the difficulty of mixing immigrant stories with popular fiction and film.

To fully understand the controversy surrounding *The Joy Luck Club*, it's helpful to understand the history of Hollywood's profoundly troubled portrayal of Asian people in film. The 1923 *Mystery of Dr. Fu Man Chu* introduced filmgoers to what became an archetypal supervillain, the evil Chinese mastermind. For the next two decades, Fu Man Chu plotted to kill white men and kidnap white women for nefarious sexual purposes. The character embodied "yellow peril" in that he was fundamentally "other" and dangerous to "real" Americans. The Fu Man Chu archetype was reproduced in countless films and became one of two main stereotypes Hollywood employed when portraying Asian men. The other stereotype functioned as Fu Man Chu's opposite: the emasculated, passive, eager to please Chinese servant type personified by the Hop Sing character in television's *Bonanza* (Frayling 2014).

Representations of Asian women were no less stereotypical and repugnant. "madame butterflies" or "China dolls" were characters willing to sacrifice themselves for their white lovers or betray their own country or culture to some white protagonist. These "good" Asian women, not unlike the Pocahontas myth, consciously or subconsciously recognized the superiority of white culture and white men and submitted themselves to that superiority. In their submission, these stereotypical female types are docile, fragile, and attractive in a manner that meets Western standards of femininity (Lee 2018; Leong 2005).

The "dragon lady" stereotype stands in opposition to madame butterfly and the China doll. Coldly beautiful and sociopathically unfeeling, the dragon lady schemes, seduces, and murders to accomplish her goals, which are always self-serving (Lee 2018). Anna May Wong, the first Chinese American actress of note, made her living playing dragon ladies, slinking from scene to scene, plotting deeds as nefarious as any ever carried out by Dr. Fu Man Chu. She also played plenty of China dolls, as seen in her a seemingly endless parade of slave girls and prostitutes with a hearts of gold characters (Hodges 2004).

In the 1920s and 1930s, Anna May Wong became the best-known Asian actor in America in spite of, or perhaps because of, the stereotypical nature of her roles. The Chinese American community criticized Wong for taking demeaning roles, but in reality, Wong had little choice. Like Hattie McDaniel, the first Black actor to win an Oscar for her portrayal of Mammy in Gone with the Wind (1939), another racist stereotype, Wong did not have the cultural power to shift Hollywood off racial stereotyping. Despite Wong's fame, Metro-Goldwyn Mayer (MGM) declined to cast her for the lead role in Pearl Buck's *The Good Earth*. Instead, MGM cast Luise Rainer, a white woman made up to look Chinese—a practice called yellow face. Wong left Hollywood for a time but returned to lobby for the Chinese war effort. In 1951, she became the first Chinese American actor to star in a television series, playing a detective in *The Gallery of Madame Liu-Tsong* (Hodges 2004).

The practice of yellow face was common in Hollywood. White actors played both Charlie Chan and Fu Man Chu in the years before World War II. The 1944 film *Dragon Seed*, based on another Pearl Buck novel, featured seven white actors playing Chinese characters, most notably Katharine Hepburn and Walter Huston (Leong 2005). The practice continued well into the late twentieth century. English actor Peter Sellers played Fu Man Chu in two movies, one in 1976 and another in 1980.

Like Wong, but more recently, Lucy Liu made a living playing dragon lady types, including her mafia dominatrix in *Payback* (1996), the ruthless lawyer in *Ally McBeal* (1997–2002), and Deadly Viper O-Ren in *Kill Bill, Volume 1* (2003). Liu is no more to blame for these roles than Wong was fifty years previous. Modern American cinema is rife with stereotypical images of Asian and Asian American women, from *Rush Hour 2* (2001) to *Miss Saigon* (2009), which is based on Puccini's *Madame Butterfly*, a film that enjoyed massive success and popularity in its Broadway Play version.

All these stereotypes share a sense of Asians and Asian Americans as the mysterious and exotic "other" best described as orientalist. First described by Edward Said in his 1978 book, *Orientalism*, the conceptual tool that is orientalism helps the West define itself in opposition to the Asian (and Middle-Eastern) "other." "Orientals" were seen (and to a great extent still are) as culturally backward, illogical, and either excessively violent or sexual or both (Rajgopal 2010).

On the other hand, the "model minority" is also an insidious stereotype about Asian Americans. This stereotype holds that Asian Americans are hard workers, educational strivers, conscientious, and law-abiding. Asian Americans share white middle-class values, or so says the "model-minority" stereotype, thus they are "good" immigrants. The model-minority stereotype holds that Asian Americans are hard-working or studious to the detriment of life's more frivolous pursuits, portraying Asian Americans in films as humorless fulfills that stereotype.

Even the book and film's use of mahjong has come under attack as so stereotypically Chinese as to be orientalist. The novel is structured like a mahjong game, with four sections, or "players," and one chapter titled "Rules of the Game." Tara Fickle argues that Tan's use of mahjong is less about playing to stereotypes and more about the characters using mahjong as a bridge between their old and new worlds. According to Fickle, the game also signifies the competition between these women, as well as their sisterhood as players in the same game. Moreover, the game becomes a device by which each older character tells her story and then her daughter's story. Fundamentally, mahjong becomes a literary and film device for storytelling, but the fact that the use of the game was so controversial for critics reveals the complicated nature of critical response to both the book and the film.

At least in initial reactions to the film, white or majority culture viewers and critics loved the film because they believed it avoided stereotypes and portrayed Chinese American women as assertive and even feminist. Roger Ebert called the film "a celebration of the richness of Asian American acting talent," and lauded the fact that the actors were "human and universal" (Ebert 1993). Certainly, the film's box office success suggests mainstream moviegoers enjoyed the film as much as some film critics did. Other critics pointed to the film's "universal" characters and stories as well. Communications Scholar Jing Yin points out that this claim of universality is in and of itself troubling. "Asian Americans are not 'human and universal' until they become acceptable to the mainstream (dominant culture). The claim for universality works as a mechanism for exclusion that perpetuates existing social hierarchies and power structures" (Yin 2005). Yin was not alone in this criticism. When white critics said the film is "universal," what they meant was that it was accessible to them as members of a dominant culture that has long demonized Asians and Asian Americans. Jing Yin points out it is hardly the movie's fault that mainstream America anointed the film as representative of Chinese American and even Asian American culture in general. Yet, that very fact demands scholars unpack the film's wide appeal to non–Asian Americans.

To be fair, one of the reasons literary critics dismissed both the novel and film is the same reason audiences loved both so much—the series of happy endings. That's not cool, at least not in scholarly circles. According to literary scholars, Asian American literature has three phases. The first, from the 1850s to 1960s, is a period of mostly non–Asian American writing about Asian Americans through the lens of the deviant "other." The second phase, in which most literary scholars put Tan's first book, reflects the first flowering of authentic Asian American writers who were mostly concerned with self-definition and self-representation. The third period, from the 1990s to the present, emphasizes the multiplicity of Asian American experience and identity politics that accompany those experiences (Adams 2006). Thus, to many critics, *The Joy Luck Club* represents an immature and outmoded phase of Asian-American literature.

The answer to that criticism is twofold. First, it is hardly Tan's fault that she wrote a book that not only encouraged an entire generation of writers but also created a wide audience for books by and about Asian Americans. And Tan never purported to represent the entirely of the Asian American experience. The book and the film tell the story of a specific Asian American group: post–World War II Chinese immigrant women and their American-born daughters. If viewers ignorant of Asian American culture thought it spoke to the entirety of Asian American experience, that's not the film's or Tan's fault. Rather, it's a problem best chalked up to poorly taught American history and the nation's ongoing struggle with white supremacy.

Also, why can't a film about Chinese immigrants have a happy ending? The HEA, or happily ever after, is a staple of both screenwriting and novel writing for a reason—*many* readers and viewers like it. The romance of the HEA is escapist and pleasant because it's not real. A more identity, politics-driven film, one that placed greater emphasis on the difficulties of the Chinese immigrant experience, would not have had such a wide appeal and would not have given birth to a market for Asian American–themed novels and films.

And make no mistake, *The Joy Luck Club* did just that. The novel's success suggested to book publishers that other Asian American themed novels might do as well. Dutton Books financed Gus Lee's first novel *China Boy* (1991) for an initial print run of seventy-five thousand, an unheard-of number for a first-time Asian American author. David Hwang's 1988 play *M. Butterfly* found both an audiobook and movie deal after *The Joy Luck Club*'s success, and David Wong's short story collection *Pangs of Love* (1990) won a *Los Angeles Times* book award. This is not to say that Tan singlehandedly invented Asian American literature. Maxine Hong Kingston's *Warrior Woman* made a splash a good decade before *The Joy Luck Club* and paved the way for Tan's work.

Contemporary Asian American writers acknowledge their debt to Hong and Tan. As far back as 2003, Korean American journalist and novelist, Suki Kim says, "Amy Tan and Maxine Hong Kingston paved the way for a new kind of writing. They did that whole immigrant thing. I no longer have to explain that Koreans are not the same as Japanese" (Reynolds 2003).

It's not just that *The Joy Luck Club* ties up the characters' stories into happy endings that upsets its detractors. Critics of the film also point out that it does not avoid stereotypes as thoroughly as mainstream critics would have us believe. At least two of the daughter characters fall into the China doll stereotype, in that they are slim, beautiful, soft-spoken, and subservient to men and the wives of white men, as are nearly all the mother characters in their youthful iterations. The mature mothers, on the other hand, fall into the tiger mom stereotype, with their strict and demanding parenting style (Wong 1997).

Others point out that while the female characters in the film are fully realized, the male characters are shadowy at best. Suyuan's first husband never appears in the movie, and her second husband doesn't speak until near the end of the film. Two of the Chinese husbands conform to "the gangster" stereotype in that they are rich and powerful and sexually violent. Except for June's father, all the Chinese husbands are flawed in some way. Lena's husband, for example, is a controlling and clueless jerk. The two white husbands, on the other hand, are portrayed sympathetically (Wong 1997).

For all the criticisms, the film avoids portraying Asian American women as one-dimensional types. As Shoba Rajgopal pointed out nearly twenty years after *The Joy Luck Club*'s premiere, the problem of one-dimensionality has not gone away. "The humanity of Asian and Arab women as daughters, sisters, and often as professionals . . . is hardly ever represented in the Western media. Where they do appear, it is as mindless, persecuted victims of their own culture who need to be rescued." Rajgopal also suggests the "rescue" mythologies enjoyed in American films are often of white men rescuing brown women, a narrative that reinforces orientalism by justifying the notion that overly patriarchal Asian and Middle-Eastern cultures require Western intervention (Rajgopal 2010). This fantasy overlooks the very real patriarchal exploitation of women in Western cultures and imagines that only brown women who live elsewhere are subject to oppression. To be fair, two of the daughters in *The Joy Luck Club* do marry white men, but one would be hard-pressed to argue that either woman is "saved" by their white husbands or that the white husbands are portrayed as superior to Asian American husbands. Indeed, the most sympathetic husband in the film is June's Chinese immigrant father.

Nor does *The Joy Luck Club* transform any of the women into hypersexual vamps. Anna May Wong immortalized this stereotype in *Shanghai Express* (1932). Wong plays opposite Marlene Dietrich, and both women play women who make their living from their sexuality. Unlike other movies where Wong played sexually charged characters, she did not have to die at the end of the film to atone for her sins. Instead, she walks away, into the dark, in a film-noir style more familiarly played by loner detectives. The scenes between Wong and Dietrich sizzled to such an extent that rumors the two had a love affair swirled around the film (Leong 2005). Lucy Liu steeped her portrayal of Ling Woo in *Ally McBeal* in Wong's *Shanghai Express* personae, becoming nearly a parody of the heartless and sexually powerful dragon lady. Activists argued over Liu's character. Some saw it as a reboot of a decades-old, racist stereotype, while others pointed out that Ling Woo was a powerful, central character in a television universe that had few roles of any kind for Asian American actors. A decade after *Ally McBeal*, Sandra Oh played Dr. Cristina Yang on *Grey's Anatomy*, yet another powerful but emotionally cold character that to too many critics, hearkens to the "inscrutable oriental" stereotype that underwrites the dragon lady (Rajgopal 2010).

The Joy Luck Club didn't change Hollywood immediately or even permanently, but it did suggest there was a "mainstream" (i.e., white) audience for films about Asian Americans. *Harold & Kumar Go to White Castle* (2004) transformed Asian American men into two stoner dudes trying to get a hamburger and, in so doing, subverted a whole bag of racial stereotypes. The film made $24 million and spawned a franchise of Harold and Kumar films. More recently *Seoul Searching* (2016) explored Korean America youth culture. In 2019, Mindy Kaling wrote and starred in *Late Night*, while the romantic comedy *Always Be My Maybe* won Ali Wong a People's Choice Award for Best Comedy Actor. And Lucy Liu got to retire from dragon lady roles when she played Dr. Joan Watson on the television drama *Elementary*, a character so smart and capable that she sometimes outthinks Sherlock Holmes. No longer a sidekick, Sandra Oh won a starring role in the television spy series, *Killing Eve* (2017–2020), where she plays a British intelligence investigator on the trail of a female assassin. Oh's performance has garnered her three Emmy nominations (as of 2021) for Outstanding Lead Actress in a drama, making her the first Asian American actress to be so recognized. Without a doubt, *Crazy Rich Asians* is the biggest box office success in recent years, suggesting the market for films by and about Asians still exists.

The Joy Luck Club was a notable box office success not just because it was a film about Chinese immigrants but also because it was a movie about female immigrants and the mother-daughter connection. Tan wrote the book for just this reason. "When I was writing it was so much for my mother and myself. I wanted her to know what I thought about China and what I thought about growing up in this country. And I wanted those words to almost fall off the page. . . . so the language would be simple enough, almost like a little curtain that would fall away" (Heung 1993). Tan juxtaposes the importance of mother-daughter stories against a cultural background where daughters are not nearly so important as sons and where even mothers are valued primarily for their ability to produce boy children. Each of the aunties has a tenuous and fraught relationship with her own mother or mother-in-law, but each auntie also expresses strong feelings of attachment to her daughters. Indeed, the aunties are attached to their American-born daughters as a result of the family ruptures and dislocations that led to their leaving China. And it is the three aunties who act like stand-in mothers for June, urging her to go to China to visit her dead mother's rediscovered twins. June must go to tell the twins of their mother's death and, more importantly, their mother's life. No mother is left out of the story, and even the once-lost twins deserve a "mother story."

While all of this mother-daughter narrative is the stuff of literature and literary criticism, it is not generally the stuff of popular American films. Films about women and women's stories are rare in American cinema, both in the 1990s when this film was made, and still today. Indeed, the Bechdel Test suggests the dearth of women in American movies. Popularized by an Alison Bechdel comic in 1985, the test asks only a few questions of a movie. Does the film have more than one named female character? Do the two named female characters talk to each other? And if so, do they speak of anything other than men? The test isn't designed to determine film quality or even if a film is feminist. It measures only one thing: real female characters (Bechdel 2005). And 40 percent of movies fail the test. Imagine a world where 40 percent of movies didn't have at least two male characters who talked to each other about something other than women.

A 2014 study determined that worldwide, only 31 percent of named characters in movies were women, and only 22 percent had a female protagonist or coprotagonist. A 2016 study of the top two thousand commercially successful films found that men have more dialogue than women in 78 percent of films, and a shocking number of films have no female dialogue. Men speak more even in films about female characters—men speak more than women in both Mulan and Little Mermaid. And films with women are overwhelmingly films about young women—even female doctors and lawyers are nearly always young. For women with speaking roles, the majority are twenty-one to thirty-one years old, while men forty-two to sixty-five speak the majority of male lines. Women in that same age group speak just 20 percent of the dialogue spoken by women in films (Swanson 2016). So it's not just that there aren't very many films primarily about women, but that women, especially older women, don't stand for much in American films.

And yet, in 1993, *The Joy Luck Club* experienced modest commercial success as a film about women, with primarily female characters, many of them quite a bit older than thirty-one. It's full of mother-daughter, crisscrossing narratives and women talk, talk, talk—which may be why some critics didn't like the film. It's unusual, to say the least, to have a film so relentlessly female and not hetero-normative-romance centered. The film is also nonchronological, shifting time frames and generations every time it shifts the narrative point of view. In that, perhaps, the novel and film's form mimic the nonlinear nature of matriarchy and the reciprocity of mothering (Heung 1993). Maybe that's why some people, particularly female viewers, enjoyed the film so much. The film invites the viewer into not just family stories, but mother-daughter stories and, in so doing, creates a fairy tale of a sisterhood that seems to transcend racial and class boundaries.

> ### *CRAZY RICH ASIANS*: THE CONTROVERSIES
>
> The romantic comedy *Crazy Rich Asians* took the 2018 film season by storm. Like *The Joy Luck Club*, the film was based on a novel, the first of novelist Kevin Kwan's trilogy of Singaporean stories. The film won a Golden Globe nomination for Best Film in a Musical or Comedy, as well as a Best Actress nomination for Constance Wu. The film also won nominations from the Screen Actor's Guild and the NAACP Image Awards. Perhaps more importantly, the film grossed $174.5 million in the United States and $239 million worldwide. The film's popularity spawned two sequels (still in development in 2020) based on Kwan's other two novels.
>
> Like *The Joy Luck Club* twenty-five years previous, *Crazy Rich Asians* utilized a primarily Asian cast, but the film's casting was not without its controversies. Some critics suggested the film plays to contemporary stereotypes by portraying its characters as rich, addicted to vulgar displays of materialism, and good at math and science. Others objected to the film's use of biracial, non-Chinese actors to play Chinese characters. Henry Golding, the film's Chinese male lead is Malaysian-British, while Japanese British Sonoya Mizuno played a Chinese heiress. Some critics took umbrage at the film's portrayal of Singapore as a primarily Chinese place. Malays and Indians are the second- and third-largest ethnic groups in Singapore, yet they are missing from the film. Ja Ian Chong, a professor at a Singapore university, said the film did worse than that—it erased the poor and marginalized people of Singapore so that it would appeal to East Asians and white Americans. The filmmakers responded to these criticisms by pointing out that the book and film are about superrich Singaporeans, and minorities play only a small role in that world. Kevin Kwan says the books and the film are satiric criticisms of excessive wealth, not representations of an authentic Singapore.

FURTHER READING

Adams, Bella. 2006. "Identity Difference: Regenerating Debate about Intergenerational Relationships in Amy Tan's *The Joy Luck Club*." *Studies in the Literary Imagination* 39, no. 2 (Fall): 79–94.

Bechdel, Alison. 2005. "The Rule." *Dykes to Watch Out For*, August 16, 2005. https://dykestowatchoutfor.com/the-rule/.

Borja, Melissa, Russell Jeung, Aggie Yellow Horse, Jacob Givson, Sarah Gowing, Nelson Lin, Amelia Nevins, and Emahlia Power. 2020. "Anti-Chinese Rhetoric Tied to Racism against Asian Americans." *Stop AIIPI Hate Report*, June 2020. https://www.asianpacificpolicyandplanningcouncil.org/wp-content/uploads/Anti-China_Rhetoric_Report_6_17_20.pdf.

Chang, Iris. 2003. *The Chinese in America*. New York: Penguin Books.

Chow, Andrew. 2018. "In 1993, 'Joy Luck Club' Changed Hollywood. Until It Didn't." *New York Times*, September 9, 2018. https://www.nytimes.com/2018/09/09/movies/joy-luck-club-crazy-rich-asians.html.

Ebert, Roger. 1993. "The Joy Luck Club." September 17, 1993. https://www.rogerebert.com/reviews/the-joy-luck-club-1993.

Fickle, Tara. 2014. "American Rules and Chinese Faces: The Games of Amy Tan's *The Joy Luck Club*." *Multi-Ethnic Literary Texts* 39, no. 3 (Fall): 68–88.

Frayling, Christopher. 2014. *The Yellow Peril: Dr. Fu Man Chu and the Rise of Chinophobia*. London: Thames and Hudson.

Heung, Marina. 1993. "Daughter-Text/Mother-Text: Matrilineage in Amy Tan's *The Joy Luck Club*." *Feminist Studies* 19 (3): 596–616.

Hodges, Graham Russell Gao. 2004. *Anna May Wong: From Laundryman's Daughter to Hollywood Legend*. New York: Palgrave Macmillan.

Hsiung, James C. 1992. *China's Bitter Victory: The War with Japan, 1937–1945*. New York: M.E. Sharpe.

Johnston, Sheila. 1994. "The Tears of Living Dangerously." *Independent*, March 11, 1994. https://www.independent.co.uk/arts-entertainment/film-the-tears-of-living-dangerously-wayne-wang-called-oliver-stones-films-evil-stone-called-wangs-1428383.html.

Lee, Joey. 2018. "East Asian 'China Doll' or 'Dragon Lady'?" *Bridges: A Journal of Contemporary Connections* 1 (3): 2–9.

Leong, Karen J. 2005. *The China Mystique: Pearl S. Buck, Anna May Wong, and Mayling Soong and the Transformation of American Orientalism*. Berkeley: University of California Press.

Ong, Paul M. 1985. "The Central Pacific Railroad and Exploitation of Chinese Labor." *Journal of Ethnic Studies* 13 (2): 119–124.

Rajgopal, Shoba Sharad. 2010. "The Daughter of Fu Manchu: The Pedagogy of Deconstructing Representation of Asian American Women in Film and Fiction." *Feminism, Race, and Transnationalism* 10, no. 2 (April): 141–162.

Reynolds, Susan Salter. 2003. "That Was 'Joy Luck,' This Is Now." *Los Angeles Times*, June 29, 2003. https://www.latimes.com/archives/la-xpm-2003-jun-29-ca-sreynolds29-story.html.

Swanson, Ana. 2016. "The Problem with Almost All Movies." *The Washington Post*, April 12, 2016.

Wong, Al. 1997. "Why *Joy Luck Club* Sucks." https://www.eskimo.com/~webguy/writings/joysucks.html#introduction.

Yin, Jing. 2005. "Constructing the Other: A Critical Reading of *The Joy Luck Club*." *The Howard Journal of Communications* 16: 149–175.

Chapter 5

G. I. Jane (1997)

Written by Danielle Alexandra and David Twohy;
Directed by Ridley Scott
Buena Vista Pictures, 1997, 2 hr., 4 min.

INTRODUCTION

Hollywood makes a lot of military/war films, in great part because there's always a market for them. War films allow viewers to safely engage in the drama, danger, and excitement of land, air, and naval warfare, all while exploring themes of sacrifice, morality, and the nature of masculinity. *G. I. Jane* is a rare military/war film with a female protagonist and, thus, is a film that implicitly and explicitly explores the gendered nature of military service. As Ridley Scott's biographer Vincent LoBrutto puts it, "*G. I. Jane* is a 'what if' film that has its heart in the right place about the continuing struggle of women to achieve equality and function in what is strictly a man's terrain" (2019).

Danielle Alexandra developed the story and an early iteration of the script for *G. I. Jane* in the early 1990s in response to the political controversy over allowing women in American military branches to serve in combat. Though primarily a producer at the time (*G. I. Jane* is her only film screenwriting credit), Alexandra wrote the script in the hope that it would convince Americans that female soldiers could be combat proficient. Indeed, she spent time with sources in Congress and the Pentagon who encouraged her to tell just such a story. Alexandra wrote the Jordan O'Neill character specifically for Demi Moore, whose controversial project choices had caused her several box office setbacks in the mid-1990s. Moore agreed to the project and began lobbying to get the film made. Twentieth Century Fox took a look at Alexandra's script and brought in David Twohy to hone the film's action elements. At the time, Twohy was best known for writing *The Fugitive* (1993), *Terminal Velocity* (1994), and *Waterworld* (1995). Meanwhile, Moore approached Ridley Scott to direct the film. Scott's history of directing strong female characters, from Ripley in *Alien* (1979) to *Thelma & Louise* (1991), made him a good choice for *G. I. Jane*. "A lot of men have a problem with strong women," he said at the American Film Institute in 1997, "But I never have" (Ollove 1997).

While the studio and Tuohy polished the script and put together a production team, Moore hit the gym. She put on twenty-five pounds of muscle for the role in a workout regimen that included one hour of running and two hours of weightlifting each day. One of her two trainers was an ex-SEAL instructor who taught her the secret to one-armed push-ups, a talent she used on the talk show circuit while promoting the film. Moore also met with Scott several times before filming began. Both the actor and the director agreed that the film's timing couldn't be better. The navy's sexual abuse scandal Tailhook was still in the news, and, just as filming began, the hazing of female students at the Citadel, a military college became public. The studio, Scott, and Moore all made overtures to the Department of Defense for technical advice on the script. Military advisors objected to the use of curse words by actors playing naval officers, though not as vociferously as they objected to the film's portrayal of sexist hazing. Scott ignored much of the military's advice, particularly after Moore tried and failed to use her political connection to President Bill Clinton to get access to SEAL training facilities.

Scott cast Viggo Mortensen, pre-*Lord of the Rings* and relatively unknown, as the SEAL Command Master Chief Urgayle. Fellow director and younger brother Tony Scott had directed Mortenson in *Crimson Tide* (1995) and recommended the actor to Ridley Scott for his ability to combine artistry with macho action. Hollywood legend Anne Bancroft was cast as Senator Lillian DeHaven. Bancroft won an Academy Award for her starring role in *The Miracle Worker* (1962) and nominations for Best Actress for *The Turning Point* (1977) and *Agnes of God* (1995) before appearing in *G. I. Jane*. Scott filmed many of the military scenes at Camp Blanding in Florida, while other scenes were filmed in Beaufort, South Carolina; Washington, D.C.; and Richmond, Virginia. Once the bulk of the filming was done, Scott wrapped for seven weeks while the production team prepped for the Libyan combat scenes. The high desert outside Lone Pine, California, famed for being the filming site for hundreds of westerns in the twentieth century, stood in for Libya, and the film used the *SS Lane Victory*, docked at San Pedro, California, for the film's shipboard scenes.

Filming took place from April to August 1996. Ridley Scott injured his knee while filming, but after a brief hiatus, during which he had surgery, filming resumed. The crew filmed two endings, one where Moore's character survives the Libyan gun battle unscathed and another in which she dies in the helicopter from a bullet wound. Both endings tested well, but Scott chose a happy ending because he thought the character deserved it.

SUMMARY

The film opens on a senate hearing for the confirmation of a new secretary of the navy. Senator Lillian DeHaven (Anne Bancroft), who chairs the committee complains about the navy's treatment of women. In a press conference, she suggests women don't have enough opportunity in the navy. The navy holds a conference where it plans on full gender integration within three years, but, in the next scene, navy officials plot to scuttle gender integration.

Enter Lieutenant Jordan O'Neill (Demi Moore), a topographic analyst with Naval Intelligence. There's a rescue underway, and she clashes with the male officers in the room. Reluctantly, they do as she suggests, and the mission succeeds. Senator DeHaven examines candidate files, looking for a woman to nominate for SEAL combined reconnaissance training (CRT) training. The Senator likes O'Neill because she's attractive and doesn't look like a lesbian. O'Neill is called to Washington, where DeHaven tells her she's been approved for SEAL training as long as she's heterosexual.

In the bath with her boyfriend, also a naval officer, O'Neill says she's "not interested in being some poster girl for women's rights," but she does point out he's made more progress in the navy because he's had combat opportunities that she hasn't.

O'Neill reports for training. The base commander wants her training to go smoothly. She tells him she expects a certain amount of pain, and she's not there to make a statement. She's given her own barracks, and, when she appears in the mess hall, the male trainees give her a hard time. Thus begins a long CRT training sequence designed to wash out all but the strongest candidates. Command Master Urgayle (Viggo Mortensen) hollers, quotes poetry, and hollers some more.

At an obstacle course training, Urgayle tells her there are special steps for her. She says she doesn't want any special treatment. In a rain of gunfire and explosions, she and the men run the course. She pushes aside the steps intended to make the task easier for a woman and helps her team up and over. They leave her behind. She goes to the camp commander to insist she be treated equally. He mocks her. Frustrated, O'Neill goes to the camp barbershop and shaves her own head. Then she moves her gear to the men's barracks. They're woken up with mock gunfire and are unhappy to find her in their midst.

Meanwhile, male navy officials meet and mock gender integration. The assistant secretary of the navy is upset that the news about O'Neill's treatment at CRT training has leaked to the press, and Senator DeHaven calls the secretary of the navy to express her displeasure with the Navy's treatment of O'Neill. In response, navy officials plan to close bases in Texas to make Senator DeHaven's reelection all but impossible.

Back at base, during survival, evasion, resistance, and escape (SERE) training, O'Neill continues to push herself physically and is made crew leader. While leading the team through a jungle scape, they are captured and tortured by instructors. In front of the men, Urgayle beats her up and simulates a rape to get her team to talk. She gets away from Urgayle and starts kicking him, even though her arms are tied behind her back. The men yell encouragement. Urgayle knocks her out, telling the men, "I'm saving her life, and yours." She gets up and yells at Urgayle, "Suck my d—." The men cheer. He nods and walks away and later tells another instructor, "She's not the problem. We are."

O'Neill goes out drinking with her crew and meets some of the female naval officers at the beach for a barbeque afterward. Pictures are taken. Navy officials accuse her of being a lesbian and force her to quit. She goes home, where her boyfriend helps her figure out that Senator DeHaven leaked the news of her alleged sexual orientation to force her out, in return for the Navy's promise to not close Texas naval bases. O'Neill confronts DeHaven and threatens to tell the press what the senator has done. The senator relents, and a triumphant O'Neil returns to CRT training.

On a shipboard training mission, Urgayle's trainees are diverted to Libya to rescue a team of Rangers who've retrieved a plutonium-laden satellite. They make land, and O'Neill and Urgayle run into a Libyan soldier, whom Urgayle shoots just before the man discovers O'Neill. As all hell breaks loose, Urgayle finds himself behind enemy lines. The SEALs set up an ambush, Urgayle is injured, and O'Neill rescues him. After helicopters extract the team, one of the men yells, "Hey, O'Neill, I'd go to war with you any day."

In the film's final scenes, the SEAL class graduates from training, and everyone gets a medallion. Afterward, O'Neill goes to her locker, where she finds Urgayle's book of poetry with his Navy Cross tucked inside it. They smile at each other from across the room as the film ends.

Released in August 1997, *G. I. Jane* held the number-one box office position the first and second weeks in theaters, eventually grossing just over $48 million. Though the film's box office gross fell $2 million below its $50 million budget, the film made another $22 million in DVD, Blu-ray, and LaserDisc releases.

Critics had mixed feelings about the film. Roger Ebert called it "good cinema ... because Demi Moore, having bitten off a great deal here, proves she can chew it. The wrong casting in her role could have tilted the movie toward Private Benjamin but Moore is serious, focused, and effective." Anticipating some reviewers' negative reaction to the film, in part because Moore had fallen out of box office favor, Ebert noted, "Demi Moore remains one of the most venturesome of current stars and though her films do not always succeed ... [her roles] test the tension between a woman's body and a woman's ambition and will" (Ebert 1997). Like others, Ebert took issue with the film's shift from training to battle scenes, finding the action sequence "choreographed" and "uncertain," and the shift in plot more about "audience satisfaction" than reality. Kenneth Turan's review of the movie made it clear he admired Moore a lot less than Ebert, calling the actress's determination "unintentionally funny," and, like many other reviewers, expressed discomfort with the film's graphic violence (Turan 1997). *The Rolling Stone* called *G. I. Jane* "Surprisingly scrappy" and "bound to disappoint those who are drooling to see the star in Top Gun Barbie." The same review called Viggo Mortensen's performance "star-making" (Travers 1997). The film garners a 53 percent on Rotten Tomatoes, though viewers' take on the film appear to be directly connected to how they view women in the military and how much the like or dislike Demi Moore. Both Moore and Mortenson earned Razzie nominations, hers for Worst Actress, and his for Worst Fake Accent. Razzies aside, many critics thought Moore's performance elevated what was otherwise a predictable film.

HISTORICAL CONTEXT

Every American war has been fought by both men and women. The nation's refusal to recognize this fact may erase our historical memory of women's military service, but the reality remains. Moreover, women have served in every facet of war, from support work to nursing to combat. Thus, the cultural argument of the 1990s about women's ability to serve in combat was a moot one. Women had already proven they could.

Even before the American Revolution women served in colonial armies. Native American women like Nanyehi, or Nancy Ward, served with the British Army during the French and Indian War (or Seven Years War) in the 1760s, as did many Seneca women. Ten years later, when the American Revolution began, women served in both the Continental and British Armies. Many women went to war as auxiliary workers, cooking, laundering, and nursing enlisted male soldiers. Some of these "camp followers" participated in battles as well. For example, Margaret Corbin was with the army at Fort Washington in Manhattan in 1776 when her artilleryman husband was killed in battle. She took his place at the cannon, firing upon the British, until she too was injured. Corbin was one of the many women who cooked for soldiers and often carried water to them during and after battles, earning her the sobriquet "Molly Pitcher." Many other women served as spies during the American Revolution, including indigenous and slave women.

In 1782, Deborah Sampson disguised herself as a man and enlisted as Robert Shurtliff (spelling varies). She served in the Fourth Massachusetts Regiment in the Light Infantry Company. Her elite unit faced several skirmishes and battles before Sampson was injured in battle near Tarrytown, New York. She doctored herself and continued to fight until the summer of 1783, when she was discovered. The Continental Army honorably discharged her and, in 1792, Massachusetts awarded her back pay. In 1809, the U.S. Congress, responding to Sampson's petition, approved back pay for her military pension, thus putting the final official seal of approval on her military service (Young 2005). Sampson and Corbin were by no means singular women but, rather, serve as examples of the hundreds of women who served in varied capacities in the Continental and British armies during the Revolutionary War.

In the 1830s, women officially began serving at U.S. Naval hospitals. In the 1840s, many women served in the Mexican American War (1946–1948). Elizabeth Newcom enlisted as Bill Newcom and served in the army in 1846, and Sarah Borginnes fought at both Fort Brown, after which soldiers called her the Heroine of Fort Brown, and at the Battle of Buena Vista, where she served on an artillery crew, firing a canon and doctored injured soldiers. At her death, the U.S. Army make her an honorary colonel and buried her with full military honors. At the same time, Indigenous women fought intertribal wars all over what would become the American West. In the 1840s, Kulix led a party of Pend d'Oreilles in raids on the Blackfeet and Crow people (Johannsen 1988).

Women engaged in significant and varied military work during America's largest military conflict, the Civil War. Harriet Tubman served as a spy and scout for the U.S. Army for the duration of the war. More than twenty-one thousand women served as nurses and relief workers with the U.S. Sanitary Commission, U.S. Army, and U.S. Navy, many of them poor women and women of color. Southern women did much the same, though they often did so outside the bounds of official organizations and are thus difficult to count. Hundreds of nuns, many of them Sisters of Charity, also served as nurses and did so without pay. And while it would be easy to dismiss nursing as nonmilitary work, it would be wrong to do so. Military nurses often served near the front lines and often found themselves in the middle of battles (Schultz 2004). Dr. Mary Walker volunteered for the U.S. Army when the war began and served at the First Battle of Bull Run and at the battles of Fredericksburg, Chattanooga, and Chickamauga as an army surgeon. In 1864, the Confederate Army captured her and held her as a prisoner of war for four months (Blanton and Cook 2002). She is the only American woman to win a National Medal of Honor.

Upward of six hundred women disguised themselves as men and fought in the Civil War for both the United States and the Confederacy. Pauline Cushman, Sarah Edmonds, and Albert (Jennie) Cashier are among the best known, but there were many more. Missouri slave Cathay Williams fought as William Cathay, both during the war and after. She enlisted in the Thirty-Eighth Infantry Regiment, better known as the Buffalo Soldiers, until she was discovered and discharged in 1868. Cuban-born Loreta Velázquez enlisted in the Confederate Army as Lieutenant Harry Buford and fought in a handful of battles before hiring herself out to the U.S. Army as a spy in 1862 (Leonard 1999).

In the 1870s and 1880s, Native American women continued to fight in battles. Cheyenne woman Ehyophsta fought against the U.S. Army in the 1868 Battle of Beecher Island. Women fought on both sides of the Battle of Rosebud (1876) and the Battle of Little Bighorn (Custer's Last Stand) the same year. During the Spanish American War (1898), the U.S. Army officially contracted female nurses, including thirty-two Black nurses. Dr. Anita McGee served in the Spanish American War as a surgeon and later played an important role in the Army Reorganization Act (1901), which established the Army Nurse Corps. The navy established its own Nurse Corps in 1908 with the "Sacred Twenty," the first women to officially serve in the U.S. Navy. During World War I, twenty thousand women served as army nurses in fifty-eight military hospitals (Monahan and Neidel-Greenlee 2000). Army and navy nurses played a crucial role in combatting the Spanish influenza epidemic of 1918–1819. About half the nurses who died in active duty were killed by the flu, which also killed more American soldiers than did battles.

During World War I, women also served in the Army Signal Corps as switchboard operators. The U.S. Navy authorized the enlistment of women in 1917 as "yeomanettes," or yeoman (F) and authorized women enlistees to be paid at the same rate as men, a first in American Armed services. The Marine Corps and coast guard also admitted women to active duty during World War I. All branches of the U.S. military considered that women enlistees could work at noncombat jobs and thus free up men to fight.

The tradition of using women in noncombat roles continued during World War II. Indeed, all branches of the U.S. military expanded roles for women. Auxiliary military units for women included the Women's Army Corps (WAC), the Women's Reserve of the Coast Guard (SPARs), Women's Airforce Service Pilots (WASP), Marine Corps Women's Reserve (MCWR), the Naval Women's Reserve (WAVEs), and both the Army and Navy Nurse Corps. In total more than three hundred and fifty thousand women served in the U.S. armed services (Wright-Peterson 2020).

Sixty-six army nurses and eleven navy nurses were taken as prisoners of war in the Philippines at the beginning of the war after General Douglas MacArthur fled the island, leaving behind thousands of American military personnel. The "Angels of Bataan" served as a nursing unit to fellow prisoners of war for the next four years, until the U.S. Army and Navy retook the Philippines. Major Maude Davison received a posthumous Distinguished

Service Medal in 2001 for her efforts to keep both nurses and other prisoners alive under a brutal Japanese prison system (Norman 1999).

The postwar years saw an expanding role for women in all branches of the American military. Each branch made inroads in the enlistment of women of color and in allowing women access to the upper echelons of officer rankings. Five hundred U.S. Army nurses served in combat zones in the Korean War. Flight nurse Captain Lillian Keil made 175 evacuation flights (in addition to the 250 she flew in World War II) in that war, making her the most decorated military nurse of her era. Seven thousand women served in the Vietnam War, most but not all of them as nurses. CDR Elizabeth Barret was the first female naval officer to assume a command post in a combat zone and became the highest-ranking female naval line officer of that conflict.

By the 1970s, the army had its first female general in Brigadier General Anna Mae Hays and the Navy its first female admiral, Alene Duerk. Each military branch began mixed-gender basic training, and all official American military academies became coeducational. In 1978, a U.S. District Court ruled that the navy's rule banning women from both support and combat ships was unconstitutional, and, soon after, naval women began to appear on ships. By the 1990s, women made up 18 percent of American military personnel, with the Air Force's 24 percent being the highest of all the services

In the twenty-first century, women had broken nearly every gender-based barrier in the U.S. military, but one: combat service. More than forty thousand women served in Desert Shield and Desert Storm, though officially in noncombat positions. The reality of those conflicts pointed out the ridiculousness of the official stance on women in combat. Front lines and combat zones did not exist in either Middle-East conflict the way they had in earlier wars, and female soldiers found themselves in combat, whether officials approved of it or not. American military women argued that excluding them from combat also unfairly excluded them from military career advancement. Opponents of women in combat argued that women could not stand the stress and rigors of combat, ignoring a long historical record that said otherwise. Others argued that women in combat units would fracture unit cohesion, an argument that had also been made against integrating Black soldiers into regular military units.

In 2013, Secretary of Defense Leon Panetta, on recommendations from the Joint Chiefs of Staff and senior defense officials, lifted the ban on women serving in combat. The army and Marines immediately announced plans to open combat positions for women by May 2013. Panetta and other Department of Defense officials cited women's record of bravery and heroism on the battlefields of Afghanistan and Iraq for the policy change (Londono 2013). Opponents of women in combat continue to argue against the policy on the grounds that women cause the military to accept lower standards for training and fitness, but officials in every branch of the military say there is no evidence for such claims.

In 1997, when *G. I. Jane* premiered, women were allowed in neither combat units in general nor the Navy SEALs in specific. The SEALs have their history in a World War II commando unit. In 1942, in preparation for the Allied invasion of North Africa, the navy formed two special mission units at the Amphibious Training Base in Norfolk, Virginia. The Amphibious Scouts and Raiders (S&R) that resulted engaged in pre-assault reconnoitering of beaches in Normandy before D-Day (June 1944) and the invasion of Southern France two months later. A specialized Naval Demolition Unit also came out of the Norfolk base. Made up of Navy salvage divers, the demolition unit's single mission was to remove a cable that blocked a Moroccan river so that U.S. ships could attack.

Recognizing the utility of highly trained demolition and scouting teams, the Office of Strategic Services (OSS) established a maritime unit that cooperated with the navy to sabotage enemy targets and support resistance groups. The navy continued to use demolition teams in the Korean War and with such success that President John F. Kennedy's administration encouraged the formation of the SEALs in response to both the Vietnam War and the crisis in Cuba. In 1961, Admiral Arleigh Burke recommended the SEALs be formed from members of the Underwater Demolition Team (Mann and Burton 2019).

SEAL training is considered among the most rigorous in the U.S. Armed Forces. Candidates must take eight weeks of naval recruit training, eight weeks of Naval Special Warfare Prep School, twenty-four weeks of underwater demolition training, five weeks of Parachute Jump School, and twenty-six weeks of SEAL qualification training. In August 2015, the U.S. Navy announced it would open SEAL team training to women, making it clear that women were expected to pass the same training regimen as male SEALs. In 2019, the first woman completed the SEAL training, but she was not selected for a SEAL contract because she chose another placement within the navy.

DEPICTION AND CULTURAL CONTEXT

G. I. Jane is a Hollywood film, not a documentary, and makes the sort of factual errors that come from transforming real life into story narrative. Nominally, the story is based on the experiences of Jane Parkhurst, though no one involved in *G. I. Jane* told Parkhurst until the film had been made. Parkhurst volunteered for the army at the beginning of Desert Storm (1991), when she was thirty-two years old. Three years into her service, and getting high marks for leadership and physical training, her commanding officers asked her to volunteer for occupational skills training, an all-male army special training course that would land her in the army equivalent of a SWAT team. Parkhurst notes that she stood out in the training not only because she was female but also because she was a good ten years older than the other candidates. Like Lieutenant O'Neill in the film, Parkhurst asked for and received no special accommodations for her gender. She also shaved her head and had a near-perfect fitness score and said the hazing and training violence was about 80 percent accurate. Like Moore's character, Parkhurst felt a sense of duty to her country and enjoyed her military service. "The Army has been exceptionally good for me in so many ways," Jane Parkhurst says. "Jobwise, they train you—I could be a surgical technician in any hospital, a paramedic. I'm a weapons expert. It gives you three squares (meals), a roof over your head, stability, medical, and dental" (Huizenga 2011).

The film makes dozens of small mistakes of the sort the average moviegoer wouldn't notice, but which bother military experts and, in particular, navy personnel. In one scene meant to be Naval Amphibious Base at Coronado, there are F-14s in the background, but no F-14s are stationed at Coronado. In another scene, an enlisted man tells O'Neill, who's a lieutenant, to "carry on," but no enlisted sailor would give that kind of direction to an officer. In numerous scenes, people talk around or in helicopters, even though helicopters are far too loud to allow for conversation. Many of the SEAL details are incorrect as well. First, SEALs are navy. SEAL teams and training are not open to Marines, Rangers, Delta Force, or any other military personnel. Moreover, there is no such thing as a CRT or combined reconnaissance team. SEALS are SEALS, and those in SEAL training are training to become SEALS. Also, the film suggests that Lieutenant O'Neill is a naval intelligence officer who had already passed Jump School and Dive School and thus could proceed straight to SEAL training. But naval intelligence candidates are not tracked through either training. Though the survival school portion of SERE does take one week, SERE training is a three-week course, not a one-week course as the film claims. Finally, the badge given to O'Neill and her team at the end of training is not a SEAL badge, nor does it exist in the navy pantheon of badges, ribbons, or medals. Navy SEALs wear the special warfare insignia, also known as the trident, though the badge features a rifle, anchor, wings, and the trident. Moreover, the other officers in the scene are wearing the trident, as is O'Neill in the movie's final scene. Finally, there is little or no chance the navy would send trainees, not even SEAL trainees, on a nontraining mission, particularly to a war zone (Szoldra 2015).

Military critics weren't the only group to take issue with the film and its premise. The American Arab Anti-Discrimination Committee (ADC) said Disney, who distributed the movie, "is apparently on a holy war against Arabs." The ADC particularly objected to the "gratuitous end sequence with star Demi Moore and her Navy Seal chums on a rampage killing Arabs.... Once again, scores of faceless Arabs bit the dust and the world is better off for their extermination." Disney fired back, saying, "*G.I. Jane* depicts activity in the Gulf region, where action involving the United States has taken place over the past several years. There was no intent to disparage any people in this film" (Ryan 1997). Nonetheless, the film's demonization and destruction of anonymous Middle-Easterners is a bad habit not uncommon to American combat and action-adventure films.

At its most basic, the film is an argument for the inclusion of women in not only the military but also in combat units. And the film may have helped the nation make some headway in that arena, particularly when paired with *Courage Under Fire*, which premiered the year before *G. I. Jane*. *Courage* tells the story of Captain Karen Walden (Meg Ryan), whose combat bravery in the Gulf War causes her commanding officer (Denzel Washington) to consider her for a posthumous Medal of Honor. While the film is a bit of a tearjerker, it makes a strong case for the inclusion of women in combat military units.

Nearly twenty years after these two film's debuts, women make up 14 percent of active military personnel. There are more military/war films with women protagonists, as well as documentaries examining the issues that face women in the military. *Home of the Brave* (2006) follows four Iraq War National Guard soldiers, one of them a woman, while a year later, *The Kingdom* told a thrilling tale of a CIA deployment team's efforts to find the men responsible for a bombing in Saudi Arabia. Technically, Special Agent Janet Mayes (Jennifer Garner) isn't U.S. military, but the CIA team appears on screen dressed and acting like military personnel. *The Reader* (2008) tells the story of a German woman who was a guard in a Nazi concentration camp. *Return* (2011) focuses on the difficulties of a woman's soldier's reentry to home life after serving in the Middle East, and *Zero Dark Thirty* (2012) integrates several female military characters into the story of the hunt for Osama bin Laden. The semi-biographical film *Megan Leavy* (2017) tells the story of the real-life U.S. Marine, Megan Leavy, and her dog Rex who served two deployments in Iraq. Each of these films, along with *G. I. Jane*, normalize the inclusion of women in American military units and allow women a range of legitimate career choices unprecedented in American history.

And while films portraying military women have become more common in the twenty-first century, as have women's real-world inclusion in American military units, the problems women face in the military have not changed much. The documentary, *The Invisible War* (2012), focused on sexual assault in the U.S. military. The film, which won an Oscar nomination for best documentary, examined the experiences of veterans from all branches of the U.S. military. The veterans, regardless of race or gender or branch of service, reported similar problems with reportage, judicial treatment, and retaliation, as well as inadequate psychological care, hindered career advancement after reporting, and even forced removal from service (Dick 2012).

While all these issues are serious, *G. I. Jane's* treatment of sexual harassment and abuse suggests it is merely something female military personnel need to get through to gain admittance to the military boys' club. In one cathartic scene, Master Chief Urgayle hits and punches O'Neill before simulating a rape. The film makes it clear that O'Neill suffers this violence both because she is a SEAL trainee and because she is a woman. O'Neill breaks away from Urgayle and, though her arms are tied behind her back, attacks him. The scene culminates when O'Neill yells, "Suck my d—," at her abuser, to the great delight of her male training team. O'Neill's claim of male sexual equipment at this particular moment suggests not only a refusal of womanhood but a refusal of the notion that women ought to be allowed in such units. Only a woman who can accept sexual abuse and become "one of the boys" is allowed entry.

The navy decried the violence, both sexual and otherwise in *G. I. Jane*, but their outrage can only be termed disingenuous. Or rather, the navy's considerable troubles with sexual harassment make their objections ridiculous. Take the Tailhook Scandal, for example. In 1991, at a navy symposium in Las Vegas, more than a hundred navy and Marine officers sexually assaulted or behaved "indecently" toward eighty-three women and men. Men wore T-shirts that read, "Women are Property," and, most infamously, forced women to "walk the gauntlet," by lining the hall with men who yelled, hit, and grabbed the women who walked down it. The navy initially tried to cover up the mass assaults by saying no men of rank had been involved and suggesting overly sensitive women were as much to blame as anyone. In the end, the cover-up took down as many high-ranking men as the initial accusations did. In the aftermath, many male naval officials continued to contend that good officers had been sacrificed to the scandal for the sake of "political correctness and not because they were sexual predators."

In fact, Secretary of the Navy John Lehman claimed "male swagger" was an essential facet of the navy culture and that integrating women weakened the institution (Scarborough 2011). The Tailhook Scandal broke the same year as the Anita Hill-Clarence Thomas hearings (see Confirmation chapter), but, thirty years later, the events that spawned the #MeToo movement and the military statistics on sexual violence explored in *The Invisible War* suggest the military's ongoing struggle with sexual harassment and sexual abuse.

While *G. I. Jane* is ostensibly a feminist film, or at least a film about equal opportunity for women, it is also a film about manhood and masculinity. First, and foremost, it falls squarely amid the military/war film genre, a genre as anchored in manly men doing manly things as the western. There's a super-elite military training course fraught with action, explosions, and military hardware, and that's before the film shifts to a defeating the bad guys abroad film. The film is also an action-blockbuster film, another genre known for its obvious displays of exaggerated masculinity and manly violence. And a military rite-of passage film that highlights the violent and competitive nature of SEAL training.

As one scholar put it, "*GI Jane* is a deconstruction of what it means to be a man and what exactly masculinity is. We start with something that *isn't a man at all* . . . and *make it into one*" (Carver 2007). While Lieutenant O'Neill is the obvious "something" made into a man, in reality, all the male recruits are made over, from some flavor of "regular man" to an uber-masculine, fighting, killing alpha male. And they are all told at the beginning that most of them will fail. The first day's training is only allowed to end when someone "rings out" and quits the training. In both the military scenes and the political scenes, men act like men, and part of that act is the denigration of all military women and any man who does not see the futility of women in the military.

Even Senator DeHaven's character suffers from masculinizing. She's an attractive older woman, but she swears, verbally dominates people, drinks hard liquor, and otherwise enacts dozens of stereotypical masculine behaviors. This is not to say that no woman has ever cursed or enjoyed scotch or that they should not but rather that the senator's character embodies fairly stereotypical "feminist as faux-man" archetypes. Feminism, these stereotypes suggest, strangles femininity and creates "outlaw" women. Indeed, DeHaven's character is troubling for several reasons, not the least of which is that her brand of feminism falls squarely into the "angry feminist" category. The senator is also clearly not as interested in women's equality as she is power. O'Neill, on the other hand, says several times that she's not interested in being a poster girl for the movement or in making a statement. She just wants to be a SEAL. The message? There's no good feminist in the film, perhaps because there's no such thing as a good feminist—or so the film suggests. When O'Neill perfects her manhood performance, she is accepted by the other men and, presumably, lives happily ever after.

As with many films in the genre, *G. I. Jane* is also strongly homosocial. That is, men have nonsexual relationships with other men in the fundamentally male-dominated worlds of the military and American politics. This all-male sociability reinforces male dominance of those worlds and insists upon the normative nature of male dominance. Whether its naval officers standing around a pool table discussing ways to ensure O'Neill's failure or the all-male training teams who refuse to include O'Neill, *G. I. Jane* highlights the near-hysteric insistence on patriarchal control. Terrell Carver argues the film slips from homosocial interaction to queer, particularly in the body of Master Chief Urgayle. "He is queer in the sense of different and utterly singular (as O'Neill is). While she is marked anatomically, albeit in minimized ways, so he is marked intellectually . . . and by his wardrobe" (Carver 2007). From his short shorts to his fondness for poetry, Urgayle straddles the space between uber-macho military manhood and mustachioed gay icon.

It's no surprise that a blockbuster action film that confused gender roles and challenged masculinity should be directed by Ridley Scott. He likes stories with strong female characters and has since the beginning of his directing career. Fresh from directing his first feature film, *The Duelists* (1977), Scott went looking for his next project. Both *Star Wars* (1977) and *Close Encounters of the Third Kind* (1977) changed the movie landscape in the 1970s and made audiences hungry for big-budget extravaganzas. Scott scuttled his plans to make medieval romance and went looking for a big space picture. Scott liked Dan O'Bannon's script for *Alien*, which featured a female protagonist in a time when most female movie characters were secondary or submissive. Instead, Ripley (Sigourney Weaver) survives the predations wrought upon the mostly male spaceship crew and kills the alien in the film's final scenes.

Scholars and critics alike consider Ripley a feminist archetype, both for her toughness and her leadership. Her fight against the monstrous alien functions as a "metaphor for the feminist struggle against sexual violence" (Zeitz 2016). But Ripley is more than a male hero in a female body. She embodied a new kind of female hero, one with an empathetic, nurturing sensibility that made her both strong and likable. Initially, critics didn't know what to make of the film, finding both its violence and its female hero disconcerting, but forty years later, the film is considered one of the best science fiction/horror movies ever made (it often shows up on lists right above or below another Ripley Scott classic, *Blade Runner*).

Scott returned to the female hero archetype with *Thelma & Louise* (1991). He optioned the script, written by Callie Khouri, intending to produce it but liked it so much he decided to direct it as well. In the film, two female friends embark on vacation but shoot a man in a bar parking lot after he tries to rape Thelma (Geena Davis). The women embark on a road trip where they take revenge on bad men. In the film's iconic final scene, Louise (Susan Sarandon) drives their car into the Grand Canyon rather than surrender to the authorities.

Some critics thought *Thelma & Louise* unfairly picked on men. A review for *Time* called it "a male-bashing feminist screed in which [men] are portrayed as leering, overbearing, violent swine who deserve what they get" (Carlson 1991). Other critics pointed out that Hollywood has a long history of making films featuring violence against women or films that made women look stupid, inferior, and ridiculous. Others pointed out that those whining about the ill-treatment of men in the film missed the point. Not only did the film have two strong, empathetic male characters, Louise's boyfriend (Michael Madsen) and the detective who pursued the two women (Harvey Keitel), but the script reimagined the road/buddy film, a story genre generally only told with male characters. Raina Lipsitz called it "the last great film about women and connected its cultural resonance with a backlash against patriarchy caused in part by the Hill-Thomas hearings" (see *Confirmation* chapter).

Even the neo-noir, dystopian *Blade Runner* (1982), Ridley Scott's second big film (after *Alien*) took a nontraditional approach to female characters. They are "other" in the film, not just because they are women but because they are replicants, from Rachael (Sean Young), Deckard's (Harrison Ford) love interest to Zhora (Joanna Cassidy) and Pris (Daryl Hannah), the characters struggle to assert themselves against the patriarchal systems intent on destroying them. In one scene, Rachael saves Deckard's life when she shoots another replicant, thus reversing the "damsel in distress" trope. This is not to suggest *Blade Runner* is a feminist film, but it is a film that challenges film stereotypes of women (Zeitz 2016). Much the same could be said about *G. I. Jane*, made ten years later and after *Alien* and *Thelma & Louise*.

In many ways, *G.I. Jane* functioned as a referendum on how movie viewers and critics felt about Demi Moore as a person. It is difficult to overstate how controversial the actress became in the 1990s. She came to stardom in the 1980s as a member of the so-called Brat Pack, a nickname given to a group of young actors including Molly Ringwald, Emilio Estevez, Rob Lowe, and Judd Nelson. Moore appeared in *St. Elmo's Fire* and *About Last Night*, both considered classic Brat Pack films, but it was her 1990 performance in *Ghost,* costarring with Patrick Swayze, that made her a bona fide movie star and an American sweetheart. The nation's uncritical love affair with Moore came to an end in 1991 when the actress appeared naked and seven months pregnant on the cover of *Vanity Fair. Time Magazine* now considers the Annie Leibovitz photograph one of the hundred most influential images of all time, but in 1991, many people found it obscene, exploitive, and just plain disgusting. A year later, she again appeared naked on a *Vanity Fair* cover, this time covered only by a painted-on man's pinstripe suit. The gender dissonance of that image made nearly as many Americans uncomfortable as the statement of unashamed femaleness of the pregnant and nude Demi from the previous year.

Despite the controversy, Moore's box office successes continued with *A Few Good Men* (1992), *Indecent Proposal* (1993), and *Disclosure* (1994), making her one of Hollywood's most marketable commodities. Her high-visibility marriage to Bruce Willis only enhanced Moore's visibility, as did her insistence on pay equality for female actors. In 1996, she was paid a record-breaking amount to appear in *Striptease*. Though she had done nude scenes in other movies, much was made of the actor's willingness to dance topless in the film. *Striptease* flopped both with critics and audiences, making several "worst films ever" lists. Significantly, though the film was written and directed by Andrew Bergman, Moore received the lion's share of blame for the film's narrative and structural weaknesses. A year later, she produced and starred in *If These Walls Could Talk*, an HBO three-part series about abortion. Though the series, which also starred Sissy Spacek and Cher, was critically well-received, conservatives again took aim at Moore for the controversial topic.

Thus, Moore's appearance in *G. I. Jane*, a film directed by a man with a string of box office successes, was at least in part an effort to salvage her career, and a largely unsuccessful effort at that. Not only did the film's topic ruffle the feathers of conservative Americans, but her insistence she be paid in the same range as male stars bought her a reputation for being difficult. *G. I. Jane* suffered at the box office because some viewers didn't care for the star's assertive feminism or her willingness to transgress gender boundaries.

Consider the attention the head-shaving scene garnered in the press. Moore's willingness to shave her head astounded and offended people in equal measure. Yet, if a man had shaved his head on screen, no one would have remarked on it at all. Moore promoted *Striptease* while filming *G. I. Jane* and appeared on talk and award shows with her shorn head. She did one-armed pushups on the *Late Show* with David Letterman to prove she really could. For a nation fresh from twelve years of the neo-conservative Reagan-Bush years and still divided over the Hill-Thomas hearings, Moore's iconoclasm made her a cultural lightning rod for all sorts of cultural issues, from the ongoing controversy about women in the military to more general anxieties about equality for women. The film upsets people who don't think women should be in the military, but on a broader scale, it challenges cultural notions of what's appropriate for women, both as actors and as humans.

PRIVATE BENJAMIN

Long before *G. I. Jane* and *Courage Under Fire*, there was *Private Benjamin* (1980). Written by Nancy Meyers, Charles Shyer, and Harvey Miller, the comedy tells the story of a spoiled society woman Judy Benjamin (Goldie Hawn) who enlists in the army after her husband dies during honeymoon sex. The film is a comedy farce, as Judy finds out the army isn't the "spa vacation" the army recruiter told her it would be. The film takes a more serious note when Judy decides to take her training seriously and eventually volunteers for the elite "Thornbirds," fends off sexual harassment, and refuses an assignment in Greenland for a preferable one in Belgium. Along the way, she meets and eventually gets engaged to a French doctor, but, in the end, she decides she'd rather be independent and leaves him at the altar. The "feminist fable" benefits from Goldie Hawn's comic genius (she won a rare Oscar nomination for an appearance in a comedy), and while a comedy, the film takes women's right to a military career seriously.

FURTHER READING

Blanton, DeAnne, and Lauren M. Cook. 2002. *They Fought Like Demons: Women Soldiers in the Civil War*. New York: Random House.

Burkett, Abra. 2014. "Beyond GI Jane: Representation and Portrayal of Women Armed Services Members in Modern Military Movies." (Thesis, American University).

Carlson, Margaret. 1991. "Is This What Feminism Is All About?" *Time*, June 24, 1991. http://content.time.com/time/subscriber/article/0,33009,973242-2,00.html.

Carver, Terrell. 2007. "GI Jane: What Are 'Manners' That 'Maketh a Man'?" *BJPIR* 9: 313–317.

Christian, Alexander. 2017. "Is Ellen Ripley a Feminist?" In *Alien and Philosophy: I Infest, Therefore I Am*, edited by Jeffrey A. Ewing, Kevin S. Decker, and William Decker, 155–166. New York: Blackwell.

Dick, Kirby. 2012. *The Invisible War*.

Donald, Ralph, and Karen MacDonald. 2014. *Women in War Films: From Helpless Heroine to GI Jane*. Washington, DC: Rowman and Littlefield.

Ebert, Roger. 1997. "G.I. Jane." https://www.rogerebert.com/reviews/gi-jane-1997.

Geoghegan, Michael. 1945. "A Salute to GI Jane." *American Journal of Nursing* 45 (4): 297–299.

Hagelin, Sarah. 2013. *Reel Vulnerability: Power, Pain, and Gender in Contemporary Films and Television*. New Brunswick, NJ: Rutgers University Press.

Huizenga, Beth. 2011. "A Veterans Day Visit with Novato's Own G. I. Jane." *Patch*, November 11, 2011. https://patch.com/california/novato/a-visit-with-novato-s-own-g-i-jane.

Johannsen, Robert. 1988. *To the Halls of Montezuma: The Mexican American War in the American Imagination*. New York: Oxford University Press.

Leonard, Elizabeth D. 1999. *All the Daring of a Soldier: Women of the Civil War Armies*. New York: W.W. Norton & Company.

Lichtenstein, Therese. 1993. "Thelma and Louise, Trouble in Paradise." *Psychoanalytic Psychology* 10 (3): 487–491.

Lipsitz, Raina. 2011. "'Thelma & Louise': The Last Great Film about Women." *The Atlantic*, August 21, 2011. https://www.theatlantic.com/entertainment/archive/2011/08/thelma-louise-the-last-great-film-about-women/244336/.

LoBrutto, Vincent. 2019. *Ridley Scott: A Biography*. Lexington: University of Kentucky Press.

Londono, Ernesto. 2013. "Pentagon Removes Ban on Women in Combat." *Washington Post*, January 24, 2013. https://www.washingtonpost.com/world/national-security/pentagon-to-remove-ban-on-women-in-combat/2013/01/23/6cba86f6-659e-11e2-85f5-a8a9228e55e7_story.html.

Mann, Don, and Lance Burton. 2019. *Navy Seals: The Combat History of the Deadliest Warriors on the Planet*. New York: Simon and Schuster.

Monahan, Evelyn M., and Rosemary Neidel-Greenlee. 2000. *All This Hell: U.S. Nurses Imprisoned by the Japanese*. Lexington: University of Kentucky Press.

Norman, Elizabeth M. 1999. *We Band of Angels: The Untold Story of American Nurses Trapped on Bataan by the Japanese*. New York: Pocket Books.

Ollove, Michael. 1997. "Filmmaker Enjoys Role as Feminist Director." *The Baltimore Sun*, August 17, 1997. https://www.baltimoresun.com/news/bs-xpm-1997-08-17-1997229065-story.html.

Ryan, Joal. 1997. "Moore Controversy for Disney." E News, August 22, 1997. https://www.eonline.com/news/35059/moore-controversy-for-disney.

Scarborough, Rowan. 2011. "Ex-Secretary Says Navigation Needs Swagger." *Washington Times*, September 11, 2011. https://www.washingtontimes.com/news/2011/sep/18/lehman-rocks-navy-complaints-about-political-corre/.

Schultz, Jane E. 2004. *Women at the Front: Hospital Workers in Civil War America*. Chapel Hill: University of North Carolina Press.

Szoldra, Paul. 2015. "39 Horrible Technical Errors in G. I. Jane." *We Are the Mighty*, June 2015. https://www.wearethemighty.com/articles/gi-jane-errors.

Travers, Peter. 1997. "G.I. Jane." *Rolling Stone*, August 1997. https://www.rollingstone.com/movies/movie-reviews/g-i-jane-101359/.

Turan, Kenneth. 1997. "Shipping Out with Demi." *Los Angeles Times*, August 22, 1997. https://www.latimes.com/archives/la-xpm-1997-aug-22-ca-24686-story.html.

U.S. Department of Defense. 2011. *Department of Defense Annual Report on Sexual Abuse in the Military: Fiscal Year 2010*. Washington, DC: Author.

Wright-Peterson, Virginia. 2020. *A Woman's War, Too: Women at Work during World War II*. Minneapolis: Minnesota Historical Society Press.

Young, Albert. 2005. *Masquerade: The Life and Times of Deborah Sampson, Continental Soldier*. New York: Vintage Books.

Zeitz, Christian David. 2016. "Dreaming of Electric Femme Fatales: Ridley Scott's Blade Runner, Final Cut and Images of Women in Film Noir." *Gender Forum* 60: 11–22.

Chapter 6

Monster (2003)

Written and directed by Patty Jenkins
Denver & Delilah Films, 1 hr., 49 min.

INTRODUCTION

American culture finds serial killers fascinating and repugnant in equal measure. The public eagerly consumes books, television shows, documentaries, and movies about real and fictional serial killers, from *Silence of the Lambs* to *Dexter*. Patty Jenkins's 2003 film *Monster* joins the pantheon of serial killer films in telling the Aileen Wuornos story, or at least part of it. Real-life serial killer Wuornos killed six men in a ten-month period from November 1989 to September 1990. Jenkins's film suggests Wuornos wasn't born a monster; she was made one.

Jenkins was a freshman in college when a Florida court convicted Wuornos for murdering six men. The trial garnered national attention, both because female serial killers are uncommon and because Wuornos claimed she killed in self-defense. Only three weeks after Wuornos's arrest, filmmaker Jacqueline Giroux talked Wuornos into signing over film rights. Wuornos's lawyer Russell Armstrong cosigned the contract. Soon after, Wuornos realized Russell was more interested in profiting from his connection to her than defending her and fired him. Giroux went on to write a script for the made-for-TV movie, *Damsel of Death*.

Tyria Moore, Aileen's one-time partner, also tried to cash in on the media frenzy surrounding Wuornos. Moore and three policemen who'd been instrumental in getting Moore to elicit Wuornos's confession tried to work out a deal with Republic Pictures to make a movie about the hunt for and capture of Wuornos that would become *Overkill*. The police department for which the officers worked launched an investigation. At issue was whether their interest in profiting from Wuornos's story encouraged them to ignore Moore's part in the murders. The investigation also considered whether or not Wuornos received a fair trial given the story was most saleable if she were portrayed as a lone killer. Eventually, two of the policemen were demoted and one resigned, but the film did get made.

To make matters worse, Wuornos's new lawyer, Steven Glazer, also acted as her media consultant, securing paid appearances for her that were supposed to pay for her defense. Under the so-called "Son of Sam" laws, Wuornos could not personally profit from books or movies about her crime, but no law made it illegal for other people to cash in on her story. Glazer teamed up with Arlene Pralle, a Florida woman who adopted the adult Wuornos, and the pair raked in profits from several books about Wuornos.

Meanwhile, Patty Jenkins began exchanging letters with Wuornos in 2001 and 2002. Jenkins, who had a deal to write a low-budget, straight-to-video movie, backed out of the project after she became convinced Wuornos's story deserved better treatment. "To my complete surprise, I ended up getting sucked into her story," Jenkins later said. Jenkins had little screenwriting experience previous to *Monster*, though she had spent ten years working as a cameraperson. In 2001, she directed a short film that played at film festivals, but nothing on the scale that would suggest she could get *Monster* made. The deal coalesced after Charlize Theron agreed to produce the film and play the lead. Theron, whose previous work included *The Devil's Advocate* (1997), *Cider House Rules* (1998), and *The Italian Job* (2003), said she almost turned down the role. "I didn't think I could do it." Theron ultimately took the role because, "The guys always get to play grey characters, but somehow women always tend to be black and white. So I knew this was something very unusual" (Epstein 2009).

Christina Ricci, a former child actress best known for her portrayal of Wednesday Addams in *Addams Family* (1991) and *Addams Family Values* (1993), played Selby Wall, a fictionalized character loosely based on Wuornos's real-life partner Tyria Moore. Acting legend Bruce Dern took on the role of Wuornos's only real friend, Thomas, while Annie Corley played Donna, an aunt who has temporary care of Selby before she runs off with Aileen.

SUMMARY

The film opens with a shot of Aileen sitting under a freeway overpass, sheltered from the pouring rain. Down to her last $5, Aileen decides to buy one last drink before killing herself. At the bar, she meets Selby, a young woman eager to talk. Selby buys a pitcher of beer, and the two women get to know each other. Selby invites Aileen back to her room, where Aileen showers and spends a platonic night with her young friend. They're discovered by Selby's aunt Donna, with whom Selby's staying, who warns Selby to "stay away from people like that." The next night, Aileen cleans up in a gas station bathroom and meets Selby at a roller rink. They kiss for the first time. After a frantic alley make-out session, Aileen promises to get together the money for the two of them to be together.

In an effort to make some money, Aileen picks up a man, who drives her into the woods for sex. He tells her he hates women and, in a brutal scene, knocks her unconscious, ties her up, and rapes her with a pipe. She gets loose, grabs his gun, and shoots him over and over again. Screaming and covered in blood, Aileen hits him with the gun over and over, crying out her pain and rage. The camera takes it all in, making sure the viewer understands this rape scene is different from the hundreds viewers have seen before. The female victim has become a killer but has not escaped her victimhood.

Aileen cleans up and goes to get Selby, who is angry because Aileen missed their date. Aileen gets on her knees and begs her, "Give me a week. You'll never meet someone like me again." They drive off together in the dead man's car.

Aileen tries to get a regular job, but she has no education, no work experience outside of prostitution, and though she's pathetically eager, she doesn't understand the rules of middle-class society. After a disastrous job interview, a policeman picks her up, calls her a whore, and forces her to have sex with him. Back at the hotel room, Selby wants Aileen to go back to sex work. Aileen doesn't want to and tells Selby she killed a guy who raped her. They fight, and Aileen relents and reluctantly returns to hooking. In a voice-over, Aileen says, "People always look down their noses at hookers. They won't give you a chance because they think you took the easy way out. You can't imagine the real power it took to do what we do. Walk in the street, night after night, taking the hits and still getting back up. But I did."

Aileen kills several customers, each one more sympathetic than the last. One afternoon, as Selby drives a stolen red car, Aileen tells Selby a semifictional version of her life story, where she's forced into prostitution to support her siblings. Selby drives off the road. An older couple sees them as they abandon the car and run away. As they pack to leave their apartment, Aileen tells Selby she killed the man who owned the car. Selby professes horror and surprise. Aileen says, "I've done everything in the whole wide world so you wouldn't have to know." Selby tells her, "You can't kill people," to which Aileen responds, "Says who?"

In an emotional scene, Aileen sends Selby away to protect her. At a biker bar, Aileen's friend Tom (Bruce Dern) knows she's about to be arrested and tries to get her away. She's too drunk to listen, and the cops arrest her.

From jail, Aileen talks to Selby on the phone. As the two talk, it becomes clear that Aileen knows Selby is cooperating with the police. With policemen in the background, Aileen tells Selby, "It was me. All me. It's over for me now. . . . I'm gonna die. I'll never forget you. Bye baby." In court, Selby testifies against Aileen, though the audience cannot hear her words. As Selby points at Aileen, the screen fades to white, and the viewer is told Selby and Aileen never spoke again and that Aileen was executed after twelve years in jail.

The film opened to nearly instant critical and box office success, grossing over $58 million, a considerable return on its $8 million budget. Critics loved the film nearly as much as they loved Theron's performance. Ebert, like many Americans, did not recognize the former Australian model Theron, so transformative was her portrayal of Wuornos, saying the movie "isn't a performance, but an embodiment." Ebert went on to call Theron's work in *Monster* "one of the greatest performances in the history of the cinema." While some critics criticized Ricci's performance, Ebert notes that what others mistake for bad acting is Ricci portraying her character as a clueless teenager, "cobbling her behavior out of notions borrowed from bad movies, old songs, and barroom romances" (Ebert 2004).

Ebert was not alone in his high accolades for the film and its performances. Theron garnered best acting awards from the Screen Actors Guild (SAG), the Golden Globes, the Independent Spirit Awards, and Critics Choice. Theron's triumph culminated with a Best Actress Academy Award. The American Film Institute named *Monster* one of the top ten films of 2003, and, in 2009, Ebert put it third on his list of best films of the decade.

HISTORICAL CONTEXT

Aileen Wuornos's childhood was a nightmarish parade of emotional, physical, and sexual abuse at the hands of mentally unstable and criminally abusive family members. Her mother, Diane Wuornos, married Leo Pittman in 1954 when Aileen was fourteen years old. Leo regularly beat Diane and controlled her behavior to such an extent that he did not allow her to hang laundry outside where another man might see her. In 1955, she gave birth to her first child, Keith. When Diane became pregnant a second time, Leo abandoned his family. By the time Aileen was born in 1956, he was in prison for a slate of sex crimes. A schizophrenic, he also spent time in mental hospitals in Kansas and Michigan. Released from the second mental hospital, he raped a seven-year-old girl. Facing lengthy prison sentence in the Kansas State Penitentiary, he killed himself in 1969. By then, Diane had abandoned both children, leaving them with her parents and disappearing for years. She would remarry and started a new family, but never retrieved her first two children.

The dysfunction in Diane's family didn't stop at allowing a mentally ill sexual predator access to a teenage daughter. Diane's father, Lauri Wuornos, was an alcoholic with a predilection for physical and sexual abuse. He often forced his granddaughter Aileen to take her clothes off and then beat her with a belt, sometimes using the buckle end on her tender flesh. The beatings transformed into rapes before Aileen was eleven years old. Almost certainly, Lauri terrorized his daughter Diane and other female children under his care, though the family remained notably silent on the issue, even while Aileen was on trial for her life.

Not long after her grandfather began raping her, Aileen learned to trade sex with neighborhood boys for money and gifts. The boys were only too glad to use Aileen but expressed nothing but contempt for her, calling her "Cigarette Pig." At some point Lauri allowed at least one of his friends, a man old enough to have grandchildren, sexual access to Aileen. When she was fourteen years old, she discovered she was pregnant. Aileen hid the pregnancy as long as she could but eventually had to tell the family. Her grandfather beat her and turned her out of the house.

Aileen gave birth to a son in a Detroit home for unwed mothers. She released her baby boy for adoption and returned to Lauri's house because she had nowhere else to go. Her wild behavior escalated and had her in and out of juvenile hall and a school for delinquent girls. Lauri's wife, Britta, herself an alcoholic and domestic abuse victim, not only allowed Lauri's abuse (which she must have known about) but joined her husband in emotionally abusing Aileen. Family lore has it that Lauri beat Britta just before she died and perhaps hastened her death from cirrhosis by choking her to death.

When Britta died, Lauri kicked Aileen out of the house for good. She was fifteen and homeless, already dragging a long history of sexual and physical abuse behind her. Her mental problems were entirely in keeping with the behaviors of a sexually and physically abused child. Friends and family reported she had a volatile temper, stole things large and small, and may have set fires. She also abused alcohol and drugs and dropped out of high school well before she graduated. High school counselors noted she had an average intelligence, but well below average verbal abilities and recommended her for psychiatric help. Nothing ever came of the report.

By the time Aileen was eighteen, she'd been hitchhiking around the country for years, prostituting herself to earn a living. In Colorado, authorities arrested her for drunk driving, firing a gun at a moving vehicle, and disorderly conduct. Released on bail, she left the state and headed for Florida. There she met and married sixty-nine-year-old Lewis Fell, a prosperous yacht club president, who was about the same age as her abusive grandfather. During their nine-week marriage, she participated in several bar fights and assaulted Fell with his cane. He took out a restraining order against her and began proceedings to have the marriage annulled.

While in Florida, Aileen inherited $10,000 from her twenty-one-year-old brother Keith, who had died of esophageal cancer. On a trip home to Michigan, she visited her sexual predator grandfather and was once again arrested for disturbing the peace. Several years later, Lauri hung himself in his oldest son's basement. Aileen returned to Florida, where her problems only escalated. She robbed a convenience store at gunpoint, taking $35 and two packs of cigarettes. After thirteen months in prison, Aileen returned to a life of drug use, prostitution, and car theft. She was twenty years old. For the next ten years, she drifted up and down the nation's freeways, selling herself to make enough money for food, cigarettes, and booze. By her count, she had sex with over two hundred thousand men and was raped nine times (Wuornos and Berry-Dee 2004).

Sometime in 1986, Aileen met Tyria Moore in a Daytona Beach bar. Moore, a sometimes hotel maid, moved from Ohio to Daytona Beach, a town with a small but vibrant gay culture, not long before meeting Wuornos. The two lived together for three years. Though Moore could work, she chose not to, preferring Aileen support them by prostituting herself. In 1989, Aileen picked up Richard Mallory, an electronics store owner who, according to Wuornos, beat her and raped her. Mallory had been convicted of rape in 1957 and spent four years in prison and another ten in a psychiatric prison. During Wuornos's first trial, for the murder of Mallory, her lawyer neglected to enter Mallory's history into the record. Later, when another lawyer sought to use this legal misstep to justify a retrial, an assistant state prosecutor called the defense's stance that Wuornos most probably had been attacked and raped by Mallory "contrived." The prosecutor went on to say Wuornos was a "predatory prostitute" and a "ruthless murderess," making it clear he didn't believe she'd been the victim of a violent crime (Russell 2002).

Over the next year, Wuornos killed six more men, each of whom intended to pay her for sex. She shot Charles Carskaddon in May and construction worker David Andrew Spears in June. In July, she killed Peter Siems. His body was never found, but it was his car that Tyria and Wuornos abandoned after a car accident. Authorities found Troy Burress's body in August 1990 and Charles Humphreys's a month later, and later determined they'd both been killed by Wuornos. She killed her last man (and john), Walter Antonio, in November and left his body on a logging road.

Florida authorities spent the summer hunting the "highway killer." Witnesses saw Moore and Wuornos in Siems's car and described the pair to authorities. That, combined with fingerprints on several of the dead men's pawned belongings, led to Wuornos. Sensing the authorities were closing in, Wuornos either sent Moore home to Pennsylvania or Moore went on her own. On January 9, 1991, Florida authorities located Wuornos in a biker bar and arrested her. They also found Moore and convinced her to help them trick a confession from Wuornos. After her capture, when asked by a policeman why she killed her johns Wuornos said, "They crossed the line. They were gonna rape me, kill me, strangle me" (Clary 1991).

While Wuornos was awaiting trial, born-again Christian and horse trainer Alene Pralle read an interview Wuornos gave to the *Orlando Sentinel*. "I'm not a man-hater. I'm so used to being treated like dirt I guess it's become a way of life." The sentiment struck Pralle as notable when so much of the media coverage portrayed Wuornos as a psychopathic, remorseless killer. Pralle began to visit Wuornos in jail and eventually adopted her. As with Moore, Wuornos was loyal to Pralle until her death, and, also like Moore, Pralle had ulterior motives. Before and after Wuornos's execution, Pralle profited from her adoptive daughter's story, most notably when she wrung $10,000 from documentary filmmaker Nick Broomfield (Petrakis 1994).

The state of Florida first prosecuted Wuornos for Mallory's murder. The prosecution was allowed to introduce evidence of Aileen's other crimes, and her lawyer, Steven Glazer, failed to expose Mallory as a convicted rapist. He also failed to introduce Wuornos's history of family sexual and physical violence. Moore testified against her former lover as part of her immunity deal. Though psychiatrists testified to Wuornos's multiple psychiatric issues, a jury found her guilty and sentenced her to death.

In March 1992 and facing trials for Humphreys, Burress, and Spears's murders, Glazer and Pralle convinced Wuornos to plead no contest to each murder charge, an unprecedented move in a capital case. Wuornos collected three more death sentences. Three months later, she pled guilty to the murder of Carskaddon, earning her a fifth death sentence. In both instances, Wuornos's lawyer tried to make the case that her first victim had violently raped her, thus setting his client off on a murderous spree, but the judge refused to allow Mallory's criminal history into the court record.

Wuornos spent the next twelve years of her life at Broward Correctional Institution. Over time, her mental status deteriorated. In 2001, she petitioned the Florida Supreme Court to fire her lawyers and end all outstanding appeals. A year later, she'd become so mentally ill that she continually heard voices and believed prison matrons were trying to poison her. The state of Florida put Aileen Wuornos to death on October 9, 2002. Her body was cremated, and her ashes given to her childhood friend Dawn Botkins. Not long after, Botkins published Wuornos's letters in a book titled *Dear Dawn*.

DEPICTION AND CULTURAL CONTEXT

Monster turned out far better than it had a right to, considering the sort of low budget films made about serial killers. It is also far and away the best of all the Wuornos films. Republic Pictures's *Overkill: The Aileen Wuornos Story* predates *Monster* by ten years, coming out in 1992, while Wuornos was still alive. Jean Smart, best known at the time for her comedic role in the television series *Designing Woman*, earned good reviews for her portrayal of a serial killer. Documentary filmmaker Nick Broomfield made two documentaries, *Aileen Wuornos: The Selling of a Serial Killer* (1992), and *Aileen: Life and Death of a Serial Killer* (2003). Both films focus on the mismanagement of Wuornos's legal cases and the way her lawyer, Steve Glazer, and adoptive mother, Arleen Pralle, took financial advantage of Wuornos. Television shows on A&E, Court TV, and an episode of *60 Minutes* also plumbed the Aileen Wuornos story, though most are little more than prurient tours through titillating female-serial-killer land.

Monster takes great pains to portray Wuornos as both a victim of society and a psychologically unhinged murderer. Wuornos claimed all seven of the men (and sex-for-hire customers) she killed raped or tried to rape her, but there is little evidence to support this claim for any of the men she killed but the first, Richard Mallory. Given his criminal history, it is all too likely that Richard Mallory raped her, and it's just as likely he raped many other prostitutes and got away with it. The film suggests Wuornos, a victim of post-rape trauma, felt threatened by all the men she picked up after Mallory, even if they did nothing more threatening than pay her for sex. The film walks a fine line, portraying Wuornos as a woman so psychologically overburdened she saw began to see all her johns as men who would hurt her if she didn't hurt them first.

As it turns out, statistically, she wasn't wrong. Prostitution is America's dirty little secret. Every year, thousands of women are arrested for prostitution, though the connections between prostitution, the illegal drug trade, human sex trafficking, and violence against sex workers are undisputed. Prostitution is the most dangerous job in America. A prostitute is twice as likely to die on the job as an Alaskan fisherman or an oilrig worker. To put it more plainly, twenty-four of every one hundred thousand prostitutes in America are murdered, 80 to 90 percent have been victims of violence, and nearly 70 percent have been raped more than once (Anklesaria and Gentile). On average, a prostitute can expect to be attacked by a "client" once a month, though only 10 percent of prostitution arrests are johns. Women make up 80 percent of the world's forty million prostitutes, one to two million of whom work in the United States—only China and India have more prostitutes than the United States.

For all that, American has trouble confronting the reality that sex work is dangerous for the people forced to do it, making it fundamentally abusive and oppressive. And make no mistake, most of the sex workers in America are forced into it, if only that they have no other life choices. Aileen Wuornos, for example, never graduated from high school, and not because she was too lazy or too stupid. She didn't graduate from high school because she was homeless by the time she was fifteen years old, thrown out by a sexually abusive grandfather who'd been raping her for years. And lest we forget, her grandfather was never prosecuted or even arrested. He abused two generations of women in his family and died a respected member of his community.

Aileen Wuornos prostituted herself to stay alive. Plenty of men were willing to pay her small amounts of money to service their sexual needs. Men who, if the statistics can be believed, verbally abused her for doing the exact thing they paid her to do. Studies say sex work shatters people's psyches. Anxiety and mood syndromes are common among sex workers, as is post-traumatic stress disorder (PTSD). Most sex workers begin their lives with an established case of PTSD as a legacy of childhood sexual trauma and self-medicate with alcohol or street drugs (Anklesaria and Gentile 2012).

Studies suggest that until fairly recently Americans, including law enforcement personnel, have viewed sex workers as "bad girls," women with an unhealthy sexual appetite who willingly chose sex work and were thus undeserving of legal protection. Prostitutes sell sex as a way to monetize their nymphomania, or so went the not uncommon theory. Of course, many people also believe either that prostitutes can't be raped or that it doesn't matter if they are. The first group believes sex workers are so sexually rapacious that they'd never say no to a sexual advance, while the second holds to the old "if you're not a nice girl you get what's coming to you" school of sexist thinking. *Monster* never explicitly comments on American attitudes towards prostitutes, but the scenes where Aileen contracts with strange men for sex are tension-filled, communicating, if only a little bit, how it must have felt for Aileen to earn her living by such dangerous means.

The largest, but most understandable inaccuracy in the film lies with Christina Ricci's character, Selby Wall. Ricci did an admirable job playing Selby as both clueless and venal in equal measures, and though Tyria Moore may or may not have had some of those qualities, Selby is nothing like Tyria. The difference was purposeful. Moore was notoriously litigious, and understandably so. Legally, a person who helps another person commit murder can also be prosecuted for murder under felony murder statutes. That is, it is possible in the United States (and other countries) to be prosecuted for murder without ever murdering anyone. While theoretically, the law applies to anyone assisting in a crime, it is most often applied to murder, robbery, and rape (Thompson 2015). Moore escaped prosecution by cooperating with the FBI and maintaining a decades-long silence about her years with Wuornos.

Unable to write a genuine version of Tyria Moore, Jenkins fictionalized a version. While Selby's age isn't specified in the film, it is clear she's much younger than Wuornos, perhaps just out of high school. Selby's youth explains her insensitivity in pushing Aileen back to prostitution, as well as her stubborn ignorance of what Aileen had to do for the wads of cash and cars that showed up at the house. Tyria Moore, on the other hand, was four years younger than Aileen. The two met, not in a lesbian bar but in a biker bar Moore frequented before and after she met Wuornos. While Selby wants Aileen to prostitute herself, Moore said in interviews and under oath that she disapproved of Wuornos's sex work. That said, Moore worked only sporadically as a hotel maid, and allowed Wuornos to support her for long periods of their relationship.

In the movie, Wuornos tells Selby about the first murder but not the others, or at least not until she's about to be arrested. In reality, Wuornos told Moore about all the murders. Moore said she didn't want to hear the details, but she had no trouble pawning the dead men's personal items and living off the proceeds or driving their cars. Moore agreed to work with the police to elicit a confession from Wuornos, though, in reality, it took Moore six phone calls, not the one shown in the film, to get the job done. In return, Moore received immunity from prosecution and avoided the repercussions that should have come from personally profiting from the work of a serial killer.

While *Monster's* portrayal of Wuornos's lover is understandably inaccurate, the film's claim that Wuornos was the first female serial killer is not. Some sources say any person who kills two or more people in separate events is a serial killer, while others say it takes at least three victims. By either definition, Aileen Wuornos was a serial killer. She was not, though, the first female serial killer (or even the first American serial killer), though the FBI erroneously called her such on several occasions. This bit of misinformation gets repeated over and over again in websites, books, and documentaries, until one can hardly mention Wuornos without seeing the phrase, "first female serial killer." While Wuornos shows up at the top of many "worst female serial killers" lists, her seven murders are nothing compared to the four hundred babies Amelia Dyer killed in the mid-1800s or the six hundred young women murdered by Elizabeth Bathory in the last 1500s. The title for the first American female serial killer belongs to either Lavinia Fisher or Jane Toppan. An innkeeper, Fisher and her husband may have killed dozens of travelers in the first decades of the 1800s, though the evidence is scanty. Toppan, who worked as a nurse, confessed to murdering thirty-one patients in the late 1800s, is the most likely candidate for the first (known) American female serial killer (Schechter 2003).

Women make up between 10 and 17 percent of all serial killers and have done so for as long as humans have been killing humans (Skrapec 1994). The point here isn't that Wuornos's crimes were not significant, but that all the effort the media has put into demonizing her is not really about her crimes. Many American women have engaged in serial murder, and female serial murders are not a modern phenomenon. Ninety percent of all female serial killers kill people they know, with over half of the convicted female murders in the United States killing an abusive domestic partner, whether boyfriend or husband. Female serial killers who kill people outside their families tend to kill relatively vulnerable people, mostly the elderly and children. Moreover, the bulk of women who kill do so in homes or home-like spaces and kill an average of nine people. Lastly, 88 percent of female serial killers are white, and over 90 percent identify as Christian (Harrison et al. 2015).

So, what is it about Aileen Wuornos that makes her exceptional enough to be widely reviled while so many female serial killers remain relatively anonymous? She killed fewer people than the average female serial killer, didn't kill people she knew, and didn't kill children. That may be the problem. Wuornos's family history suggests an ugly reality about America. While we profess to abhor violence against children, we also believe families are sacrosanct, and what goes on in them is private and acceptable. Thus, the violence against Wuornos was (and largely still is) invisible. Also, Wuornos killed men who solicited her for sex and did so while roaming the highways looking for men who solicit sex from prostitutes. In both her sex work and her unsettled life, she put herself well outside the boundaries of "respectable womanhood" and, to all too many Americans, got what she deserved.

In many ways, the Wuornos portrayal in *Monster* fits in with the "deadly dolls" subsection of American film. Movies like *Kill Bill*, *Thelma and Louise*, *The Hand That Rocks the Cradle*, and *Basic Instinct* all promoted the idea of vengeful feminism—violent women striking a blow against men for women everywhere (Holmlund). While *Monster* does not explicitly make feminist claims, the film does suggest Aileen's murderous violence was, if not acceptable, then understandable in the crucible of a society blind to violence against children and women (McCaughey and King). This is not a stance all Americans find comfortable or acceptable. Indeed, one study found that the majority of American female serial killers are not charged with murder at all, in part because, as a society, we are unwilling to admit women can be killers, and, when we do, we prefer to think of them as victims acting in self-defense (Farrell et al. 2011).

Both these realities suggest why the media and the legal system could not see Wuornos, at least in part, as a victim. She certainly saw herself as one, claiming self-defense for all the murders for which she was convicted. There can be little doubt she had a nightmare childhood, chock-full of the kind of violence that leaves permanent psychological scars. Also, like the bulk of American murderers, Wuornos was most assuredly mentally ill. Prison psychologists diagnosed her with antisocial personality disorder and, like her father, schizophrenia. And all the research on rape and incest survivors suggest she surely suffered from post-traumatic stress disorder, including flashbacks to violent episodes in her life, chronic anxiety, and fear of abandonment. Aileen lived with alcohol, cigarette, and drug addiction. Sexual abuse survivors are twenty-six times more likely to have substance abuse problems than the general population (Korte et al. 2010). It is no accident that the only feminist organization that came to Wuornos's defense was WHISPER, a group that seeks to abolish prostitution and create alternatives for sex workers.

But the media frenzy around Wuornos is more complicated than American ambivalence about sexual violence and prostitution. Responses to Wuornos and her killing spree suggest considerable cultural anxiety about female violence against men and considerably comfort with male violence against women. Men who pick up sex workers are, at least according to the law, themselves criminals, as are the men who pimp prostitutes. But very few johns and pimps are ever arrested, and society spends little time demonizing the men who buy and sell women's bodies. The notion that women might fight back is an anathema in a society that sees women's bodies, particularly the bodies of poor women and women of color, as commodities for the nastier elements of male privilege. This may explain why none of the four anti–death penalty organizations would take Wuornos's case. Women who kill in self-defense or because they were raped are defensible, in part because they fall within normative gender expectations of women as victims of male violence, but women who take revenge make us uncomfortable. And until recently, few people believed or cared about the violence, including rape, inflicted upon prostitutes in the United States.

Wuornos's media notoriety may also have something to do with her preferred method of murder. More than half of female serial killers kill with poison and only about 10 percent use guns. Guns, to put it bluntly, are considered a man's tool, and women who use them also fall outside society's ideas of the feminine ideal (Harrison, et al. 2015; Farrell et al. 2011). Wuornos shot her victims multiple times, demonstrating a level of violence even seasoned anti–death penalty advocates found unacceptable in a woman. Indeed, the fact that she shot her victims more than once has always been important in the Wuornos reporting, with each victim generally listed by occupation, and then the number of times shot. This preoccupation with gunshots is not shared in the reporting of male serial killers, suggesting a uniquely gendered approach to thinking about female killers. Wuornos's notoriety might be put down to a combination of all of the above, particularly when we consider that at the time of her trials, everyone in America "knew" she was gun-toting, lesbian prostitute, but no one knew she'd been raped by the first man she murdered, nor that she'd been physically and sexually abused as a child.

Monster makes short shrift of Wuornos's trials, and probably for good reason. The movie is an exploration of her year as a serial killer, not a trial drama. But if the film had covered the trial, Jenkins surely would have exposed Wuornos's lawyers as inept. Tricia Jenkins, a public defense lawyer for Volusia County, Florida, defended Wuornos in her first trial, where she was tried for killing sociopath rapist Richard Mallory. Jenkins failed to introduce any evidence of Mallory's sexual predator past or any evidence of her client's past sexual traumas. Friends and neighbors later said they offered to testify about the family dysfunction, but no one at the public defender's office responded to their offers. Jenkins's defense consisted of only one witness—her client. Wuornos described Mallory's rape in great detail, as well as his threats to kill her, but the prosecution's cross-examination and suggestion she was lying about the rape so upset Wuornos that she lost her temper and refused to speak anymore. Not long after the first trial, an NBC reporter (not the police or her lawyer) discovered Mallory's criminal past. The judge refused to admit this evidence in post-trial proceedings and also refused to hear arguments for a retrial.

Aileen Wuornos's second trial was even worse. Often referred to as the "hippy lawyer," Steven Glazer vaulted to the big time when Arleen Pralle hired him to handle her adoptive daughter's ongoing legal issues. Jenkins, the first lawyer, later testified that Glazer never picked up the files for the Wuornos case and told her he only took the case because he needed "media exposure" (Capital Punishment). He convinced Wuornos to plead "no contest" to the next four murders, earning his client four more death sentences with no trial—despite of the fact that no-contest pleas are virtually unheard of in murder trials. Meanwhile, Arleen Pralle, who never missed an opportunity to pat herself on the back in front of the television and newspapers reporters for her Christian charity, took $10,000 from Nick Broomfield (she asked for $25,000), a documentary filmmaker, and split it with Glazer (Ansen 1994). Pralle helped Glazer avoid doing his job by encouraging Wuornos to skip the trials so she could "get right with God" (Capital Punishment).

Wuornos's appeal lawyers were better, but it hardly mattered. Her mental condition deteriorated to such an extent that she fired her attorneys and dropped her clemency appeal, publicly stating her wish to be executed. At the Florida Supreme Court, the fired lawyers argued their former client wasn't competent to make such a decision. The court disagreed. In one of her last interviews, she said, "A raped woman got executed so people could sell books" (Wuornos and Berry-Dee 2004). She wasn't entirely wrong.

It is hard not to ask how Wuornos's story might turn out if replayed in the twenty-first century. The #MeToo Movement, born in 2006 but fully flowered in 2016 in the wake of then-candidate Trump's "grab them by the p—" scandal and the crimes of Hollywood moguls like Harvey Weinstein, which contributed much to American understanding of sexual violence. As one legal scholar put it:

> It's hard not to draw comparisons between [Aileen Wuornos's case] and the violence being done to women all over the world in the name of religion, from women in the Middle East being executed after being raped because they're "unclean," to the cults in the US . . . that serve as a front for sex trafficking, rape, and child abuse. Even organizations that explicitly forbid rape and sexual abuse, like the Catholic church, often protect the sex offenders within their ranks, disregarding the suffering of their powerless or voiceless members in favor of maintaining the illusion of structural integrity. (Wells 2018)

Neither the film nor scholars argue that Wuornos was wrongly convicted. There's little doubt she killed seven men. The question comes in searching for motivations and justifications for her execution. Her father, a sexual predator, ended up in a psychiatric hospital, as did Richard Mallory, the man who most certainly raped her and began her murder spree. Society offered the men who helped make a "monster" psychiatric help, but that same help was never extended to Aileen Wuornos.

Far too many people in Wuornos's life abused her, betrayed her, or treated her as a cash cow. And the people around her stood by and let it happen. Family members and neighbors ignored the abuse. School officials did nothing about the dirty, ragged child who showed up at school, unable to concentrate on the work. The woman Wuornos loved betrayed her to keep her freedom, and her first lawyer couldn't be bothered to mount a real defense. Once in jail, her adopted "mother" and second lawyer treated her like a paycheck and opportunity for fame, and the legal system never gave a darn about any of it. Instead, they put her down, like a dog with rabies, which, metaphorically, was pretty much what she'd become. A civilized society takes care of those who can't or won't take care of themselves, and that goes doubly for children. Until America takes care of abused children, we can expect the cycle of violence, like the one that made Aileen Wuornos, to continue.

A PAIR OF DUBIOUS FIRSTS: MARY SURRATT AND MARTHA PLACE

In 1865, Mary Jenkins Surratt became the first woman executed by the U.S. government for her part in the Lincoln assassination. Surratt owned and ran the Washington, D.C., boarding house frequented by John Wilkes Booth and his gang of conspirators, including at least one of her sons. The plan was that Booth would kill President Abraham Lincoln, while George Atzerodt would kill Vice-President Andrew Johnson, and Lewis Powell would kill Secretary of State William Seward. Mary Surratt's son John Jr., who worked as a spy for the Confederate government, collaborated in the plot but fled to Canada, and then Europe and Egypt to avoid prosecution. Though Mary Surratt claimed to know nothing of the assassination plot, historical evidence says otherwise. She stored guns and binoculars, later used in the assassination, at her house and knew of (and probably participated in) several meetings of the conspirators in her home. Moreover, Lewis Powell returned to her house after his attempt on Seward's life failed and was there when she was arrested two days after Lincoln's murder. Surratt was charged with aiding and abetting the conspirators in a trial that began just three weeks after the assassination. On June 20, a military tribunal found Surratt guilty and sentenced her to be hanged. Surratt and her convicted male coconspirators were hung simultaneously on July 7, 1865, less than three months after Lincoln's assassination.

Thirty-four years after Mary Surratt's hanging, Martha Garretson Place became the first woman to be executed by electric chair. Place was convicted of killing her step-daughter Ida in February 1898. Martha, who'd sustained a traumatic head injury in her twenties and suffered from diminished mental capacity, married William Place after his wife died, though she was the household maid at the time. William and Ida routinely mocked Martha for her lack of education and refused to let her son from a previous marriage live with them. The night of the murder police found Martha on her bedroom floor, her clothes skirts over her head, and the gas jets turned on but not lit. The police determined that Martha's husband William was not culpable in the murder, though acid from his photograph studio had been used in the attack on Ida. At her trial, William testified against her, saying she attacked him with an ax after she murdered Ida. Martha refused to defend herself and never said a word about the events of that night. The governor of New York, Theodore Roosevelt, declined to commute her death sentence, and on March 20, 1899, authorities at Sing Azeroth prison strapped Martha into the electric chair and pulled the switch.

FURTHER READING

Anklesaria, Ariz, and Julie P. Gentile. 2012. "Psychotherapy with Women Who Have Worked in the Sex Industry." *Innovations in Clinical Neuroscience* 9, no. 10 (October): 27–33.

Ansen, David. 1994. "Profit Sharing, American Style." *Newsweek*, March 6, 1994. https://www.newsweek.com/profit-sharing-american-style-186104.

Capital Punishment in Context. "Aileen Wuornos: The Post-Trial Period." Accessed June 13, 2022. https://capitalpunishmentincontext.org/node/77456.

Clary, Mike. 1991. "A Mother's Love." *Los Angeles Times*, December 17, 1991.

Ebert, Roger. 2004. "Theron Turns in Powerhouse Performance." January 1. https://www.rogerebert.com/reviews/monster-2003.

Epstein, Rachel. 2009. "Charlize Theron Had Doubts about Playing a Serial Killer in 'Monster.'" *Marie Claire*, May 1, 2009. https://www.marieclaire.com/celebrity/a27330771/charlize-theron-monster-movie-doubts/.

Farrell, Amanda, Robert Keppel, and Victoria Titterington. 2011. "Lethal Ladies: Revisiting What We Know about Female Serial Killers." *Homicide Studies* 15 (3): 228–252.

Gottlieb, Daphne, and Lisa Kester. 2011. *Dear Dawn: Aileen Wuornos in Her Own Words*. New York: Soft Skull Press.

Harrison, Marissa, Erin Murphy, Y. R. Lavina, Thomas Bowers, and Claire Flaherty. 2015. "Female Serial Killers in the United States: Means, Motives and Makings." *The Journal of Forensic Psychiatry & Psychology* 26 (3): 383–406.

Holmlund, Christine. 1994. "A Decade of Deadly Dolls." In *Moving Targets: Women, Murder, and Representation*, edited by Helen Birch. Berkeley: University of California.

Korte, Jeffrey, Therese Killeen, Susan Sonne, Louise Haynes, Angela Malek, and Kathleen Brady. 2010. "Gender Differences in History of Sexual and Physical Abuse in Relation to Addiction Severity." *Drug and Alcohol Dependence* 156 (1): 117–129.

McCaughey, Martha, and Neal King, eds. 2001. *Reel Knockouts: Violent Women in the Movies* Austin: University of Texas Press.

Petrakis, John. 1994. "Hypocrisy Imbues the Tale of Aileen Wuornos." *Chicago Tribune*, March 25, 1994.

"Prostitution in the U.S." Legal Resources, https://www.hg.org/legal-articles/prostitution-in-the-united-states-30997.

Russell, Sue. 2002. *Lethal Intent: The Shocking Story of One of America's Most Notorious Female Serial Killers*. New York: Pinnacle Books (Kensington Publishing Corp).

Schechter, Harold. 2003. *Fatal: The Poisonous Life of a Female Serial Killer*. New York: Gallery Books.

Skrapec, Candice. 1994. "The Female Serial Killer: An Evolving Criminality." In *Moving Targets: Women, Murder, and Representation*, edited by Helen Birch, 241–268. Berkeley: University of California.

Thompson, Christie. 2015. "Charged with Murder: The Paradox of 'Felony Murder.'" The Marshall Project, September 24, 2015. https://www.themarshallproject.org/2015/09/24/a-person-can-be-charged-with-murder-even-if-they-haven-t-killed-anyone.

Wells, Ashley. 2018. "Revisiting Aileen Wuornos in Light of #MeToo." May 11. https://medium.com/@misswellstoyou/revisiting-aileen-wuornos-in-light-of-metoo-835fac5aa51d.

Wuornos, Aileen, and Christopher Berry-Dee. 2004. *Monster: My Story*. London: John Blake Publishing.

Chapter 7
Iron Jawed Angels (2004)

Written by Jennifer Friedes, Sally Robinson, and
Eugenia Bostwick-Singer; Directed by Katja von Garnier
HBO Films, 2 hr., 5 min.

INTRODUCTION

Iron Jawed Angels chronicles the last three years of the political movement to gain American women the right to vote. Focusing on the young radicals who energized the movement, the film takes a nearly two-century effort of steps forward and back and turns it into an energizing two-hour film. The film was written as collaboration, with Jennifer Friedes getting credit for the story and sharing teleplay-writing credits with Sally Robinson, Eugenia Bostwick-Singer, and Raymond Singer. *Iron Jawed Angels* is Friedes's only writing credit. Bostwick-Singer and Singer also cowrote *Mulan* (1998), and Sally Robinson is a long-time television writer who's worked on a variety of television shows and movies, while also working as an English professor at Texas A&M.

HBO tapped German film director Katja von Garnier to direct *Iron Jawed Angels* because the director's previous work proved she could make films that attracted young viewers. In 1993, Garnier made a short film that won her considerable accolades. Hollywood took notice and hired her to direct *Moonlight and Valentino*, starring Gwyneth Paltrow and Whoopi Goldberg. Garnier canceled her contract for the film due to "artistic differences" when the studio wouldn't let her make the movie she envisioned. The film was eventually made and tanked at the box office and with critics.

In 1997, Garnier cowrote, directed, and acted in *Bandits*, a German coming-of-age/underdog band makes good/road movie for young women (think *Thelma & Louise* meets *This Thing You Do!*). Garnier and her costars also wrote and performed the music for the film, and the soundtrack climbed to number one in Germany not long after the film's premiere. A *New York Times* critic called *Bandits* "a celebration of liberated sisterhood and the rebellions, anarchic spirit of youth" (Van Gelder 1999). As a result, Hollywood beckoned for the second time. However unlikely the choice of Garnier, it seems clear HBO wanted a director who could take a staid historical topic and make it relevant to twenty-first-century audiences. To ensure the film's success, HBO signed a handful of notable film stars to the film, including Angelica Huston, Margo Martindale, Hilary Swank, Julia Ormond, and Patrick Dempsey.

SUMMARY

The film opens on two young women walking down an early 1900s city street. They stop to admire a hat in a store window, and, while they talk, we learn they are activists recently returned from England, where they met British suffragettes Emmeline and Christabel Pankhurst. Alice Paul (Hilary Swank) and Lucy Burns (Frances O'Connor) agree they should present an action plan for women's right to vote to the National American Women's Suffrage Association (NAWSA).

In Washington, D.C., Paul and Burns meet with Carrie Chapman Catt (Angelica Huston) and Anna Howard Shaw (Lois Smith). The women's discussion reveals a generational divide, with the older women, represented by Catt, determined to take a cautious, state-by-state approach to winning the vote for women. Paul and Burns, on the other hand, want an amendment and more active campaigning. Catt agrees they can set up the NAWSA Congressional Committee if they raise their own money to support the endeavor. The two set up an office and begin to organize a women's suffrage parade to be held just before President Woodrow Wilson's inauguration. Along the way, they collect an enthusiastic team of volunteers, including Mabel Vernon (Brooke Smith) and Doris Stevens (Laura Fraser). At a strike meeting of immigrant women workers, they convince factory worker Ruza Wenclawska (Vera Farmiga) to join the cause, arguing that if women could vote, they could vote for better working conditions.

At an art gallery opening Alice meets labor lawyer and antiwar activist Inez Milholland (Julia Ormond) and asks her to lead the parade, dressed as Winged Victory on a white horse. The idea is to have a parade that is beautiful and exciting. Alice also meets *Washington Post* cartoonist Ben Weissman (Patrick Dempsey), a man both sympathetic to women's suffrage and romantically interested in Alice Paul.

Before the parade, Black activist Ida Wells-Barnett (Adilah Barnes) asks for a contingent of Black women to march in the Parade. Alice explains that they can't anger Southern, prosegregation politicians who might not vote for the amendment if the right to vote was extended to Black women. Wells-Barnett leaves, rightly dissatisfied with this strategy.

The parade begins well enough, with Inez at the front and women marching in groups. The crowd is large and mostly enthusiastic at first but turns ugly as some men begin to jeer the women. "You should be home with your mother," one man calls out. "My mother is here," a parade participant responds. Mid-parade, Ida Wells-Barnett steps into the parade, earning a smile from Alice. A bottle is thrown, and antisuffrage men attack the parade participants. The police do nothing to stop the violence against the women, one man telling them none of this would have happened if they'd just stayed home.

Meanwhile President Wilson arrives at the train station to find it empty. He has been upstaged by the suffrage parade. Alice and Lucy meet with Catt and tell her the parade violence has turned public opinion toward the women. Catt does not agree. The young suffragettes meet with President Wilson, who puts them off with hollow promises. Meanwhile, Emily Leighton (Molly Parker), wife of congressman Tom Leighton, volunteers with the suffragettes against her husband's wishes. NAWSA leaders force Paul and Burns out of the organization, and the two found the National Women's Party (NWP), an organization that will take a significantly more aggressive approach to women's suffrage.

News of the United States' entry into World War I causes controversy within the NWP women. Should they put aside their politicking to work for the war effort? They agree that they can do both. While giving a speech, the overworked Inez Milholland collapses and dies. Alice has a crisis of conscience and retreats to her parents' farm. Lucy finds her there and convinces her to return to political activism. The NWP develops a bold plan to picket the White House. President Wilson has been making much of the war as a fight for democracy, but, at home, there is no democracy if women can't vote.

Women appear in front of the White House gates, holding signs that read things like, "Mr. President, How Long Must Women Wait for Liberty?" Dubbed "the Silent Sentinels," the protesters are directed by Paul to not respond to hecklers or do anything at all but stand before the gates, holding their signs. The police begin arresting the protesters for "obstructing traffic." Alice Paul goes out on the picket line and is arrested, as is Emily Leighton, whose husband has taken her children away from her for her activism. The suffragettes are sent to Occoquan Workhouse, where they are physically and psychologically abused. Alice and several other women go on a hunger strike. In a startlingly violent scene, guards force-feed Paul. News of the women's treatment reaches the press after Emily passes her husband a note from Alice during a prison visit. A psychiatrist examines Alice and tells the president she is not crazy, just determined.

Public disapproval of the treatment of the suffragettes mounts, and the press dubs them "the Iron Jawed Angels." Frustrated, Wilson meets with Catt but continues to stall on supporting a women's suffrage amendment. After the women are finally released from prison, Wilson announces he will support the Nineteenth Amendment.

In the final scenes, we see both Houses of Congress pass the amendment. The suffragettes turn their efforts to the state-by-state ratification process. It comes down to one state, Tennessee, and the vote is close. The women fear they will lose the vote, but a young conservative state senator receives a letter from his mother telling him to vote yes. He does, and the amendment passes and becomes law. The film ends as the suffragettes rejoice, and we see a montage of women, young and old, voting for the first time.

The film premiered at the Sundance Film Festival in January 2004, where it garnered a standing ovation from viewers, while the festival's critic called it "visually stunning and cinematically breathtaking" (Fischer 2004). The film appeared on television immediately after the last *Sex and the City* episode in February and appeared in limited theater release soon after. *Iron Jawed Angels* did well at awards season, garnering several Emmy and Golden Globe nominations in a variety of categories. Angelica Huston won a Golden Globe for Best Supporting Actress, and Robbie Greenberg won a Best Cinematography award from the American Society of Cinematographers. The writers also won recognition with a Humanitas Prize nomination and PEN Center award for Best Teleplay.

HISTORICAL CONTEXT

The fight to get American women the right to vote goes back to the birth of the nation. In 1776, as the Continental Congress met in Philadelphia to discuss the formation of a new nation, Abigail Adams wrote her husband the now famous "Remember the Ladies" letter. In it, she urged lawmakers to "not put such unlimited power into the hands of Husbands. Remember, all Men would be tyrants if they could. If particular care and attention is not paid to the ladies we are determined to foment a rebellion and will not hold ourselves bound by any Laws in which we have no voice or Representation" (Holton 2009). Though the letter makes no specific claim to voting rights, voting not having yet been legally established, Adams's insistence that women have a voice in governance began a decades-long national struggle to include women in the governance of the United States.

The 1776 New Jersey state constitution enfranchised all property owners and referred to voters as "he and she" until disenfranchising women in 1807. Kentucky voted in 1838 to allow white widows who headed households to vote, but otherwise, all American women were exempted from the vote. The 1830s and 1840s saw a groundswell of activism by women, most of it aimed at temperance reform, the abolition of slavery, and married women's property rights. The philosophical works of Englishwoman Mary Wollstonecraft underwrote much of the early women's rights movement and inspired South Carolina abolitionist Sarah Grimké to write *The Equality of the Sexes and the Condition of Women* in 1838. Sarah and her sister Angelina Grimke traveled the country giving speeches supporting both the abolition of slavery and voting rights for women in the 1830s, inspiring other women to join the cause.

In the 1840s, increasing numbers of women joined the abolition movement, but they grew dissatisfied by the way the movement, while advocating for Black rights, dismissed women's rights. Elizabeth Cady Stanton and Lucretia Mott traveled to the World Anti-Slavery Convention in London in 1840 with their husbands but were not allowed to speak, vote, or even appear on the floor. Mott, who was a Quaker, organized other Quaker women into planning a women's rights meeting and, along with Stanton, planned the Seneca Falls Convention. The 1848 meeting produced the Declaration of Sentiments, modeled on the Declaration of Independence. Among the document's demands was the right of women to vote.

Other conventions followed in the 1850s, most of them organized by state or city affiliation. Susan B. Anthony met Elizabeth Cady Stanton in 1851. Anthony was the organizer, while Stanton was the writer, and between the two of them, they led the movement until their deaths. At the beginning of the Civil War, women's rights activists met and agreed to suspend their political agitation until the war's end in favor of working for Union victory and the end of slavery. They formed the Women's Loyal National League and together collected over three hundred thousand signatures on a petition to present an abolition amendment (the Thirteenth Amendment) to the U.S. Congress.

At the war's end, the Thirteenth Amendment passed, signaling the end of two hundred years of American slavery. The New England Woman Suffrage Association (later the American Woman Suffrage Association or AWSA), led by Lucy Stone, formed to work for universal suffrage (the vote for both Black men and all women), but as the Fifteenth Amendment stalled in congress, Stone agreed to drop the demand for women's suffrage in favor of Black male suffrage. Objecting to this, Stanton and Anthony formed the National Woman Suffrage Association (NWSA). The NWSA and AWSA split on the issue of voting for decades, but each organization brought its own tactics and adherents to the fight to gain all American women the right to vote (Dubois 1978).

The movement lost momentum during the 1860s as the nation reconstructed itself in the wake of the Civil War and argued over what to do with four million freed persons. In 1872, Susan B. Anthony revitalized the movement when she was arrested for attempting to vote in the presidential election. The subsequent trial created a platform where Anthony argued for the enfranchisement of women. When found guilty and ordered to pay a $100 fine, she declared she would "never pay a dollar of your unjust penalty," adding that "resistance to tyranny is obedience to God" (Hull 2012).

By the turn of the twentieth century, the suffrage movement struggled to make significant gains. In 1869, Wyoming Territory enfranchised women, with Utah following suit a year later. Washington and Montana Territories followed suit in the 1880s. Less a move toward women's rights and more a practical need to have more voters in sparsely populated territories, these victories gave the movement new life. In 1890, the AWSA and NWSA merged to form the monolithic National American Woman Suffrage Association (NAWSA), with Elizabeth Cady Stanton at its head. Stanton retired in 1892 to focus on her book, *The Woman's Bible*, leaving the post to her sister-activist Susan B. Anthony, who held it until her retirement in 1900.

Carrie Chapman Catt took the helm and distanced the NAWSA from Black and immigrant voting, particularly that block of immigrant women in labor unions, as well as controversial issues like divorce reform. Instead, Catt pursued middle- and elite-class women. Anna Howard Shaw replaced Catt in 1904, after Catt resigned to organize a European suffrage organization. Shaw resisted racist Southern demands to work for the enfranchisement of only white women. Catt returned to the American suffrage movement to found the Woman Suffrage Party in New York, which functioned under the NAWSA umbrella. By 1910, the NAWSA had nearly one hundred and twenty thousand members, and by 1914, eleven states, all of them western states, had enfranchised women. Meanwhile, efforts to enfranchise women in Eastern and Southern states stalled (Weiss 2019).

Alice Paul returned from England in 1910, galvanized by the radical tactics she learned there. While in England, Paul was arrested at a protest and responded with a hunger strike. As would happen later in the United States, prison officials instituted forced feedings that functioned as little more than prison torture (Adams and Keene 2008). While she was in England, Paul met Lucy Burns, an American who had also joined the British suffragettes. Burns and Paul bonded over their shared frustration with the NAWSA's conservative approach to women's suffrage. After Paul completed her doctorate in 1912, she and Burns began lobbying the Shaw and the NAWSA for a national suffrage amendment, but with no success. Venerable social reformer Jane Addams interceded for Paul and Burns with Shaw and got Paul appointed to the chair of the NAWSA's Congressional Committee (Adams and Keene 2008).

After their experience in England, Paul and Burns believed that only direct action would result in any forward progress on the stalled suffrage fight. Rather than written rhetoric, the two wanted visual rhetoric and so planned the first Washington, D.C., suffrage parade to coincide with President-elect Wilson's March 1912 inauguration. Nearly 130 women attended the first parade-planning meeting in January. Theater producer Hazel MacKaye designed the floats, as well as an allegorical pageant that would be staged outside the Treasury Building. Parade coorganizer Doris Stevens wrote a statement for the parade, saying the parade was to protest "the present political organization of society" and "to dramatize in numbers and beauty the fact that women want to vote" (Brown 1913).

A week before the parade, suffragists from Southern states protested the inclusion of Black participants. Some state delegations allowed Black women to march, and some did not, while a delegation from Howard University, a Black college, marched as a group near the rear of the parade. Ida B. Wells antilynching activist and founder of the Alpha Suffrage Club was asked not to march with the Illinois state delegation, but join the Black women at the rear of the parade. Wells declined to do so and, instead, waited until the parade was underway to join the all-white Illinois delegation (Zahniser and Fry 2014).

Suffrage activists faced significant opposition from the lobbies. Chief among these were the powerful brewers' and distillers' organizations, who worried that once women had the vote, they'd vote to prohibit alcohol, a reasonable concern given the long connection between female activism and the temperance movement. Factory owners also opposed women's suffrage, worried that enfranchised women would both move to protect women workers and outlaw child labor. Conservative religious institutions also opposed women's suffrage, contending women who voted would upset patriarchal order (Maddux 2004). Some of those opposing women's suffrage blocked the March 3 parade along its route, and then hecklers and others surged into the street. The mounted police did little to stop the melee, though a few arrests were made. A group of Boy Scouts and some soldier spectators stepped in to push back the crowd, before young men from a nearby college formed a human chain to keep the marchers safe (Dodd 2008).

In a speech the evening of the parade, Anna Howard Shaw decried the police brutality and commended the marchers. She joined Alice Paul in recognizing the publicity advantage of the day. Public opinion favored the suffragists, and donations poured into the NAWSA. Nonetheless, Shaw's dislike of radical tactics led to her resignation in 1915. Carrie Chapman Catt stepped back into the presidency, a post she held until soon after the passage of the Nineteenth Amendment in 1920.

In 1916, Paul, Burns, and others split from the NAWSA to create the National Women's Party (NWP). Alva Belmont, millionaire widow of two exceedingly rich men, donated the money to make the new, more radical party possible. Belmont also helped the NWP's largest and most effective protest, the picketing of the White House, and, in 1917, she became the NWP's president, an office she held until her death in 1933. In January 1917, the NWP began picketing the White House. Known as the "Silent Sentinels," the picket lines were peaceful at first. Women stood silent and still in front of the White House gates, holding signs that beseeched the president to support women's right to vote. Picketing changed with the United States entry into World War I in March 1917. The NWP both refused to take a pro- or antiwar stance and declined to suspend political activities in favor of war work. The decision was a controversial one, but women's rights activists had learned their lesson in the Civil War and kept up the picketing. The police began arresting the Silent Sentinels for obstructing traffic, but volunteers continued to take their posts before the White House gates each day.

Alice Paul went out on the picket line in October 1917, carrying a sign that read, "The Time has come to conquer or submit, for us there can be but on choice. We have made it" (Adams and Keene 2008). She was arrested and sent to the district jail. Many other arrested picketers were sent to Occoquan Workhouse. As she did in England, Paul went on a hunger strike, taking nothing but bread and water. Sentinels on the picket line in November were arrested and suffered what is now known as the "Night of Terror" for the police abuse the protesters suffered. Lucy burns was chained and beaten, and Alice Cosu had a heart attack. The story got out, and, in late November 1917, the women were released from jail and their convictions vacated (Dodd 2008).

Activists kept up the pressure and resumed picketing for another year. In August 1918, the police began arresting picketers again. The NWP also ran a campaign against antisuffrage senators up for election in the fall of 1918. Wilson relented and announced his support for the Nineteenth Amendment, and in May 1919, the House of Representatives passed the Amendment. The U.S. Senate followed suit two weeks later. Suffrage activists from NAWSA, NWP, and other groups immediately began work on state-by-state ratification. Within two months, Illinois, Wisconsin, Michigan, Montana, Arkansas, and Nebraska had ratified the amendment. Texas and four border states voted no on ratification. Western states, all of which had already legalized voting for women, hastened to ratify the amendment by the early months of 1920. By March the Nineteenth Amendment had been ratified by thirty-five states. Suffrage activists needed one more state and turned their eye on Tennessee, a southern border state. Both pro- and antisuffrage forces pulled out all the political stops in Tennessee, and, on August 12, the Tennessee state senate ratified the amendment. The state House of Representatives voted six days later in favor of the amendment, and though the Speaker of the House tried to file a motion for a revote, the vote stood and the Nineteenth Amendment became national law in August 1920 (Weiss 2019). After more than a hundred years of American democracy, American women could finally exercise that most vital civil right, the right to vote.

DEPICTION AND CULTURAL CONTEXT

HBO decided to make *Iron Jawed Angels* after voting statistics revealed that more than half of women eighteen to twenty-four years old did not vote in the 2000 election, an election of such closeness that women's votes could have changed the outcome. The evening of the election, the nation did not know which man had won the election. Al Gore won the popular vote, but electoral votes were less clear. The results came down to the votes in Wisconsin, Oregon, and Florida. Wisconsin and Oregon went to Gore, giving him 270 electoral votes to Bush's 246. Florida's 25 electoral votes would determine the election. Bush won by a margin so small it triggered a recount, and then after a month of discoveries of voter irregularity in Florida, the U.S. Supreme Court voted to end the recount and give the presidency to Bush. So, for the fourth time (of five overall), a man who did not win the popular vote became president.

Why did this matter to women voters or, more appropriately, nonvoters? Since 1980, female voters have overwhelmingly support Democratic candidates, while men are more likely to vote Republican. This "gender gap," reflects the reality that Democrats are more likely to fund projects that help or support women while being proreproductive rights. One of George W. Bush's campaign slogans was, "the W. stands for woman," but his conservative and evangelical background made him hostile to even the most basic issues of women's rights. Bush's "stealth misogyny" meant he put women in his cabinet, and then undercut family leave; closed the Women's Bureau in the Labor Department; and defunded agencies that monitored sex discrimination, including cutting funding for the Equal Employment Opportunity Commission (the same place where future U.S. Supreme Court Justice and uber-conservative Clarence Thomas once sexually harassed at least four women—See *Confirmation* chapter). The Bush administration also promoted "abstinence-only" sexual education in schools, despite numerous studies that demonstrated the policy caused higher teen pregnancy rates, while engaging in an ongoing attack on women's reproductive rights (Yarrow 2019). None of this would have happened if women eighteen to twenty-four had all voted in the 2000 election because women, and this is doubly so for young women, are more likely to vote for Democrats.

For HBO executives, the question was how they could use their considerable media power to overcome the ambivalence young women (and men) feel about voting. It's not an inconsiderable problem. Rock the Vote, an organization dedicated to encouraging the youth vote, has determined there are several reasons young people don't vote. First, we used to teach "civics" or "government" in high schools, but conservative education programs like No Child Left Behind have eradicated classes likely to familiarize students with government and their place in it. Moreover, teachers, particularly history teachers, are often underprepared or unwilling to talk about politics in the classroom (Rock the Vote). Rock the Vote events include popular music and Hollywood speakers to energize youth voters, and the success of such events undoubtedly played a role in HBO's production decisions for *Iron Jawed Angels*. They hired a hip, young director who made a movie aimed at Generation X sensibilities, complete with a super-sexy love interest for Alice Paul, fast paced montages, and a contemporary music soundtrack. It's not your mother's history documentary, rife with boring talking heads and earnest reenactors.

So HBO purposefully set out to make a film about women's suffrage that would attract young women and get them excited about voting. And they never pretended otherwise. The studio's promotional literature for the film makes it abundantly clear:

> Katja von Garnier's *Iron Jawed Angels* tells the remarkable and little-known story of a group of passionate and dynamic young women, led by Alice Paul (Hilary Swank) and her friend Lucy Burns (Frances O'Connor), who put their lives on the line to fight for American women's right to vote. This true story had parallels to today, as the young activists struggle with issues such as the challenges of protesting a popular president during wartime and the perennial balancing act between love and career. Utilizing a pulsing soundtrack, vivid colors, and a freewheeling camera, Katja von Garnier's driving filmmaking style shapes up preconceptions of the period film and gives history a vibrant contemporary energy and relevance.—Synopsis

But all that contemporary energy and relevance comes at a price.

To be fair, *Iron Jawed Angels* gets most of the large historical events and issues right, and what it gets wrong is sometimes understandable from a historical storytelling point of view. The parade, for example, is reproduced much as it was back in 1917. From Inez Milholland's headpiece and horse to the floats and ladies marching in graduation gowns, the film gets the look right. It is startling to see women of the period wearing color, but that's because all the photo and film images from that period are in black and white. But Alice Paul did not plan the parade, per se. She planned for *a* parade, but not the actual parade. As happens so often in large organizations, the NWP formed a committee to plan what they called "The White House Procession." Dora Lewis, who would later be arrested four times for picketing the White House; Mary Ritter Beard, a historian who organized a number of suffrage rallies; and journalist Crystal Eastman headed up the committee, and Jane Burleson acted as grand marshall. It was Burleson, not Inez Milholland, who led the parade, accompanied by a paper-mache model of the Liberty Bell. Like Milholland, Burleson rode a white horse, though in the real parade, Milholland carried a banner that read, "Forward Into the Light" (Zahniser and Fry 2014).

The film also correctly portrays Milholland's tragic death while on the speaking circuit, though she did not die of overwork, as the film suggests. Like Paul, Milholland was a college graduate, though Milholland's advanced degree made her a lawyer. While finishing her undergraduate degree at Vassar, the college briefly suspended her for organizing a women's suffrage meeting. She used her law degree to work for prison reform and child labor reform, believing that if women could vote, they would vote to address the vexing social problems caused by both. She was in Europe when World War I began in 1914 and developed a horror of war after seeing it up close. She was diagnosed with pernicious anemia, an autoimmune disease that causes the body to make insufficient red blood cells, and refused to stop campaigning for suffrage. In her last speech, she said, "Mr. President, how long must women wait for liberty?" and collapsed. She lingered for a month, supported by blood transfusions, but died in November 1916 (Cooney 2015).

The film's larger narrative is essentially historically accurate, from Paul and Burn's proposal to Catt and the NAWSA, though the parade, riot, beginning of the war, picketing the White House, arrests and prison abuse, and then the final votes to secure the amendment. The picketing signs are exact replicas of signs women carried in 1917–1918, prison conditions really were that bad, and force-feeding is gruesomely like rape. And the Amendment really did was ratified by a one state margin, where the vote was won by one vote, when one mother wrote her politician son a letter. It's almost too Hollywood to believe, but sometimes the truth really is stranger than fiction.

The film falters a little with the prison and hunger-strike scenes. For example, Alice Paul wasn't jailed in the Occoquan Workhouse with the other picketers. She was in the district jail. It makes sense that the writers and director decided to combine the two jails into one, both for storytelling drama and the sheer impracticality of filming two different jails in one movie that had a lot of ground to cover in two hours. More troubling is the film's suggestion that the women went on hunger strikes to protest prison conditions. Nothing could be further from the truth. The arrests and hunger strikes were political and purposeful tools in the women's fight for to gain the vote.

The hunger strike is a classic nonviolent resistance technique dating back centuries. Protesters in India used hunger strikes in the 1860s, hearkening back to a resistance tradition going back to 750 BCE. British suffragettes adopted the practice in 1909, and by the 1910s, dozens of imprisoned activists undertook hunger strikes and endured forced feedings. Emmeline Pankhurst's sister Mary Clarke died on Christmas Day 1910 as a result of force-feeding. The violence of force-feeding is hard to overstate. Prisoners are tied down, and their mouths forced open with clamps. Tubes are then inserted through the mouth, down the esophagus to the stomach, and liquid food is poured in via funnels. The process is so violent that prisoners are often injured, and afterward, in response to the physical and emotional trauma, regurgitate the liquid food. Britain outlawed force-feeding in 1913, but prison officials in the United States continue the practice to the present day.

Paul, Burns, and other American activists learned nonviolent tactics from their British counterparts, including the practice of engaging in some protest behavior that resulted in arrest, followed by hunger strikes. As the film suggests, Paul's National Women's Party purposefully sent picketers to the White House during wartime to gain publicity for their cause. They planned for arrests, and arrested they were. By October, 1917, more than seventy picketers were held in Occoquan Workhouse and the district jail. They began their incarceration by first refusing to pay fines, thus ensuring jail time, and then, once ordered to jail, petitioning to be treated as political prisoners and thus excused from prison uniforms and prison work. An October 15, 1917 petition for political prisoner status outlined the suffragette's demands. "We . . . refuse to work while in prison . . . This action is a necessary protest against an unjust sentence . . . we were exercising the right of peaceful petition, guaranteed by the Constitution of the United States" (Adams and Keene 2008). Paul and the others understood the United States didn't recognize political prisons, but they also understood that in asking for political prisoner status, they were asking for a special kind of legal status. In forcing the government to deny them special status, they constructed themselves as "unrepresented protesters that had not been allowed to vote on the laws and regulations for which they were being held accountable" (Adams and Keene 2008). Having made it clear they considered themselves political prisoners, they set the stage for the hunger strikes and resultant force-feedings that so outraged the public.

Paul didn't hunger strike alone either. Many women undertook a hunger strike, leading to the nickname "Iron Jawed Angels" for their lock-jawed resistance to force-feeding. Rose Winslow and Alice Paul began their hunger strikes the same day, after alerting their lawyers to spread the word, and prison officials force-fed them at the same time, though they were separated into adjoining rooms. It was Winslow who got the word out about the abuse Paul suffered because Paul was in solitary confinement in the prison mental ward, with friendly prison guard to pass her notes (as the movie suggests). When Paul continued to refuse to eat, the prison doctor ordered prison nurses to wake her every hour and began force-feeding her three times a day. The same doctor thought force-feeding might also cure Paul of a number of psychological problems, including her refusal to marry and have children and her pursuit of higher education.

Nor were the conditions and treatment of the suffrage activists secret until Alice Paul got a note out via Emily Leighton's politician husband, as the film portrays. First, both the Leightons are fictional characters, though she is a stand-in for the sort of upper-class women who worked for women's suffrage, and he was representative of an otherwise politically progressive politician who did not support the vote for women. More to the point, Paul and the other women didn't go off to jail without a plan. They recruited women from across the country, women who understood they'd be away from their families and, for some, jobs, for quite some time. Each woman knew that by picketing, she volunteered for arrest and prison abuse. Each woman knew they could hunger strike, and each one of them understood the dangers inherent in that course. They did it anyway, knowing they could get their stories out to the public and turn the tide of public opinion toward their cause. Lawyers for the NWP collected jail stories, as did husbands, prison doctors, and others. They were all published in the NWP's newspaper *Suffragist* and, from there, picked up by mainstream newspapers (Adams and Keene 2008). And, as the film suggests, the NWP's tactics succeeded in changing the national dialogue and pushed Congress to vote on the Nineteenth Amendment.

Which is not to say that it was the NWP alone that got the Nineteenth Amendment before Congress or that the hunger strikes had immediate effect on Congress. In spite of what the film suggests, there was a year and a half between Paul's release from prison and the congressional vote, and it was the combined effort of dozens of suffrage organizations over decades and decades that got the job done, not one group of renegade activists. Women's war work had something to do with the final success as well. Women played a crucial role in America's victory, filling in tens of thousands of jobs that freed up men for the front. Women also volunteered for war service in women's auxiliary branches of the U.S. military, serving as telegraph operators, truck drivers, spies, nurses, and more. Women working for the Red Cross and Salvation Army also provided crucial war work. President Wilson acknowledged the nation's debt to women in a September 1918 speech before Congress. "We have made partners of women in this war. . . . Shall we admit them only to a partnership of suffering and sacrifice and toil and not to a partnership of privilege?" (History.com). A great combination of efforts and factors came together to make 1919 the year Americans decided it would be a good idea if women could vote.

Perhaps the most egregious error the film makes is not so much in getting historical details wrong, but in adding historical details that never existed. The most marked of these is the addition of a love interest for Alice Paul. First, we see Burns and Paul gushing over a cute hat. They wear pretty dresses and know how to accessorize. Feminists, we are assured, are fashion conscious and like to be pretty. A *New York Times* reviewer likened that aspect of the film to "Legally Blonde III: The Suffragette Years" (Keith 2014).

The masturbation scene bothers critics and historians alike, and for good reason. It's not that academics and critics disapprove of sex but, rather, an issue of the real purpose of such a scene in a film about political activists working on the greatest expansion of democracy in American history. The director, Katja Von Garnier, said she (and presumably the writers) added the romance and sex elements on purpose. "There is this cliché that women who fight for their rights can't love, that they have no sense of humor, they aren't attractive. I think we are trying to break that cliché and portray women who are fun to watch" (Keith 2014). She's not wrong. The stereotypes about feminists are brutal. Feminists, we are told over and over again by those on the right, are humorless, man-haters who wear ugly shoes and hate families, heterosexuality, Christianity, and monogamy. Feminists are angry, hateful women who stay home with their children and have a grudge against bras. It's no wonder young women don't want to be identified as feminists. The social stigma is daunting. It's also effective. In not self-identifying as "feminist," young women can't fully embrace the realities of sexism or the struggle to overcome it. Also, studies show that young women who do not self-identify as feminist have lower self-esteem and are less likely to graduate from college than young women who do (Roy et al. 2007). There are real-world consequences to this cultural notion that "feminists are bad."

That said, it's a big leap from on-screen masturbation to "feminists not good," and one perhaps not worthy of the effort, particularly as filmmakers used the Alice Paul character for the scene. Paul never married, nor did she ever have a romantic relationship with anyone, man or woman. Lucy Burns and she were close, like Stanton and Anthony two generations before (Anthony may have been a lesbian, but Stanton was not), but they did not have a romantic relationship (Adams and Keene 2008). Alice Paul doesn't appear to have structured her life so that she had time to moon around in the bathtub fantasizing about anyone, let alone a fictional male reporter. Paul was scholarly and driven. People who knew her commented on her seriousness and the machine-like precision of her mind. She was, for example, willing to sacrifice the vote for Black women if she could achieve the larger goal of suffrage for white women, not because she was a racist, but because she was an unsentimental, practical thinker who embraced political expediency (Keith 2014).

The film suggests Progressive Era young women worried about balancing love and work. They simply didn't think in those categories. It's appealing to young twentieth- and twenty-first-century viewers, who've been told over and over again that balancing home/love and work is something *they* should worry about. It's a film made by third-wave feminists for third-wave feminists, or at least those who might become third-wave feminists. This is particularly seen in the "girly feminism" the film promotes. The suffrage activists wear cute clothes, get dressed up for parties, and like pink hats. They are slim, attractive, and funny. It's a kind of "lipstick feminism," a la *Sex and the City*. In this version of feminism, women are empowered by beauty and sexual liberation (Groeneveld 2009)—which is fine, except that it's not a feminist any suffragette would have recognized.

Also, the Ben Weissman character suggests even the most independent woman needs help from a man. He teaches Alice Paul to drive and dance and helps her with publicity for the movement. Maybe someone had to teach the real Alice Paul how to drive and dance, but no one had to help her with publicity by this stage in her career. She was a master at the game. She planned a parade that overshadowed the presidential inauguration both in its size and the riot it encouraged. And then there was Paul's long-range plan to set up picketers, have them be arrested, resist arrest, be abused, and get the word out about that abuse to sway public opinion (Lumsden 2019). Alice Paul didn't need anyone's help getting publicity for the movement, not even a super-hot journalist with mad dance moves.

Nonetheless, there's little doubt the film succeeds in energizing young viewers. As Laura Mayhall points out, "While arguably struggling beneath a rock-and-roll sensibility, it nevertheless captures the emotional resonance of an important chapter in American history and does so for a young, post-feminist audience in sore need of the message." Like others, she notes that the "MTV aesthetic" may offend serious historians, but "perhaps a little historical license should be excused" when engaging young American women viewers (Mayhall 2004). Writing for the *Journal of American History*, Carla Bittel thought the film's appeal outweighs its failures. "For an audience new to women's history, it conveys the very serious barriers to women's political participation and social justice. When activists are physically attacked as the protest peacefully, the true hostility towards women's suffrage comes alive" (Bittel 2004). For many historians, particularly those teaching women's history, that's the film's great strength.

SUFFRAGE PARADES AND MARCHES: THE TRADITION CONTINUES

While the 1913 Woman Suffrage Procession is the most famous and largest suffrage parade, it was not the only one. In 1908, a group of New York women calling themselves the American Suffragettes organized a parade through the streets, terminating in Madison Square, though they could not get a permit to march. In 1910, Harriet Stanton Blatch, daughter of Elizabeth Cady Stanton, organized a parade of New York working women lobbying for equal pay. The next year, Blatch organized a larger parade, this one a combination of working women and suffragettes. At three thousand marchers strong, it was the largest suffrage parade to date. Blatch liked the parade as a lobbying and publicity tool because the public display reached "obtuse minds" and caused people to think. Like her mother, she thought that if people thought about women's suffrage, they would surely see its democratic possibilities and convert to the cause. Two months after the 1913 Washington Parade, Blatch organized a similar one, again in New York City. This parade included ten thousand women and didn't end in a riot.

Over a hundred years later, in protest of President Donald Trump's election, after he was caught on tape admitting he sexually harassed women, millions of American women marched in 673 America cities and towns. The Washington Women's March drew nearly a half million people, and the Los Angeles march exceeded half a million, while the march in Antarctica consisted of one woman. Marchers wore homemade pink "pussy" hats. Two Los Angeles women conceived the "Pussyhat Project" as a way for women who couldn't attend a march to participate by making a hat for a marcher and including a personal note in it. The nation had a pink yarn and fleece shortage as a result of all the hat making. Like the suffragettes before them, women and men used marches as a form of nonviolent protest and an exercise of free speech. The events proved so successful that they have been repeated in January 2018, 2019, and 2020. The pandemic delayed the 2021 march until October, and in 2022 women and men across the country marched in "Bans Off Our Bodies" protests against the U.S. Supreme Court's intention to overturn *Roe v. Wade* (1973). Mass marches may do little to affect a body as unresponsive to public opinion as the U.S. Supreme Court, but the peaceful protests remind American voters that the majority of Americans support full civil rights for women.

FURTHER READING

Adams, Katherine, and Michael Keene. 2008. *Alice Paul and the American Suffrage Campaign*. Urbana: University of Illinois Press.

Bittel, Carla. 2004. "Iron Jawed Angels." *Journal of American History* (December 2004): 1132–1133.

Brown, Harriet C., ed. 1913. *Official Program, Women Suffrage Procession*. Library of Congress. https://www.loc.gov/pictures/item/94507639/.

Cooney, Robert P. J., Jr., ed. 2015. *Remembering Inez: The Last Campaign of Inez Milholland, Suffrage Martyr—Selections from The Suffragist, 1916*. Half Moon Bay, CA: American Graphic Press.

Dodd, Lynda G. 2008. "Parades, Pickets and Prisons: Alice Paul and the Virtues of Unruly Constitutional Citizenship." *Journal of Law & Politics* 39 (Fall): 340–432.

Dubois, Ellen Carol. 1978. *Feminism and Suffrage: The Emergence of an Independent Women's Movement in America, 1848–1869*. Ithaca, NY: Cornell University Press.

Fischer, Paul. 2004. "Sundance Film Festival 2004." Film Monthly. https://www.filmmonthly.com/behind_the_scenes_exclusive/sundance_film_festival_2004.html.

Graham, Sally Hunter. Winter, 1993–1994. "Woodrow Wilson, Alice Paul and the Woman Suffrage Movement." *Political Science Quarterly* 98 (4): 665–679.

Groeneveld, Elizabeth. June 2009. "Be a Feminist or Just Dress Like One: BUST, Fashion and Feminism as Lifestyle." *Journal of Gender Studies* 18 (2): 179–190.

History.com. "President Wilson Speaks in Favor of Female Suffrage." Accessed May 31, 2022. https://www.history.com/this-day-in-history/president-woodrow-wilson-speaks-in-favor-of-female-suffrage.

Holton, Woody. 2009. *Abigail Adams: A Life*. New York: Free Press.

Hull, N. E. H. 2012. *The Woman Who Dared to Vote: The Trial of Susan B. Anthony*. Lawrence: University of Kansas Press.

Iron Jawed Angels. "Synopsis." Iron Jawed Angels. http://iron-jawed-angels.com/synopsis_1.htm.

Keith, Sheree. 2014. "The Pinkwashing of Alice Paul in HBO's Iron Jawed Angels." *The Journal of Popular Culture* 47 (6): 1283–1294.

Lumsden, Linda. 2019. "Historiography: Women Suffrage and the Media." *American Journalism* 36 (1): 4–31.
Maddux, Kristy. 2004. "When Patriots Protest: The Anti-Suffrage Discursive Transformation of 1917." *Rhetoric and Public Affairs* 7, no. 2 (Fall): 283–310.
Mayhall, Laura E. Nym. 2004. "Iron Jawed Angels." American Historical Association, December 2004, 1589–1590.
Rock the Vote. 2016 Annual Report. https://www.rockthevote.org/wp-content/uploads/Rock-the-Vote-2016-Annual-Report.pdf.
Roy, Robin, Kristin S. Weibust, and Carol T. Miller. June 2007. "Effects of Stereotypes about Feminists on Feminist Self-Identification." *Psychology of Women Quarterly* 31: 146–156.
Shales, Tom. 2004. "Women's Right to Vote? HBO Gets It All Wrong." *Washington Post*, February 15, 2004.
Van Gelder, Lawrence. 1999. "*Bandits*: The Saga of a Criminal Band of Runaway Musicians." *New York Times*, September 24, 1999. https://archive.nytimes.com/www.nytimes.com/library/film/092499bandits-film-review.html.
Weiss, Elaine. 2019. *The Woman's Hour: The Great Fight to Win the Vote*. New York: Penguin Books.
Yarrow, Alison. 2019. *90s Bitch: Media, Culture, and the Failed Promise of Gender Equality*. New York: Harper Perennial.
Zahniser, J. D., and Amelia R. Fry. 2014. *Alice Paul: Claiming Power*. Oxford: Oxford University Press.

Chapter 8

Confirmation (2016)

Written by Susannah Grant; Directed by Rick Famuyiwa
HBO Films, 1 hr., 50 min.

INTRODUCTION

Confirmation examines the Clarence Thomas Senate hearings of 1991 that preceded his confirmation to the U.S. Supreme Court and Anita Hill's testimony that Thomas sexually harassed her in the workplace. Released in 2016 amid the Senate's refusal to consider President Obama's U.S. Supreme Court nominee, Merrick Garland, *Confirmation* reminds viewers that hearings for Supreme Court may have always been exercises in political partisanship. More worrisome, the events and topics of the Brett Kavanaugh hearings in 2018 and a growing MeToo Movement suggest the nation's understanding of sexual harassment and sexual assault remains imperfect decades after Anita Hill's testimony.

HBO conceived of a film about the now-infamous hearings in 2014 and went shopping for a woman screenwriter. Susannah Grant, best known for her award-winning *Erin Brockovich* (2000) screenplay, agreed to write the film, in part because she had such vivid memories of the hearings. Grant brought Kerry Washington, who would go on to star in the television series *Scandal*, to the project as executive producer and to play Hill. Washington remembered watching the hearings as a teenager and seeing her parents view the testimony differently. "My dad felt one way about watching this African American man have his career and reputation stripped and maligned publicly by this panel of older white men. And my mother felt equally pulled in the direction of Anita Hill and listening to this professional African American woman talk about the challenges she faced" (Goldberg). To prepare for the role, Washington read all the books on the hearings before interviewing Anita Hill, who helped her understand the emotional journey that brought Hill to the Senate hearing.

Kerry contacted Rick Famuyiwa to direct the film. Famuyiwa, just off box office and critical success with the comedy caper *Dope* (2015), agreed because the project was different from his other films. Like Washington and Grant, Famuyiwa said the Thomas confirmation hearings were "a big part of my coming of age" (Felsenthal 2016). Famuyiwa also took the project because it examined the intersection of racial and gender politics, played out on what was then a new thing, the twenty-four-hour news cycle. Both Grant and Famuyiwa were struck by how Hill's testimony captured (and divided) the nation and how the media shaped public opinion. Indeed, Famuyiwa and HBO decided to intercut the film with a significant amount of archival footage because so much of news footage seemed designed to create a particular public message. The director also liked the "improvisational feel" the archival footage brought to the film (Berkowitz 2016). Filming began in June 2015 and the film aired on HBO on April 16, 2016 and was released on DVD four months later.

SUMMARY

Confirmation opens with archival footage of Ronald Reagan announcing he'll nominate Robert Bork for the U.S. Supreme Court, quickly followed by more footage of that failed nomination. More archival footage shows George H. Bush's election and his nomination of a conservative Black judge, Clarence Thomas, to fill a spot created by Black civil rights giant, Thurgood Marshall. Both the NAACP and women's rights organizations oppose Thomas's nomination, but conservatives want him on the court.

The film's first nonarchival footage opens on Ricki Seidman (Grace Gummer), an aide to Senator Ted Kennedy (Treat Williams) taking a call from the Alliance for Justice. They've got stories about how nominee Thomas treats women who work for him. In the next scene, we see Anita Hill (Kerry Washington) telling a friend that if she comes forward, she'll be ruined.

In the meantime, the Senate Judiciary Committee of the United States Senate winds up its ten-day examination of Thomas when Senator Joe Biden's (Greg Kinnear) assistant brings him Hill's story. "What if she's lying?" Biden asks. "Can we just let it go?" His assistant tells him they're not the only ones who know. He tells her to call the FBI, and in the next scenes, agents appear at both the Hill and Thomas homes. Thomas denies the allegations to his wife, the FBI, and senators. Biden and others want to ignore Hill's affidavit of Thomas's sexual harassment. Thomas refuses. "I'm a Black man in America. I cannot not care. This is a very different thing for me."

Nina Totenberg from NPR interviews Hill, unleashing a maelstrom of publicity. Hill gives a press conference and appears smart and credible. These two events make it impossible for the Senate to ignore the problem. Congressional women, including Pat Schroeder (Jan Radcliff), descend on a group of white male senators at lunch and insist they take Hill's allegations seriously. The men, including Biden, refuse, thus setting up one of the film's primary points, that men and women have different experiences with sexual harassment and, thus, understand the problem differently.

Republican senators, including Jack Danforth (Bill Irwin), Orrin Hatch (Dylan Baker), Arlen Specter (Malcolm Gets), and Alan Simpson (Peter McRobbie) vow to do whatever it takes to get Thomas confirmed. Again and again, men talk about sexual harassment as if it's not real, something hysterical women imagine. Simpson says if Hill wants to expose Thomas to harassment charges, "She'll be harassed. Real harassment, not the sexual kind."

Charles Ogletree (Jeffrey Wright) volunteers to act as Hill's lawyer for the hearing while several congressional women, clearly motivated to force male senators to take this issue seriously, offer support. Republican senators insist Thomas testify first, outmaneuvering Joe Biden, who chairs the committee. In his testimony, Thomas denies all allegations of sexual harassment but adds that if he did anything she might have construed as harassment, he is sorry.

Hill begins her testimony by reading a written statement. Biden then questions her, asking her for graphic details. She describes how Thomas liked to talk about group sex, sex with animals, men with large penises, and women with large breasts engaged in sex acts. He also told her of his sexual prowess, though she tried to stop him. She then describes the now-infamous incident where Thomas got himself a Coke and then loudly asked why it contained a pubic hair. Hill is uncomfortable with these sexual details, particularly after her parents are ushered into the chamber. Hill emphasizes the fact that she didn't volunteer to testify against Thomas. She was asked to testify and felt "I could not keep silent."

Senator Arlen Specter questions Hill, making it clear he does not understand sexual harassment. If she didn't do any of the things Thomas wanted her to do, what's the problem? Nor does he understand why she didn't come forward before or why she followed Thomas from the Department of Education to the EEOC. She says she doesn't know. She only knew she tried to be cordial, and she worried about her career.

Thomas testifies again, this time making the case that he's the real victim. "It's a high-tech lynching for uppity Blacks who in any way deign to think for themselves." In the next scene, another victim comes forward, saying, "I know Thomas is capable of doing these things; he did them to me."

Republican senators accuse Hill of everything from lesbianism to erotomania to discredit her. Hill volunteers to take a lie detector test. The test shows she's telling the truth, but archival footage shows President Bush dismissing the test as "stupid."

As Hill's legal team prepares for her to testify again, she tells them, "This was a mistake. They don't care. They only want to win." She withdraws her testimony, and Republicans get the votes to confirm Thomas as a justice to the U.S. Supreme Court.

Back in Oklahoma, Hill enters her office to find it chock-full of mail. She reads a letter from a woman who says her boss has sexually harassed her for years, but Hill's testimony has given her strength. Hill discovers her testimony did mean something after all. The film's end card reads, "In the wake of the hearings, the number of sexual harassment cases filed with the EEOC doubled. The number of women elected to congress was the largest of any single election in the nation's history."

The Writer's Guild of America (WGA) gave Susannah Grant the Paul Selvin Award for her *Confirmation* script for the best embodiment of "the spirit of constitutional rights and civil liberties indispensable to the survival of free writers everywhere." Grant also won the Guild's Best Long Form script award. The WGA called Grant's work on the film "a feat of research, writing, and empathy" (McNary 2017). Writing for Roger Ebert, Brian Tallerico damned the film with faint praise, calling it "fine," but adding, "The story of Clarence Thomas and Anita Hill deserves more than fine. This is a fascinating political chapter with deep issues of race, gender, and power to examine, but the production of 'Confirmation' is satisfied with a superficial, then-this-happened approach to storytelling" (Tallerico 2016). Viewers liked it more than Ebert, with the film earning an 83 percent fresh rating on Rotten Tomatoes (Confirmation). Critics also liked Kerry Washington's performance. Ben Travers at Indie Wire says Washington "makes you believe in Hill's integrity and determination, [finding] nuance in the small moments" (Travers). Travers, Ebert, and others unfavorably compared the film to HBO's recent *The People v. OJ Simpson* (2016), though, to be fair, the latter aired as a ten-episode season and, thus, had more time to explore cultural context and meaning.

HISTORICAL CONTEXT

Anita Hill came from a rural farming family and graduated from Yale Law School in 1980. She joined a District of Columbia law firm before taking a job in the Department of Education under Clarence Thomas. Thomas, who grew up in Georgia and also graduated from Yale Law School, though in 1974, began his career working for Missouri attorney general John Danforth. Danforth later became a senator and Thomas nomination supporter.

Thomas also worked briefly for Monsanto Chemical Company before Ronald Reagan appointed him assistant secretary of education for the Office of Civil Rights in the Department of Education. Reagan appointed Thomas to the post because, unlike most Black leaders, Thomas was anti-affirmative action and politically conservative. A year later, Thomas took a post at the Equal Employment Opportunity Commission (EEOC).

While at the Department of Education, Thomas began his sexual harassment campaign against Hill and other women. He often described pornographic movies to Hill and others, particularly films featuring large-breasted women. He bragged of his sexual prowess and suggested Hill would enjoy dating him. Hill said she tried to change the topic when Thomas's conversation turned sexual, worried that if she wasn't "cordial" with her boss, her career would suffer.

Hill transferred jobs when Thomas took the position at the EEOC because her professional goals included working in civil rights law. At the EEOC, Thomas continued to ask Hill for dates; discuss pornographic films, including bestiality and rape films; and describe his sexual equipment. While only Hill would later testify about Thomas's sexual harassment, four other women at the EEOC would report they'd been victimized by him or seen him victimize others.

In 1990, President George H. Bush appointed Thomas to the U.S. Court of Appeals for the District of Columbia. A year later, judicial and civil rights legend Thurgood Marshall announced his retirement from the bench. Bush, who'd previously nominated David Souter for a U.S. Supreme Court, wanted a true conservative for this vacancy and nominated Thomas. Political commentators noted the boldness of Bush's nomination because Thomas was an extreme right-wing ideologue along the lines of Robert Bork. Then-president Reagan nominated Bork in 1987, but Bork's views were so extreme, his nomination failed in the Senate. The NAACP, Urban League, and National Organization of Women immediately protested Thomas's nomination because he held extreme views on civil and reproductive rights.

Thomas came before the Senate Judicial Committee for questioning on September 10. Ten days later, the hearing ended, but senators had begun to hear rumors of Thomas's sexual malfeasance.

On October 6, Nina Totenberg, an NPR reporter, broke Hill's story in the media. This combined with Hill's press conference the next day meant the Senate Republicans did not have the votes to get Thomas confirmed. They had to reopen the nomination hearing.

Senator Joe Biden reopened the hearing on October 11. Thomas began the new hearing by denying all allegations of sexual harassment. The committee next called Hill, who began her testimony by reading a prepared statement, after which the senators questioned her. Senator Spector (R-Pennsylvania) dismissed her testimony as perjury and said, on the record, that discussing large breasts in the workplace was "Not bad," and Senator Heflin (R-Alabama) asked Hill if she was "a scorned woman" or a "zealot civil rights believer." Spector continued his questioning by insisting that as long as Thomas never explicitly asked Hill to watch pornographic movies with him or to have sex with him, no crime had been committed. Hill said Thomas continually pressured her to go out with him and would not take no for an answer, but Spector maintained that as long as Thomas never asked her for sex, there was no harassment. Senator Biden asked Hill for details about Thomas's discussions of his sexual equipment. Hill said it was "graphic," but was reluctant to say more. Biden pushed, forcing her to say, "He measured his penis in terms of length, those kinds of comments."

Senator Simpson (R-Wyoming) asked Hill why she continued to work for Thomas if he was so bad. She said she was afraid of retaliation and "damage to my professional life." Simpson maintained that if these he continued to be puzzled by her ongoing employment under Thomas, demonstrating his ignorance of the issues surrounding sexual harassment in the workplace.

On the second day of the hearing, only Clarence Thomas testified. As part of his testimony, he likened the hearing and the media circus around it to "a high-tech lynching for uppity Blacks who in any way deign to think for themselves, to have different ideas. It is a message that this is what will happen to you. You will be lynched, destroyed, caricatured by a committee of the U.S. Senate, rather than hung from a tree" (Committee 1991). Thomas ignored the fact that Anita Hill, a Black woman, had accused Thomas of sexual harassment and that the Judiciary Committee had done everything it could to avoid making her testimony public. Later that day, Senator Orin Hatch brandished a copy of *The Exorcist* and read from it a line about pubic hair. He then suggested Hill had taken her story from the horror novel but allowed her no chance to rebut his unfounded accusation.

On Sunday, October 13, the hearing saw its third and last day. Testimony began after a new conference, announcing Hill had volunteered for and passed a lie detector test. Ellen Wells, on behalf of the American Welfare Association; Susan Hoerchner, a Workers Compensation Judge; and lawyers John Carr and Joel Paul testified on Hill's behalf. So too did a handful of EEOC employees, a judicial polygraph expert, and many others. Senator Biden introduced a letter to Angela Wright and transcripts of telephone interviews with both Wright and Rose Jourdain. In her phone interview, Wright said, "Clarence Thomas did consistently pressure me to date him. Clarence Thomas made comments about women's anatomy quite often." When the interviewer tried to elicit dates from Wright, she said, "We are talking about a thing that pretty much pops out of Clarence Thomas's mouth when he feels like it" (Committee 1991). Wright and Jourdain both said Thomas harassed other women, some of whom they said would be willing to testify. Biden declined to call either Wright or Jourdain as witnesses and buried their phone interview transcripts deep in the Congressional Record of the hearing. Hatch, who had once been the chair of the Judiciary

Committee himself, also claimed Hill found the pornography references in her testimony from law cases readily available in any law library.

Judge Edward Kennedy testified that contrary to a Republican Senator's claims, Hill's voluntary polygraph test violated no laws. Alan Simpson read testimony from an unidentified prosecutor, who had never met or interviewed Hill, suggesting she might be delusional. Her delusion syndrome (which was never proven by any psychological expert) explained why she passed the lie detector test, or so Simpson theorized. Simpson also introduced testimony from John Doggett, a lawyer and Yale classmate of Thomas, claimed Hill had sexually pursued both Thomas and himself. Though Doggett had no qualifications as a psychologist and admitted he barely knew Hill, the senate allowed him to testify that Hill had erotomania or unfulfilled romantic fantasies about Thomas that caused her to make false accusations against him. Doggett demonstrated his own issues with sexual harassment when he testified that a woman he talked to the previous night told him, "Put your penis back in your pants" (Jacobs 2018).

Two days later, on October 15, the U.S. Senate confirmed Clarence Thomas as associate justice of the U.S. Supreme Court in a vote of 52–48. Eleven Democrats voted for Thomas, and two Republicans voted against his confirmation. He rarely speaks or asks questions in court, once going ten years without asking a question in oral arguments, making him the least verbal Supreme Court justice in U.S. history. While on the bench, he often appears unaware of the legal questioning taking place in the room, and though he is considered the intellectual father of many of the court's most conservative rulings, he rarely writes majority or minority opinions.

Conservatives continued to question Hill's veracity well after the hearings ended. David Brock's *The Real Anita Hill*, which appeared in 1992, made several negative assertions about Hill. The book has since been categorized as "character assassination," and Brock himself repudiated it in a second book, saying he made up many of the details (Noah 2002). Others pointed out that the Senate's poor treatment of Hill might have been avoided if the FBI had more thoroughly vetted Clarence Thomas. A better investigation would have turned up Hill, Wright, Jourdain, and Hardnett. The FBI might also have discovered that Thomas left law school with a reputation for sexual crudity or that, while separated from his wife, he decorated his apartment walls with Playboy centerfolds and posters for pornographic movies (Mayer and Abramson 1994). Of course, there is nothing illegal about having dubious decorating taste or a fondness for dirty language, but taken together, they point to a pattern of thought and behavior that makes his indignation at the charges disingenuous at best.

Anita Hill returned to her job at Oklahoma State University Law School, where conservative Oklahoma politicians demanded she resign, comparing her to Lee Harvey Oswald, the man who shot President John F. Kennedy. When that failed, politicians tried to close the law school. After five years of political harassment, Hill resigned her position at the university and accepted a visiting scholar position at the University of California, Berkeley. She also coedited an anthology of essays about the Hill-Thomas hearings and, in 1997, published her autobiography, *Speaking Truth to Power*. In late 2017, a group of female leaders in the film industry asked her to lead the Hollywood Commission to investigate widespread misconduct in the entertainment industry (Buckley 2017).

In the year after the Hill-Thomas hearing, sexual harassment claims at the EEOC were up 50 percent, and polls showed that the majority of Americans believed Hill. American women voted in record numbers the year after the hearing, pundits say in part because so many women found the all-male Senate committee and its stunning inability to understand the realities of sexual harassment untenable. Across the country, hundreds of women were elected to state legislatures and local governments. Dubbed "The Year of the Woman," 1992 saw four women elected to the U.S. Senate (upping the total number of female senators to five) and twenty-four to the U.S. House of Representatives. Newly elected Senator Patty Murray said she felt compelled to run for the Senate after seeing the "blatant sexism" of the Hill-Thomas hearings (Green).

DEPICTION AND CULTURAL CONTEXT

Though the MeToo movement was born in 2006, it became a nationwide phenomenon in the mid-2010s. In 2015, the New York district attorney's office failed to bring charges against Harvey Weinstein for sexually harassing Ambra Gutierrez, even though they had an audio recording where Weinstein admitted he'd done it. In subsequent months, dozens of women came forward with accusations against Weinstein ranging from harassment to rape. In 2016, then presidential candidate Donald Trump was caught on tape admitting he sexually harassed women. Other women came forward charging an astounding number of prominent men with sexual misconduct. The list includes actors, businessmen, politicians, and professional athletes. In 2017, actor Alyssa Milano came forward with her account of Weinstein harassment and asked women who'd had similar experiences to repeat and repost her tweet with #MeToo. By the end of the day, the hashtag had been retweeted more than two hundred thousand times. Since his 2016 election, twenty-five women have accused President Trump of sexual crimes ranging from harassment to rape. Popularity polls suggested a significant minority of Americans did not believe sex crimes were disqualifications for the presidency, further pushing the MeToo movement to prominence.

The MeToo movement demonstrated the prevalence of sexual harassment and sexual assault in the United States, as well as the nation's inability to acknowledge the size and scope of the problem. According to the United

States Equal Employment Opportunity Commission, unlawful sexual harassment is any unwelcome sexual advances, requests for sexual favors, and verbal or physical interactions of a sexual nature in the workplace. A boss or coworker's behavior escalates from casual conversation to harassment when the behavior becomes so frequent or severe that it causes a hostile or offensive work environment or results in an employee's demotion or firing.

A 2018 study by a not-for-profit foundation working in conjunction with the Centers for Disease Control found that 81 percent of women and 43 percent of men over eighteen report experience with sexual harassment. Verbal harassment was, the study found, the most common type of sexual harassment, followed by unwelcome sexual touching and cyber-harassment. An astounding 30 percent of women reported unwanted genital flashing by a coworker or boss, and another 27 percent reported the sexual harassment escalated to sexual assault (Chatterjee 2018).

HBO's decision to produce *Confirmation* came amid this national awakening to the facts of sexual harassment, in part because while the Hill-Thomas hearings brought national attention to sexual harassment, the succeeding years saw a kind of historical amnesia about both the Anita Hill and the issues she raised. *Confirmation* is the second film to cover the Hill-Thomas sexual harassment controversy. The first, a documentary titled *Anita*, came out in 2014. Director Freida Lee Mock, who won an Academy Award for her 1994 documentary *Maya Lin: A Strong, Clear Vision*, premiered *Anita* at the Sundance Film Festival to strong reviews.

Confirmation fundamentally follows the historical narrative of the Hill-Thomas hearings. The film accurately portrays Senate Judiciary chairman Joe Biden's refusal to push the accusations against Thomas. Biden has never particularly cared for controversy and prefers people to get along, but his handling of the hearings goes beyond his "Uncle Joe" personality. Again and again, as the film suggested, Biden refused to protect Hill from attacks senators from both sides of the aisle leveled at her. When Democrat Howell Heflin asked Hill if she had a "martyr complex" or was a "scorned woman," Biden sat on his hands. When Republicans openly called her a liar, Biden did nothing, nor did he object when they suggested she had a psychological problem or stole her accusations from popular novels.

Frustrated by Biden's passivity, female lawmakers headed up by Congresswoman Pat Schroeder asked Biden to be more proactive, though in a less melodramatic manner than the film portrayed. Schroeder said Biden refused to consider their plea, saying "he had given his word to [Senator John Danforth (R-Mo.), Thomas's chief sponsor] in the men's gym that this would be a very quick hearing and that he had to get it out before Columbus Day" (Mayer 2019). Schroeder and her sister lawmakers were not alone in their unhappiness with Biden's handling of the hearings. Senator Howard Metzenbaum said, "Joe bent over too far backward to accommodate the

Republicans who were going to get Thomas on the court come hell or high water." Leading Democrat Ted Kennedy who kept largely quiet during the hearings, in part because of his own troubled sexual history, had one of his aids put out a statement that read, "Biden agreed to the terms of the people who were out to disembowel Hill" (Mayer 2019).

Recognizing the political liability created by his failure to be proactive during the hearings, Biden first tried to make the episode disappear by leaving it out of his 2007 autobiography. When that failed, he blamed Senate rules for his failure to call the three additional female witnesses, though such rules do not exist. Next, he attempted several public apologies to Hill. In March 2019, only weeks before he announced his candidacy for the U.S. presidency, Biden issued a statement of "regret" for Hill's hearing experience. Weeks later in a television interview, when asked if he felt regret for how he treated Hill, Biden defended his inaction, saying, "I did everything in my power" (Culp-Ressler 2014).

Not surprisingly, Hill continues to reject Biden's half-hearted apologies. She's said his willingness to let Senate Republicans attack her truthfulness set the stage for the Republican senator's deplorable treatment of Christine Blasey Ford during the more recent Brett Kavanaugh confirmation hearings. Kavanaugh also took a petulantly angry stance in responding to the accusations of his sexual crimes, portraying himself as a victim of both Democrats and unreasonable women. It is a tactic he learned from Thomas, whose angry statements about victimhood played so well to the all-male Judiciary Committee. Hill contends Biden's apologies are essentially meaningless and useless. "I will be satisfied when I know there is real change and real accountability," she said in a *New York Times* interview. "There are women and men now who have just really lost confidence in how our government responds to the problem of gender violence" (Stolberg and Hulse 2019).

Confirmation rightly credits staffers for bringing Anita Hill's testimony before the Senate Judiciary Committee, though the characters portrayed in the film are composites of a larger number of people, many of them young women. Zoe Lister-Jones plays Carolyn Hart, a fictitious Biden aide. The Hart character is likely based on Cynthia Hogan, staff director for the Judiciary Committee, with a little Ron Klain, chief counsel for the Judiciary Committee, thrown in for good measure (Herzog 2016). On the distaff side, the film makes Senator Danforth the villain of the piece, when there was a handful of senators who were only too willing to impeach Hill's character and testimony. Senators Alan Simpson, Charles Grassley, Arlen Spector, Howell Heflin, and Orrin Hatch all accused Hill of a variety of misdeeds during the hearings. Simpson has since admitted he treated Hill badly though, in the same interview, made it clear he doesn't understand the difference between sexual harassment and sexual assault (Culp-Ressler 2014).

In one of the film's most disturbing scenes, Senator John Danforth suggested Hill suffered from erotomania. Danforth got the idea from psychologist

Park Dietz, who contacted conservative senators before the hearing. Erotomania is a delusional disorder where a person believes another person, usually of higher status, is in love with them. Danforth theorized that Hill's undiagnosed erotomania might have caused her to feel angry at Thomas's rejection of her and caused her subsequent accusations of harassment. Biden allowed Danforth's questions, even though they were founded in nothing more than conjecture and a desire to discredit and embarrass Hill.

Confirmation reveals that Hill was not the only woman Thomas victimized with sexual harassment, but, rather, Hill was the only woman allowed to testify. In the film, Angela Wright (Jennifer Hudson) volunteered to testify that Thomas had harassed her too. She came to Washington and waited to be called, but Biden ultimately made a deal with Senate Republicans to end the hearings without calling any corroborating witnesses for Hill's harassment accusations. Wright would have testified that Thomas often spoke to her about the size of her breasts and his penis, continually asked her to date him (though he was married), and once showed up at her house without an invitation.

The film does no more than mention the other women who offered to testify to Thomas's harassment. Sukari Hardnett worked with Thomas at the EEOC for two years and saw the way Thomas treated Hill. Hardnett offered to testify before the Senate Judiciary Committee about the treatment of young Black women who worked with Thomas. Likewise, Rose Jourdain offered to testify about Thomas's behavior, but, like Hardnett and Wright, she never got further than a phone interview. All three of these witnesses might have changed the course of the hearing's outcome, if for no other reason than Senate Republicans would have had a harder time portraying Hill as a psychologically damaged liar bent on destroying an innocent man's chances at the Supreme Court.

The film also captures the anger of both Clarence Thomas and his second wife Virginia Lamp Thomas. Thomas compared the hearings to a "lynching," an accusation many people thought more than a bit historically inaccurate. The about-to-be Supreme Court justice was demonstrably indignant during the hearings and denounced Hill in the strongest terms, though he failed to address the fact that she passed a lie detector test and was joined by several other accusers. Though Thomas had a lot to say during his hearings, once on the bench, he appeared to lose his voice. For his first ten years on the bench, he never once asked a question or issued an opinion, though he did ask a question in 2016 and again in 2019. He consistently votes with conservative judges, voting for measures that disenfranchise minority voters, restrict women's rights, and weaken social welfare programs. In his 2007 autobiography, Thomas called Hill a traitor and said she tended to overreact. He dismissed the other women's accusations as well, saying they'd all left the EEOC on bad terms. His book also made it clear he felt abused by the confirmation process and insisted Democrats who didn't want a Black man on the U.S. Supreme Court invented the controversy (Thomas 2008).

Anita Hill responded to Thomas's autobiography with a *New York Times* op-ed. She pointed out that Thomas offered no proof for any of his accusations against her, many of which were out-and-out lies. She also pointed out that the sorts of attacks made by Thomas against his accuser are not uncommon. "In efforts to assail their accusers' credibility, detractors routinely diminish people's professional contributions. . . . Those accused of inappropriate behavior also often portray the individuals who complain as bizarre caricatures of themselves—oversensitive, even fanatical and often immoral" (Hill 2007). In the post-MeToo era, we know this to be true. Men (and women) accused of sexual malfeasance often blame the victim or in some way suggest the victim was the inappropriate actor. The accused also often claim their accusers are oversensitive, politically correct, or on a witch-hunt designed to defame the accused. The accused, in short, commonly portray themselves as the victims to minimize the accusations and dismiss their accusers.

Clarence Thomas's wife was just as indignant at Hill's charges as was her husband. Though *Confirmation* portrays Clarence Thomas's wife, Virginia Lamp Thomas as a homemaker, in reality, she is a lawyer and conservative lobbyist. Before her husband's nomination to the U.S. Supreme Court, she worked for the Heritage Foundation, a conservative organization that played an important role in Ronald Reagan's presidency. In 2010, Lamp Thomas called Anita Hill's office at Brandeis University and left a message asking her to apologize to her and Clarence Thomas. Hill thought the call was a hoax and contacted the campus police. When questioned by the authorities, Lamp Thomas claimed the call was an "olive branch," but she continues to insist Hill owes her and her husband an apology. In 2020, Lamp Thomas worked as an advisor for Turning Point, an organization devoted to organizing conservative students, including Students for Trump. Lamp also promotes many right-wing conspiracy theories and likened the student activist survivors of the Parkland shooting to terrorists. She is also active in an organization that identified conservatives not loyal to President Trump so they could be purged from government payrolls and has been linked to the "Stop the Steal" movement, as well as the January 6, 2021 Capitol insurrection (Christian and Laila 2020).

Unfortunately, the film is also accurate in its portrayal of Republican politicians' decision to accuse Hill of psychological problems, including erotomania. Essentially, the White House claimed Hill suffered from delusions, causing her to imagine that she and Thomas were in a romantic relationship. When he did not reciprocate, or so the theory went, she became angry and tried to destroy him with lies. Republicans dug up Texas lawyer John Doggett, who signed an affidavit swearing Hill had first fixated on him, and then he testified before the hearing about his claims. A Bush advisor peddled the story of Hill's undiagnosed mental illness to several journalists, including

Washington Post columnist Ruth Marcus, who called the accusation, "one of the slimiest moments in Washington political history" (Herzog 2016).

Part of the problem was that the George Bush White House was willing to do and say anything to get Thomas on the bench. The administration's willingness to overlook Thomas's flaws lie, at least in part, in the failed Robert Bork nomination. In 1987, President Ronald Reagan nominated Bork to the U.S. Supreme Court, causing a furor in both houses of Congress and the nation. Bork's ultraconservative stances with regard to civil rights for women and minorities made him one of four Supreme Court nominees opposed by the American Civil Liberties Union (ACLU), along with William Rehnquist, Samuel Alito, and Brett Kavanaugh. Reagan subsequently nominated moderate Anthony Kennedy, but the Bork loss made Reagan's then vice president George Bush extremely eager to get an archconservative on the bench.

Conservative politicians didn't just accuse Hill of mental illness. One senator made it clear her story of Thomas's reference to "Long D— Silver" was a figment of her imagination, while another claimed the basis for her story about Thomas claiming pubic hair was in his Coke came from the horror novel *The Exorcist*. Right-wing reporter David Brock later said the administration encouraged him to write negative and nasty things about Hill. He printed derogatory allegations, no matter how far-fetched, saying he wanted Hill to seem "a little bit nutty and a little bit slutty." He later repudiated *The Real Anita Hill* (1993), saying the book was no more than "character assassination" in the service of the Republican Party, as was his book about Hillary Clinton (Brock 2002).

Some critics took issue with the film's failure to take sides. Famuyiwa said, "I was very adamant that we were going to go wherever the truth took us, whoever looks good or bad. But I didn't necessarily want to start with a point of view" (Felsenthal 2016). Nonetheless, for many people, the film is far too sympathetic to Thomas and, for others, it is not sympathetic enough to Hill. While the director may have wanted to be scrupulously fair, the Hill-Thomas imbroglio polarized a generation of Americans. People either believed her and saw his confirmation as a massive miscarriage of justice in a sexist country where women just can't get a break, or they believed him and thought she was a liar out to ruin a good Black man.

There wasn't and still isn't much middle ground on the issue. Many critics call the whole controversy a massive case of "he said, she said," suggesting the truth is impossible to know, but that's not entirely accurate. Four women came forth and corroborated Hill's claims that Thomas was a serial sexual harasser. Hill took and passed a lie detector test, one administered by the FBI's foremost authority at the time. As important, though harder to quantify, is the twenty-first-century acknowledgment that women have long been sexually harassed by powerful men and that, by and large, the American criminal justice system and courts of public opinion have been loath to hold powerful men who are also sexual predators accountable for their actions.

And while many critics and viewers thought the film was far too kind to Thomas, Republicans claimed the film was laden with "liberal bias." One review of the film from a pro-Republican newspaper went so far as to say the film leaves the impression Thomas was lying and Hill was telling the truth. The implication, of course, is that the opposite is true. Yet Hill passed a polygraph test, and several other women corroborated her testimony. Indeed, in claiming the film is biased because it portrays Hill as a truth-teller, critics reveal their own bias—one where female accusers of powerful conservative men should always be discounted as liars.

The specter of the Hill-Thomas hearings hung over the 2018 Senate Judiciary hearings to confirm Brett Kavanaugh to the U.S. Supreme Court. Soon after President Trump nominated Kavanaugh, Christine Blasey Ford wrote a letter to Senator Dianne Feinstein. Ford contended that Kavanaugh sexually assaulted her in 1982. The Senate Judiciary committee temporarily postponed the hearing to investigate the allegations. Two more women came forward, both with stories of Kavanaugh's sexual misconduct. Deborah Ramirez said Kavanaugh had pushed his penis into her face at a dorm party, while Julie Swetnick alleged Kavanaugh and his friends had planned and undertaken the gang rape of girls, including herself. Judy Munro-Leighton also accused Kavanaugh of rape, though she later recanted.

Ford testified before the Senate committee on September 27, 2018. Though her testimony was widely considered reasonable and credible, Senate Republicans questioned her veracity. Under oath, Kavanaugh denied all the charges. Kavanaugh took a page from Thomas's book by becoming belligerent and hyper-indignant during his testimony and casting himself as the real victim. An FBI investigation revealed Kavanaugh had a record of drunken and violent misbehavior in college and that he had lied to the committee while under oath. Additionally, a total of eighty-three ethics complaints were filed against Kavanaugh during the confirmation process, including lying under oath and concealing sexual misconduct crimes. The day after Ford's testimony, the Judiciary Committee voted to send Kavanaugh's nomination to the Senate for a full vote. The Senate voted 50–48 to give Kavanaugh a seat on the U.S. Supreme Court, with Republicans voting for and Democrats voting against. At Kavanaugh's swearing-in ceremony, President Trump, who has his own sexual misconduct problems, publicly apologized to Kavanaugh for his treatment during the nomination.

In the wake of his confirmation, Kavanaugh remains a controversial public figure. Many Washington insiders refuse to attend events with him, diners have jeered at him in local restaurants, and his own "drinking buddies" repudiated him as a liar. But Kavanaugh has it easy compared to his accuser. Christine Blasey Ford had to move four times in the two years since the hearings because of death threats from the radical right.

During the Kavanaugh hearings, Anita Hill wrote an opinion piece for the *New York Times*, suggesting how senators might get the hearings right. She began by noting that in 1991, the Senate Judiciary Committee failed to demonstrate a basic understanding of both sexual harassment and the public need to trust Supreme Court justices. She also pointed out that the Senate still had no procedure for vetting sexual harassment claims, demonstrating they'd learned very little since her testimony against Thomas. "With the current heightened awareness of sexual violence comes heightened accountability for our representatives," Hill wrote. "To do better, the 2018 Senate Judiciary Committee must demonstrate a clear understanding that sexual violence is a social reality to which elected representatives must respond" (Hill 2018). Kavanaugh's confirmation and reaffirmation by the president suggest to all too many Americans that powerful men don't have to care about sexual violence, let alone avoid it in their personal lives.

Anyone old enough to remember the Hill-Thomas imbroglio couldn't help but remark on the déjà vu–like experience of the Kavanaugh confirmation hearing. *Confirmation* reminds us that sexual violence, from sexual harassment to rape, is still not considered a serious crime by all too many Americans. Men who admit to sexual misconduct and men who deny sexual misconduct in the face of multiple female accusers take their places in the very highest positions of power this nation has to offer. What does this say to the countless women and men who are victimized by sexual violence each year? Nothing good. *Confirmation* is not a perfect film, but it tells a story all Americans ought to know.

THE "WEINSTEIN EFFECT" AND THE HOLLYWOOD COMMISSION

In 2016, journalist Gretchen Carlson filed a lawsuit against *Fox News* chairman, Roger Ailes, alleging sexual harassment. Carlson's suit forced Ailes's resignation and prompted other *Fox News* journalists to come forward with stories of sexual harassment. Soon after, popular conservative pundit Bill O'Reilly was also forced to resign from *Fox News* after being linked to sexual harassment. In fall 2017, *The New York Times* reported that dozens of women claimed Hollywood producer Harvey Weinstein had sexually harassed or assaulted them. Ronan Farrow's reporting in the *New Yorker* further explored Weinstein's misdeeds, including evidence the producer had raped at least three women. The media storm caused by these high-profile cases created significant public support for the victims of sexual harassment.

Called "the Weinstein Effect," the media campaigns fueled by victim testimony exposed a number of prominent Hollywood men as sexual harassers, including actors Ben Affleck, Kevin Spacey, Dustin Hoffman, Louis C.K. and Bill Cosby; animators John Lasseter and Chris Savino; and journalists Matt Lauer and Charlie Rose, among others.

> In the immediate wake of the Weinstein allegations, Kathleen Kennedy and Nina Shaw founded the Hollywood Commission to investigate sexual harassment in the entertainment industry. Anita Hill volunteered to chair the commission, explaining that "the commission is part of a long overdue journey to adopt best practices and create institutional changes that foster a culture of respect and human dignity throughout the industry" (Vlessing 2020). The commission focuses on exposing and preventing discrimination, harassment, and bullying in the entertainment industry by supporting independent film producers, creating a reporting platform for abuse and offering in-person and online training for sexual harassment prevention. According to the commission's surveys of entertainment industry workers, more than 62 percent of male workers and 67 percent of female workers report experiences with gender harassment, including behavior ranging from crude language to sexual coercion. Hill, Kennedy, and Shaw believe naming the problem and creating a clearing house for reporting harassment will lead to more equity and safety in the entertainment industry.

FURTHER READING

Berkowitz, Joe. 2016. "'Confirmation' Director Famuyiwa on Recreating Recent History." Fast Company, April 16, 2016. https://www.fastcompany.com/3058659/confirmation-director-rick-famuyiwa-on-recreating-recent-history.

Brock, David. 2002. *Blinded by the Right: The Conscience of an Ex-Conservative*. New York: Crown Publishing.

Buckley, Cara. 2017. "Hill to Lead Hollywood Commission." *New York Times*, December 15, 2017. https://www.nytimes.com/2017/12/15/movies/anita-hill-hollywood-commission-sexual-harassment.html.

Chatterjee, Rhitu. 2018. "A New Study on Sexual Harassment." *National Public Radio*, February 21, 2018. https://www.npr.org/sections/thetwo-way/2018/02/21/587671849/a-new-survey-finds-eighty-percent-of-women-have-experienced-sexual-harassment.

Christian, Carlos, and Christina Laila. 2020. "President Trump on a Warpath with a 'Deep State' Hit List to Oust 'Never Trumpers.'" February 24, 2020. https://www.axios.com/trump-memos-deep-state-white-house-ce5be95f-2418-433d-b036-2bf41c9700c3.html.

Committee on the Judiciary, Nomination of Judge Clarence Thomas to Be Associate Justice of the Supreme Court of the United States: Hearings before the Committee on the Judiciary, United States Senate, One Hundred and Second Congress. October 11, 12, 13, 1991, Parts 4 of 4. https://www.loc.gov/law/find/nominations/thomas/hearing-pt4.pdf.

Culp-Ressler, Tara. 2014. "23 Years Later, Senator Who Interrogated Anita Hill Still Doesn't Understand Sexual Harassment." *Think Progress*, May 7, 2014. https://thinkprogress.org/23-years-later-senator-who-interrogated-anita-hill-still-doesnt-understand-sexual-harassment-c82c9cd3d95e/.

Felsenthal, Julia. 2016. "Rick Famuyiwa on Making *Confirmation* and Meeting Anita Hill." *Vogue*, April 12, 2016. https://www.vogue.com/article/rick-famuyiwa-confirmation-interview.

Goldberg, Leslie. 2016. "Kerry Washington Defends 'Confirmation': It's Not a Propaganda Movie." *Hollywood Reporter*, April 14, 2016. https://www.hollywoodreporter.com/live-feed/kerry-washington-defends-hbos-confirmation-883672.

Green, Emma. September 26, 2013. "A Lot Has Changed since 1992, the 'Year of the Woman.'" *The Atlantic*. https://www.theatlantic.com/politics/archive/2013/09/a-lot-has-changed-in-congress-since-1992-the-year-of-the-woman/280046/.

Herzog, Kenny. 2016. "Fact-Checking HBO's *Confirmation*." *New York Magazine*, April 16, 2016. https://www.vulture.com/2016/04/hbo-confirmation-fact-checked.html.

Hill, Anita. 1998. *Speaking Truth to Power*. New York: Anchor Books.

Hill, Anita. 2007. "The Smear This Time." *New York Times*, October 2, 2007. https://www.nytimes.com/2007/10/02/opinion/02hill.html.

Hill, Anita. 2018. "How to Get the Kavanaugh Hearings Right." *New York Times*, September 18, 2018. https://www.nytimes.com/2018/09/18/opinion/anita-hill-brett-kavanaugh-clarence-thomas.html.

Jacobs, Julia. 2018. "Anita Hill's Testimony and Other Key Moments from the Clarence Thomas Hearings." *New York Times*, September 20, 2018. https://www.nytimes.com/2018/09/20/us/politics/anita-hill-testimony-clarence-thomas.html.

Mayer, Jane. 2019. "What Biden Hasn't Owned up to about Anita Hill." *The New Yorker*, April 27, 2019. https://www.newyorker.com/news/news-desk/what-joe-biden-hasnt-owned-up-to-about-anita-hill.

Mayer, Jane, and Jill Abramson. 1994. *Strange Justice: The Selling of Clarence Thomas*. New York: Houghton Mifflin Harcourt.

McNary, Dave. 2017. "WGA West Awards Susanna Grant for 'Confirmation' Script." *Variety*, January 19, 2017. https://variety.com/2017/film/awards/wga-west-honors-susannah-grant-confirmation-1201964037/.

Morrison, Toni, ed. 1992. *Race-ing Justice, En-gendering Power: Essays on Anita Hill, Clarence Thomas and the Construction of Social Reality*. New York: Pantheon.

Noah, Timothy. 2002. "David Brock, Liar: A Lifelong Habit Proves Hard to Break." *Slate*, March 27, 2002. https://slate.com/news-and-politics/2002/03/david-brock-liar.html.

Rotten Tomatoes. "Confirmation." Rotten Tomatoes. Accessed June 13, 2022. https://www.rottentomatoes.com/m/confirmation.

Stolberg, Sheryl Gay, and Carl Hulse. 2019. "Joe Biden Expresses Regret to Anita Hill, but She Says 'I'm Sorry' Is Not Enough." *New York Times*, April 25, 2019. https://www.nytimes.com/2019/04/25/us/politics/joe-biden-anita-hill.html

Tallerico, Brian. 2016. "Confirmation." April 16. https://www.rogerebert.com/reviews/confirmation-2016

Thomas, Clarence. 2008. *Clarence Thomas: My Grandfather's Son*. New York: Harper Perennial.

Totenberg, Nina. 1991. "Transcript of Nina Totenberg's NPR Report on Anita Hill's Charges of Sexual Harassment by Clarence Thomas." *NPR, Weekend Edition*, October 6, 1991. https://jwa.org/media/transcript-of-nina-totenbergs-npr-report-on-anita-hills-charges-of-sexual-harassment-by-0.

Travers, Ben. 2016. "Confirmation Refuses to Confirm or Deny Anything, but Kerry Washington Shines." *Indie Wire*, April 16, 2016. https://www.indiewire.com/2016/04/review-confirmation-refuses-to-confirm-or-deny-anything-but-kerry-washington-shines-289886/.

Vlessing, Etan. 2020. "Anita Hill Led Hollywood Commission Details Sexual Harassment Claims in Industry Workplaces." *Hollywood Reporter*, October 27, 2020.

Chapter 9

Hidden Figures (2016)

Written by Allison Schroeder and Theodore Melfi;
Directed by Theodore Melfi
Fox 2000 Pictures, 2016, 2 hr., 7 min.

INTRODUCTION

Hidden Figures began as a book researched and written by Margot Lee Shetterly who, upon a family visit back in Hampton, Virginia, in 2010 learned from her father about the many local African American women who worked as "computers," calculating high-end mathematical problems for the Langley Air Base when it was actively involved in the Space Race of the 1950s and 1960s. Before the laptops that are so ubiquitous today, the word computer referred to the human who did the calculating. Shetterly had visited the site when her father worked as an engineer and realized the story of these women had indeed been hidden from history. She spent the next six years interviewing the women and published her book in 2016.

The galleys, as is typical, were sent to producers for consideration as a film, and Donna Gigliotti (Oscar winner for *Shakespeare in Love* and *Silver Linings Playbook*) snagged the rights for her Levantine Films. Gigliotti wanted a female screenwriter who understood the NASA world to work with Shetterly on a script. Oxford-educated Allison Schroeder had interned at NASA's Cape Canaveral during high school. Her family was littered with relatives–male and female—who had worked at NASA. After only two and a half drafts, Gigliotti's note to Schroeder was, "This is very factual now I need you to go have some fun" (Schroeder 2021). On the strength of that script, Octavia Spencer signed on to play Dorothy Vaughan. "I thought it was fiction," says Spencer of her first reaction to the script. "Then when I met with Donna, I realized it wasn't fiction, and I was angry that no one knew this story" (McClintock 2017). Then they hired Theodore Melfi to direct, and Fox 2000 agreed to finance the production.

SUMMARY

The film opens on seven-year-old Katherine walking to school, chanting numbers, and later naming all the types of triangles in a stained-glass window. "White Sulphur Springs 1926" flashes on the screen as we learn Katherine is being promoted from sixth grade to eighth grade, which requires her parents to move to a new district, as the local one does not have a school for children of color that goes any higher. The story jumps ahead to Hampton, Virginia, 1961, where the now grown Katherine (Taraji P. Henson) is carpooling to work with Dorothy Vaughan (Octavia Spencer) and Mary Jackson (Janelle Monáe), and their car has broken down. Personalities are made clear when a white policeman drives up. Dorothy is the mechanic, Mary wants to talk back to the policeman, and Katherine doesn't want any trouble at all. When the policeman learns they work at NASA, he professes to be ready to help do anything to "keep the Commies from putting a man on the moon first" and gives them an escort to their offices at Langley.

At work, the all-white male teams of U.S. scientists watch the Russian team discuss the success of Sputnik. We meet Paul Stafford (Jim Parsons) and Al Harrison (Kevin Costner), heads of the Space Task Force, who need someone who can handle analytic geometry. That person is, of course, Katherine, but she works in another area—the West Computing Building—with a roomful of other African American "computers," which was the title given to people who computed mathematical problems for the scientists. The white female supervisor of all female computers, Mrs. Mitchell (Kirsten Dunst) comes to Dorothy (serving as interim supervisor to the segregated African American computers). Dorothy recommends Katherine, and then asks if her application for supervisor is being considered, since she has been substituting in the job for a year. Mitchell's simply responds that there has never been a full-time supervisor of color. Meanwhile, Mary is assigned to an engineering department where she meets Carl Zielinski (Olek Krupa), who asks her why she hasn't applied to an engineering training program rather than remaining a mere computer. Mary says, "I'm a negro woman. I'm not going to entertain the impossible."

In the Space Task Force room, Katherine is asked to double-check the numbers of the male scientists, something they balk at allowing, but Harrison orders it done. She also learns that the colored ladies room is in a different building, and it takes her nearly a half an hour to walk-run there and back, which makes Harrison wonder where she disappears so often during the day. On day two, she finds that the coffee table now has a second coffee pot marked "colored." She understands that is for her use alone.

Katherine returns late to the home she shares with her three daughters and her mother, who watches them all day while she is at work, since their father has died. The next day is Sunday, and the three female NASA friends attend services together. At the barbecue afterward, Mary's husband Levi doesn't believe any woman of color can be accepted into an engineering program without a fight. Katherine meets National Guard Colonel Jim Johnson (Mahershala Ali), who is a bit incredulous about women doing the taxing work of math. Katherine's response is, "They let women do some things at NASA and it's not because we wear skirts. It's because we wear glasses."

When the Mercury astronauts arrive at Langley Air Base, they are greeted by segregated sections of employees, but John Glenn insists on shaking the hands of all the lead characters. When he asks what they work on for NASA, Katherine proudly states, "We calculate the trajectories for launch and landing." More change is in the air. Dorothy walks by a new "computing" room and sees the first IBM computers arrive at the base. Comic relief comes from the fact that they are too big to fit in the room allocated to them. She asks Mitchell for information and learns the machines can do the job the female calculators have been doing in record time. Dorothy realizes this will put her and her friends out of a job. The three women discuss it at their segregated lunch table. Dorothy insists that the only thing they can do is learn as much as they can to stay useful. Similarly, Mary learns that she needs some extension courses to qualify for the engineering training program, but they are held in the evening at a segregated high school.

Dorothy takes her sons to the local library for books on Fortran, and they return home riding in the back of a bus after having witnessed a protest against segregation. At a party that weekend, Col. Johnson and Katherine dance and begin courting after he apologizes for underestimating her "or any other woman like you." The party is interrupted by a news announcement of the Russian Yuri Gagarin becoming the first human to orbit the Earth, which naturally causes tensions at work to rise.

A montage of exploding rockets follows, along with footage of the astronauts, capsules, and the new IBM being tested. Nothing the NASA scientists do seems to be working well. Mary goes to court for the right to attend the classes she needs, Dorothy teaches her female computers Fortran, and Katherine calculates while also continuing to race to her appropriate restroom, even in the rain. This leads to a confrontation with Harrison in front of the whole office when she finally admits what's going on—and heads out, assuming she'll be fired for insubordination. Instead, Harrison rips the "colored" sign off he coffee pot and proceeds to bash down the "colored" sign over the restroom.

Astronaut Alan Shepard finally enters space, with all three ladies watching the news at home. But the next launch doesn't go as smoothly. Astronaut Gus Grissom's capsule is lost in the ocean, making the following launch, John Glenn's, even more important—but the math to get the capsule out of orbit at precisely the right moment has yet to be invented. After requesting several times, Katherine is allowed in a high-level meeting over this question and provides some advanced calculations on the blackboard, impressing the men in the room. Likewise, Mary's husband supports her as she begins the evening classes she fought to attend. Finally, Dorothy is assigned to the IBM programming department but refuses to go without her whole office of African American female computers, who are, of course, ready to work as programmers, thanks to Dorothy's tutoring. Mitchell tells Dorothy she has some white female computers who would like to learn as well, and Dorothy graciously offers to be their instructor.

Katherine solves the problem of when the capsule should reenter the atmosphere by using Oiler's method, an old math formula. As things improve at work, so do they at home where Col. Johnson proposes—first to Katherine's children, and then to her. As the day of Glenn's ride approaches, the calculations are moved to Cape Canaveral, and Harrison has to tell Katherine they don't need her numbers anymore. She's given a string of pearls in honor of her engagement and leaves the office. The problem is that the IBM's calculations are off, and John Glenn refuses to leave the ground unless Katherine checks the go/no-go numbers.

Mitchell comes to finally offer Dorothy the supervisor position—over the IBM computer lab and thirty or more employees. Mitchell finally refers to Dorothy as Mrs. Vaughan instead of just "Dorothy," which reflects the respect she is now willing to share.

A montage of the whole country learning the news that Glenn's trip is endangered as his heat shield fails is followed by Mission Control suggesting he not jettison his retro pack, as its straps may hold the heat shield in place. When it is announced that "Landing coordinates are spot on," we understand that was Katherine's contribution. Harrison shakes her hand and asks her if she thinks "we can get to the moon." She responds with his own words from earlier: "We're already there, sir."

Another montage tells us the history of each astronaut as we watch our three leads begin their new careers. Katherine types up a report with the words "written by Paul Stafford and Katherine Johnson." Stafford brings a cup of coffee to her desk, takes the report, accepts the shared credit, and carries it upstairs to the Harrison's office as Katherine tidies her desk at the end of another long day of intellectual labor. We read onscreen that she went on to "perform calculations for the Apollo 11 mission to the moon and the space shuttle and that in 2016 NASA dedicated the Katherine G. Johnson Computational Building in honor of her groundbreaking work in space travel." At the time of the film, she was ninety-seven years old and had been married to Johnson for fifty-six years.

The film ends with photos of the actresses, which fade into photos of the real women they portrayed, first as young women, then middle-aged, and then with photos of the women at their ages when the film came out. At that point, the words "Hidden Figures" appears under their names, reflecting on and respecting their years of dedication to the space program.

Hidden Figures cost approximately $25 million and earned a worldwide gross of $236 million (Fleming 2017), qualifying it as successful on many fronts, including financially. It spent two weeks at the top of the box office, ahead of big-budget films like *Patriots Day*, *Live by Night*, and Oscar frontrunner *La Oleo Land* (which actually lost to *Moonlight*). Its deeper cultural success comes from the way it wrote these women back into history. While the book had begun the work of recognizing all these "hidden" women who had contributed so much to the United States space program, a film naturally creates more attention. After the film's release, Katherine Johnson received the Presidential Medal of Freedom at the age of ninety-seven from President Barack Obama. Katherine was honored with a Lego character alongside other women from NASA, including Sally Ride and Mae Jemison. She was also invited to attend the 2016 Oscar ceremony where the film had been nominated for three awards: Best Motion Picture of the Year, Octavia Spencer was nominated for Best Performance by an Actress in a Supporting Role, and Allison Schroeder and Theodore Melfi were nominated for Best Adapted Screenplay. While *Hidden Figures* did not win any Oscars, it did win for Outstanding Performance by a Cast in a Motion Picture at the 2017 Screen Actors Guild Awards and was nominated as Best Foreign Language Film at the Awards of the Japanese Academy.

Later, the Walt Disney Company partnered with the U.S. State Department to create the Hidden No More International Visitor Leadership Program. They bring fifty international women who have excelled in STEM careers to the United States, where they meet professional counterparts to discuss strategies to advance the achievements of women in STEM.

Richard Brody, in reviewing for *The New Yorker* felt the film was about "calm and bright rage at the way things were—an exemplary reproach to the very notion of political nostalgia. It depicts repugnant attitudes and practices of white supremacy that poisoned earlier generations' achievements and that are inseparable from those achievements" (Brody 2016).

For *The Undefeated*, Soraya Nadia McDonald wrote, "The pragmatism that flows through *Hidden Figures*, combined with its upbeat-yet-straightforward approach to showcasing the racist nastiness that Katherine Johnson (Taraji P. Henson), Dorothy Vaughn (Octavia Spencer), and Mary Jackson (Janelle Monáe) endured while working at NASA's racially segregated Langley Research

Center in Hampton, Virginia, in the 1960s, provides a beacon of hope in a modern era that feels marked by uncertainty and despair" (McDonald 2017).

HISTORICAL CONTEXT

(Due to marriages and name changes, Katherine Coleman Goble Johnson will be referenced as Katherine throughout this section.)

The history of women working for NASA (or its predecessors) begins in California with Barbara Canright, who joined the Jet Propulsion Laboratory (JPL) in 1939 as the first female "human computer," alongside her husband. He was a student at Caltech while she attended Occidental College and graduated in 1940. When the U.S. government invested $10,000 into the aeronautical program, JPL hired the couple as mathematicians. As with all mathematicians of the day, Canright did calculations with pencil and graph paper. Canright helped design and test rocket propellant with three of the next female mathematicians JPL hired, but when she became pregnant in 1943, Canright had to resigned, as that was the custom of the day (Holt 2017).

One of the next female hires, Macie Roberts, came to JPL via working at the Internal Revenue Service and soon became supervisor to a team of human computers. She chose to hire only women to ensure cohesion in the unit. The idea spread throughout all computers hired, including the African American units. Then the next female supervisor, Helen Ling, solved the problem of losing qualified women due to pregnancy. She simply rehired them after they had had their children, which made being a computer at JPL a long-term occupation for her staff (Holt 2017).

On the East Coast, specifically at Langley Air Base, the hiring of African Americans into federal jobs begun by President Ulysses S. Grant in Reconstruction had been ended by President Woodrow Wilson during World War I. It began again under President Franklin Delano Roosevelt during World War II, when white Americans took over most of the lucrative war work. Then civil rights activist A. Philip Randolph threatened a march on Washington to open those high-paying occupations (and the training that went with them) to African Americans. In 1941, in response to Randolph, President Roosevelt issued Executive Order 8802, which banned discriminatory employment practices by federal agencies and any unions and companies engaged in war-related work. That allowed Langley to fill their urgent need for employees by recruiting at local African American colleges. Soon a flood of well-educated African American women applied to be computers when they would likely have become high school or college math teachers (Shetterly 2016).

The boon in African American female education began in 1912 when the National Association of Colored Women's Clubs (NACWC) created a national scholarship fund for college-bound African American women. The group, which would soon become the National Association of Colored Women (NAACW), a precursor to the National Association of Colored People (NAACP) had begun in 1896. After Reconstruction ended in the Jim Crow south, it was safer for African American women to gather in groups than for African American men. Women's clubs formed all over the country; held a convention in Washington, D.C., in 1896; and consolidated into the NACWC under the guidance of women such as Harriet Tubman, Frances E. W. Harper, Ida Bell Wells-Barnett, and Mary Church Terrell, who became the organization's first president. The NACWC hoped to endorse the suffrage movement and advance opportunities for African American women through awarding scholarships.

These scholarships helped women like Goble attend college and, therefore, qualify for jobs at Langley. However, situated in Virginia, the base followed the state laws of segregation, which required Langley to house the two teams of female computers separately based on race. African American women worked out of the West Computing Building. This also involved the creation of separate bathrooms and cafeterias. This practice ended in 1959 when NASA was formed and took over the offices at Langley. Likewise, with the Supreme Court ruling in *Brown v. Board of Education* in 1954, all public schools had to desegregate, but Virginia refused the order until 1959. Even then, it took the passing of the 1964 Civil Rights Act until the Department of Health, Education, and Welfare threatened southern states with the loss of federal funding if they did not integrate their schools. Still, Virginians went to court to fight the idea until the 1970s, when the state government ended their attempts to resist desegregation.

The film is a collected biography, so it cannot give in-depth coverage to any of the three lead characters. While the film runs from 1961–1963, in fact, Dorothy Vaughan is the first to be hired at Langley, having come to the position after working as a high school math teacher. She became their first Black female supervisor in 1949 and held the position for a decade. Engineers came to her to recommend the best women for their very specific project and often chose her, which required extra work on top of her managerial duties. In the 1950s, mechanical computers entered the NASA world. Since women had been computing for so long, the operations of those new machines became their domain. Vaughan became an expert FORTRAN programmer and joined the Analysis and Computation Division (ACD), along with many of her West Computing colleagues.

When Mary Jackson came to NASA in 1951, she worked in Vaughan's department. Despite having earned a dual degree in math and physical sciences at the Hampton Institute in 1942 and being a math teacher in Maryland, Jackson held three other jobs before being accepted as a computer. She had been a USO Club receptionist during World War II, a Health Department bookkeeper, and an army secretary at Fort Monroe. After two years as a computer, Vaughan assigned Jackson to engineer Kazimierz Czarnecki in the Supersonic Pressure Tunnel. There she gained the hands-on experience that qualified her for the engineering training program. As in the film, though, Jackson had to petition for the right to attend some extra night courses at a local all-white high school. But in 1958, Jackson became NASA's first Black female engineer (NASA: Jackson).

In her earlier years, Katherine's innate abilities with high-level math secured her a place as the first woman to integrate the graduate school of West Virginia University (along with two male students). She left graduate studies to begin her family, and, in 1953, when her daughters were older, Dorothy Vaughan hired her at Langley. Her temporary job became permanent a few years later, which helped her family at a critical time because her husband died unexpectedly. Though work at Langley had focused on airplane technology, once the Russians launched the Sputnik satellite successfully a Space Task Group formed, and Katherine joined their work to calculate trajectory analysis for Alan Shepard's May 1961 mission onboard Freedom 7. Male engineers praised Katherine's work and recognized her genius. In 1960, she coauthored (with a male engineer) a report on equations for the landing position of the spacecraft, the first time a woman in the Flight Research Division received credit as an author of such a report.

The most famous example of the trust the men placed in her came when Astronaut John Glenn asked that Katherine double-check the numbers on his flight reentry, which had been calculated by the relatively new IBM computer. As Shetterly wrote in her book, "The astronaut who became a hero looked to this black woman in this still segregated South at the time as one of the key parts of making sure his mission would be a success" (Shetterly 2016). Katherine remained at NASA through the bulk of the years of the space shuttle, retiring in 1986. In 2016, NASA dedicated the Katherine Goble Johnson Computational Building in honor of her groundbreaking work in space travel.

Shetterly's book chronicles many other African American female computers, but the film only accommodated the stories of these three.

DEPICTION AND CULTURAL CONTEXT

Though *Hidden Figures is* a story set in the United States, Paul Byrnes of *The Sydney Morning Herald* took the film to task for historical errors, mostly of time and of wasting time on moments for a white hero or two to shine. He wrote, "Almost every one of the fudges makes the film more entertaining and less truthful. Don't these women deserve better? They blazed a trail much earlier than we see here; they kept doing it much later than is shown here, although the end titles at least acknowledge that. I suspect that many of the film's biggest moments never happened, or not the way they do here, which makes the movie almost worthless as history. When a film purports to be selling history, we're entitled to ask where the history went, even if it offers a good time instead" (Byrnes 2017). Megan Garber of *The Atlantic* found the film did offer up a proper history, calling it "a work of history, and a collective biopic, and a beautifully rendered drama of the small-scale victories that lead to large-scale progress" (Garber 2017).

Both critics are correct in certain ways. To adapt Shetterly's nonfiction account of the many African American female computers, screenwriter Allison Schroeder had to cut some corners—and in order to sell the film to studios (and for the studios to sell it to name actors), she had to invent ways to allow those actors to shine. The first and most obvious change was to truncate a nearly thirty-year timeline into the most exciting era for the space race: 1961–1963. This meant moving up the times when Vaughan and Jackson earned their promotions in order to parallel Katherine's work on Glenn's launch. It also required showing the three lead characters as a triumvirate of friends when they worked at different times in different departments. Also, they never carpooled (Schroeder interview).

Each main female character did encounter years of microaggressions, but, again, shrinking the timeline meant shrinking those moments, which, in turn, meant assigning them to just a few of the white characters. There was also the question of obtaining life rights to the surrounding characters, who were not as open about seeing themselves cemented into this story as the female computers had been. Therefore, the characters of Paul Stafford (Jim Parsons) and Mrs. Mitchell (Kirsten Dunst) are fictitious, while the Al Harrison character played by Kevin Costner is a composite of three different NASA directors. In terms of creating moments for white actors in the midst of a film about African American female triumphs, that was necessary to sell big-name actors like Costner (Schroeder interview). Hence, the invention of the smashing of the "colored" sign over the ladies' restroom.

In reality, Katherine didn't need to walk a half mile to a segregated bathroom. That had happened to Jackson in the engineering building. Even then, the issue was moot before the time frame of the film, since that segregation ended at Langley in 1958. In her earlier work at Langley, Katherine had not realized there were segregated bathrooms in the Space Task Force building, so she used the one reserved for whites and received only one complaint, which she ignored (Shetterly 2016). The smashing of the sign moment exists merely for the Harrison character to do something dramatic that could be conceived as heroic.

Such cinematic moments in films with predominantly African American casts are termed "white savior moments." Yet, as Richard Brody noted in his article about the film, "Al plays a heroic role, championing Katherine's work and treating her with due respect—but his heroism is a conditional and practical one, spurred by his single-minded devotion to the space program" (Brody 2016). It is not, in fact, a renouncing of segregation because it is unfair to the African Americans in his employ but because this particular segregation rule stands in the way of his own achievement. This reasoning is reminiscent of how some white abolitionists did not fight to end slavery for the benefit of the enslaved, but in order to save the souls of those who enslaved them and treated them inhumanely, thereby risking a sentence in hell. Writing for *The Undefeated*, Soraya Nadia McDonald concurred: "While *Hidden Figures* illustrates that good that can come of dismantling barriers in the pursuit of common interests, it doesn't offer white absolution" (McDonald 2017).

Though she appreciated the way the history of females of color came alive in the film, critic Megan Garber did not fail to note both the white savior moment and another syndrome worth mentioning: "*Hidden Figures*'s narrative trajectory involves not just progress that emerges, too often, from pettiness, but also thematic elements of the white savior, and of a culturally enforced tiara syndrome. All those things effectively temper the idealism of its message" (Garber 2017). Carol Frohlinger and Deborah Kolb, who train and consult professional women through their company, Negotiating Women, Inc., coined the phrase "the tiara syndrome." Then Sheryl Sandberg spread the idea to a larger audience in her book, *Lean In* (cowritten with Nell Scovell). It involves the idea that women are culturally taught to keep their heads down, deliver excellent work, and hope that the right people will notice so they can place a tiara on their head.

Considering all three lead characters publicly stood up for their own advancement—both in the script and in real life—the tiara syndrome doesn't seem to serve here. It was true that Vaughan pushed to be given the full title (and pay) of a supervisor—and won that right. It was true that women weren't allowed in high level meetings, and it is true that Katherine pushed to be allowed to attend—and won that right. It is true that Jackson pushed to be allowed to study in the all-white high school night school course—and won. The women fought two systemic prejudices—one based on race and one based on gender—and won to the extent that African Americans could win in the midst of a still evolving Civil Rights movement.

As with any piece of writing, many moments came from Schroeder's own life. For instance, when Jackson walks into a night class and she's the only woman in the room, the teacher says the curriculum isn't designed for a woman. "That happened to me," Schroeder says. "I walked into an international economics tutorial and the professor said, 'I don't know how to teach a woman.' I said, 'It's the same as teaching a man'" (Kaufman 2017). Also, when Jackson has to walk in high heels in a wind tunnel or Katherine is told that the only jewelry allowed is a pearl necklace, those moments came from stories Schroeder heard from her own grandmother's working life at NASA (Schroeder interview). However, one piece of comic relief came from a NASA reality. When Vaughan walks by a new "computing" room and sees the first IBM computers arrive at the base, they are too big to fit in the room allocated. That is true (Harris 2017).

In her review of why *Hidden Figures* engaged audiences of all races and genders, Garber wrote that beyond the empowering of females and women of color, beyond the reviving of real histories long left behind by male historians, *Hidden Figures*:

> ultimately, celebrates numbers. Not just as tools for understanding the world, but as instruments for making it better. Get the girl to check the numbers. Because lives are at stake, and that fact, right now, transcends everything else, and "the girl"—Katherine Johnson—is objectively better with those numbers than anyone else around. And what *Hidden Figures* also knows—and what the book that occasioned the film knows, as well—is that numbers, when they can be freed of their human freight, are leveling. They do not care about one's gender. They do not care about one's creed. They do not care about the color of one's skin. They can be used by anyone who cares to learn their ways. (Garber 2017)

While the film's story takes place in the Civil Rights Movement of the 1960s, it came to print and to the screen just after the founding of the BlackLives-Matter Movement. In 2013, Alicia Garza, Patrisse Cullors, and Ayo (formerly known as Opal Tometi) founded BlackLivesMatter after the acquittal of George Zimmerman in the shooting death of Trayvon Martin a year earlier. Their movement grew nationally in 2014 after the deaths of Michael Brown in Missouri and Eric Garner in New York and reached a zenith in 2020 with the murder of George Floyd by a police officer in Minneapolis (Watters 2017).

Along with that timing, *Hidden Figures* came out a year after activist April Reign created the hashtag #OscarsSoWhite since the 2012 Academy Awards did not include nominations for any person of color in either a lead or supporting actor and actress category. In response, an analysis by the *Los Angeles Times* found that membership in the Academy of Motion Picture Arts and Sciences, the body that votes for the Oscars, was 93 percent white and 76 percent male (Kang 2015). At the 2017 Academy Awards, five Black artists were among that year's winners. *Hidden Figures* earned three nominations, for Best Motion Picture of the Year, Best Adapted Screenplay, and Octavia Spencer earned a nomination for Best Performance by an Actress in a Supporting Role. She lost to another woman of color, Viola Davis in *Fences*.

As noted earlier, while the film did not win traditional awards associated with the art form, it brought to light stories of a group of women who were intrinsic in the United States success in the space race and in landing a human on the moon.

MERCURY 13

Another example of how long women have been involved in STEM fields—and been ignored—comes from the story of the Mercury 13. This group of thirteen female pilots tested for the astronaut program in the early 1960s. Dr. Randolph Lovelace, chairman of NASA's Life Sciences Committee for Project Mercury, wanted to study the effects of spaceflight and women, so he asked Jacqueline Cochran, America's premier female pilot, to invite the most prestigious female pilots she knew to test. At fifty-four, Cochrane was too old for the test herself, but she assisted the effort by helping to fund Lovelace's studies. Jerrie Cobb, a pilot who had logged over ten thousand flight hours, was the first woman selected for the first phase of the test in 1960. The preparation for the test involved running five miles a day and riding twenty more on a stationary bike. The tests were exactly the ones given to the Mercury astronauts, and Cobb matched their statistics on each test. For the isolation test, pilots were immersed up to their necks in an underground water tank. Cobb stayed there for nine hours, forty minutes, exceeding the highest male astronauts test time by just over three hours. Cobb's test results were so extraordinary, she was sent to phase two of the program, and the other twelve women began phase one.

Among the other women of the Mercury 13 were members of the Women's Air Force Service Pilots from World War II, some school teachers, and two identical twins. All test subjects accepted Cochrane's invitation, despite having to pay their own way. Overall, the women proved to be less prone to heart attacks and loneliness, cold, heat, pain, and noise. It was also discovered that NASA could save money by using female astronauts, since the cost of sending anything into space was nearly $1,000 per pound. Women weighed less and would, therefore, cost less in space.

Despite all these advantages, and although Cobb passed her second phase of testing with flying colors as well, NASA did not allow her or the other twelve members of the Mercury 13 to become full astronauts. Instead, Cobb was made a NASA consultant. The others were simply dismissed. On July 17, 1962, Cobb and a few others testified before Congress in favor of women being included in the astronaut corps. Astronaut John Glenn (a hero in the *Hidden Figures* story) testified against the idea.

NASA decided that although the women could pass the extra tests, they did not have the complete qualifications to take them. Women had never passed the jet aircraft testing at Edwards Air Force Base because women were not yet eligible for jet pilot training programs in the military (and they would not be eligible by law until 1973). Cobb requested the jet experience requirements be waived in lieu of her extensive flying hours and high scores. NASA refused to waive the requirement. The Mercury 13 lost their quest to travel in space. In July 1961, NASA canceled all further testing of women for the program.

Seventeen years after the cancellation, in 1978, NASA finally opened astronaut training to women. Among the class of thirty-five astronauts, there were six females: Sally Ride (who would become the first United States female in space), Judy Resnik, Anna Fisher, Kathy Sullivan, Shannon Lucid, and Rhea Seddon.

> Thirty-four years after the cancellation, seven of the Mercury 13 crew watched as America's first woman pilot astronaut, Lieutenant Colonel Eileen Collins, launched at Cape Kennedy on February 3, 1995, piloting the Discovery Space Shuttle on special mission STS-63.

FURTHER READING

Brody, Richard. 2016. "'Hidden Figures' Is a Subtle and Powerful Work of Counter-History." *The New Yorker*, December 23, 2016. https://www.newyorker.com/culture/richard-brody/hidden-figures-is-a-subtle-and-powerful-work-of-counter-history.

Byrnes, Paul. 2017. "Hidden Figures Review: These Trailblazing Women Deserve Better." *The Sydney Morning Herald*, February 14, 2017. https://www.smh.com.au/entertainment/movies/hidden-figures-review-these-trailblazing-women-deserve-better-20170214-gucbs5.html.

Fleming, Mike, Jr. 2017. "No. 15 'Hidden Figures' Box Office Profits—2016 Most Valuable Movie Blockbuster Tournament." *Deadline Hollywood*. https://deadline.com/2017/03/hidden-figures-box-office-profit-2016-1202048264/.

Garber, Megan. 2017. "*Hidden Figures* and the Appeal of Math in an Age of Inequality." *The Atlantic*, January 18, 2017. https://www.theatlantic.com/entertainment/archive/2017/01/hidden-figures-and-the-appeal-of-math-in-an-age-of-inequality/513434/.

Harris, Robin. 2017. "Hidden Figures and the IBM 7090 Computer." *ZD Net*. https://www.zdnet.com/article/hidden-figures-and-the-ibm-7090-computer/.

History vs. Hollywood. "*Hidden Figures* (2017)." Accessed May 31, 2022. https://www.historyvshollywood.com/reelfaces/hidden-figures/.

Holland, Bryan. "Human Computers: The Women of NASA." History. Updated August 22, 2018. Accessed May 31, 2022. https://www.history.com/news/human-computers-women-at-nasa.

Holt, Nathalia. 2017. *Rise of the Rocket Girls: The Women Who Propelled Us, from Missiles to the Moon to Mars*. New York: Back Bay Books.

Kang, Cecilia. 2015. "Oscars 2015: No Nominations for a Single Actor of Color or Female Director." *The Washington Post*. https://www.washingtonpost.com/news/business/wp/2015/01/15/oscars-2015-no-nominations-for-a-single-actor-or-director-of-color/.

Kaufman, Amy. 2017. "Meet Allison Schroeder, the NASA-Loving Writer of 'Hidden Figures' Who Was Just Nominated for an Oscar." *The Los Angeles Times*. https://www.latimes.com/entertainment/movies/la-et-mn-hidden-figures-writer-allison-schroeder-20170124-story.html.

McClintock, Pamela. 2017. "Making of 'Hidden Figures': Re-Creating the '60s to Tell an Untold Story of Space, Sexism and Civil Rights." *The Hollywood Reporter*, January 10, 2017. https://www.hollywoodreporter.com/movies/movie-features/making-hidden-figures-how-taraji-p-henson-octavia-spencer-pharrell-williams-revisited-60s-t-960650/.

McDonald, Soraya Nadia. 2017. "*Hidden Figures* and the Power of Pragmatism. Just When We Need It, a Space Movie Filled with Real, Tangible Hope." *The Undefeated*, January 5, 2017. https://theundefeated.com/features/hidden-figures-and-the-power-of-pragmatism/.
NASA. "Mary W. Jackson Biography." Accessed May 31, 2022. https://www.nasa.gov/content/mary-w-jackson-biography.
NASA. "Katherine Johnson Biography." Accessed May 31, 2022. https://www.nasa.gov/content/katherine-johnson-biography.
NASA. "Dorothy Vaughan Biography." Accessed May 31, 2022. https://www.nasa.gov/content/dorothy-vaughan-biography.
Schroeder, Allison. Author's Interview. April 7, 2021.
Shetterly, Margot Lee. 2016. *Hidden Figures*. New York: William Morrow.
Walt Disney Company. 2019. "The Walt Disney Company Partners with U.S. State Department on 'Hidden No More' Exchange Program." October 28, 2019. https://thewaltdisneycompany.com/the-walt-disney-company-partners-with-u-s-state-department-on-hidden-no-more-exchange-program/.
Watters, Jessica. 2017–2018. "Pink Hats and Black Fists: The Role of Women in the Black Lives Matter Movement." *William & Mary Journal of Race, Gender, and Social Justice* 24 (1): 199.

Chapter 10

On the Basis of Sex (2018)

Written by Daniel Stiepleman; Directed by Mimi Leder
Dreamworks Pictures, 2018, 2hr.

INTRODUCTION

While telling the story of the one case famed Supreme Court Justice Ruth Bader Ginsburg represented in tandem with her husband Martin Ginsburg, *On the Basis of Sex* provides a glimpse into their feminist marriage and how their dedication to their partner's equality—and to the law—bound them together for life. Written by their nephew Daniel Stiepleman, a lawyer in his own right, it offered a more personal look into what became a very public life.

Stiepleman brought the idea of a film about his aunt's life to a colleague, film producer Karen Loop (*Outlander* and *Second Hand Lions*). Judge Ginsburg gave legal permission for the film on the stipulation (she was a lawyer after all) that her husband, Martin, could not be made to look like the antagonist, since he had been nothing but supportive of her work across their entire relationship. At the time, Judge Ginsburg was not yet a household name, but production delays caused the project to stall. Various actresses signed on to the project; asked for script rewrites, which took time; and then booked other films, which resulted in other actresses coming onboard and asking for other rewrites. Similar situations arose in the hiring of a director. Long before it became practice to find female directors for female-driven stories, Loop and Stiepleman interviewed women and hired prolific television director Mimi Leder (*China Beach*, *ER*, and

Shameless). Finally, with the allotment of a $20 million budget, filming began. By then, by dint of her salty dissensions on the court, Judge Ginsburg had become the popular culture "Notorious RBG," complete with her own action figure.

SUMMARY

The film opens on twenty-six-year-old Ruth (Felicity Jones) among the sixth class at Harvard Law School to accept females, so she is one of only nine women among five hundred plus males, mostly all white. The wo
men and a few chosen males attend a party given by the dean, Erwin Griswold (Sam Waterston) where, instead of being lauded for their achievements, the women are asked to explain, "Why you are occupying a place at Harvard that could have gone to a man?" While other women attempt to explain their desire to do more than be teachers or nurses, Ruth snidely (but oh, so politely) explains that her husband is in the class above so she is at Harvard to learn about his work, "So I can be a more patient and understanding wife." The dean understands he's been insulted but has no ready retort.

In the middle of her first year, her husband (Armie Hammer) is stricken with testicular cancer, a disease that, at the time, had only a 5 percent survival rate. While he undergoes radiation therapy and slowly recovers, Ruth attends both his law courses and her own, takes notes, and types out papers he dictates from his sick bed. Eventually, Martin graduates and obtains a position at a prestigious firm in New York City. Ruth has one year left on her degree, so she goes to Griswold asking to finish out long distance so she can be an alumna of Harvard Law School. He denies her request, so she transfers to Columbia Law School to finish.

Then, despite stellar qualifications from being top of her class to being on staff at both the Harvard *and* Columbia law reviews, she is denied a place in a law firm due to being female, married, a mother, and Jewish—all of which were legal reasons to deny employment in 1959. She takes a position at Rutgers University teaching sex discrimination and the law to a group of burgeoning second-wave feminists. Though she has been teaching a class of feminists, Ruth needs to relearn some of the notions ingrained in her all her life. She is challenged to do so by their teenage daughter Jane, who has cut class with a fake note in order to attend a rally and hear Gloria Steinem speak. A pivotal moment in her career occurs after she and Martin attend a party hosted by Martin's law firm, where she politely ignores some of the more moronic microaggressions she has had to endure. In a rare argument with Martin, he offers respect for her academic career by saying, "You're teaching young people to change the world," but she honestly responds, "That's what I wanted to do."

Soon Martin comes home with an interesting tax case that will become *Charles E. Moritz v. Commissioner of Internal Revenue*. It seems that section 214 of the tax code allowed all women to take a tax deduction for employing a caregiver. Only men whose wives were incapacitate or dead—or divorced—could apply. The IRS denied Moritz, a bachelor with a full-time job who hired a caregiver for his live-in elderly mother, the same deduction. Ruth recognizes it as a clear case of discrimination based on sex. She insists they take the case pro bono, going so far as to recruit Mel Wulf (Justin Theroux), a childhood friend who now works with the ACLU, to have that group sign on to the brief, making for a stronger defense team. Ruth also solicits the help of an older female lawyer formerly involved in pushing first-wave feminism and women's vote. Dorothy Kenyon (Kathy Bates) proves to be a damaged dynamo, still working for women's equal treatment under the law though that causes many male lawyers to dismiss her as a crackpot.

Ruth writes the brief, and when they receive the response from the IRS lawyers, she, Martin, and Mel practice, with three friends giving them pointers. Obstacles thrown in their way include the government's ability to use a computer to collect data on all the thousands of tax codes that discriminate based on gender—a term Ruth begins to use because she thinks seeing the word *sex* all over a legal brief takes the reader's mind off of the law and turns it to less practical matters. Also an obstacle of intimidation, they learn the government's team includes Ruth's old professor from Harvard, as well as Dean Griswold, since he was promoted to solicitor general. Griswold and his team are aghast at the widespread change that this case could create while, at the same time, sure it can't be won.

Meanwhile, Ruth and Martin and their team of volunteers, including daughter Jane and some of Ruth's college students, begin the tedious task of investigating each of these cases. Ruth and Martin make it clear that Moritz is being harmed and kept from his civil rights on the basis of his sex, which is clearly unconstitutional. If the judges agree to this, they will be setting the precedent that discrimination based on gender is unconstitutional. That precedent would have to be applied to all the other many tax codes on the books and many other laws, clearly giving Ruth and Martin a chance to change the world.

While rehearsing Ruth to make this, her first presentation to a judge, Martin shows his support, as noted in the script, "without condescension . . . with trust and affection." Yet their friends think he should make the presentation instead due to his experience in court. The mutual choice is for them to share—Martin will present the tax research, and Ruth will cover the gender-discrimination argument. Another wrench comes when the government offers to settle with Moritz. The ACLU thinks it's the safer bet. Moritz asks Ruth for her legal opinion, and she admits she disagrees. With Moritz's agreement, she goes to the opposing lawyers to settle—but *only if* the government writes in the documents that her client had been discriminated against due to his gender. They decline. Ruth goes to court.

Nervous and outnumbered by all the testosterone in the courtroom, including the intimidation of her former university professor, Ruth originally stumbles at all the ridiculous questions raised by the judges. When she states, "There is nothing that women are inherently better at then men," the judge retorts, "Growing a beard?" and "Lactation?" Flustered, Ruth reserves the rest of her time for rebuttal. The government's lawyer steps forward and insists that Moritz is being used by the Ginsburgs to achieve, "Radical. Social. Change."

Everyone expects Martin to make the final rebuttal after Ruth's shaky performance, but, with one look, they agree this is Ruth's fight, and she rises. She argues that change has already happened and "We are asking you to protect the right of the country to change." When the judge balks at the idea of overturning one hundred years of precedent, Ruth reminds him it is his job to make precedent "as courts have done before when the law is outdated."

The film ends with other lawyers in later cases using Ruth's words to press their own discrimination cases. As we watch actress Felicity Jones ascend the stairs of the United States Supreme Court, she melds into footage of the real-life Supreme Court Judge Ruth Bader Ginsburg, aged eighty-four, entering the hallowed hall. Superimposed on screen, we read that Martin Ginsburg became one of America's preeminent tax attorneys and that on June 14, 1993, President Bill Clinton nominated Ruth Bader Ginsburg to the U.S. Supreme Court. The Senate confirmed her nomination 96–3.

The film opened in December 2018, and though it received no Oscar nominations, it was nominated for the Humanitas Prize, given for film and television writing intended to promote human dignity, meaning, and freedom. Nominated for several other awards, *On the Basis of Sex* won for Outstanding Feature Film at the Women's Image Network Awards. In terms of box office, the film eventually earned $38,755,900 in worldwide distribution.

Among film reviewers, many wrote that they felt Ginsburg's life had to be more dramatic than the script that attempted to contain it. They didn't seem to understand that the film was not a biopic in that it wasn't the traditional cradle-to-grave coverage of a life. Instead, as the story of a legal case that, in fact, changed the country, *On the Basis of Sex* is more akin to 2016's *Loving*, which told the story of the *Loving v. Virginia* case invalidating state laws against interracial marriage or 2017's *Marshall*, which told the story of one of Thurgood Marshall's early cases for the NAACP.

Apropos to the theme of the film, there was some difference detected in the way reviewers felt about the film based on their own genders. Writing for *The Chicago Tribune*, Katie Walsh felt the film "might be a rather broad biopic, but it beautifully argues the importance of Ginsburg's work—prior to the Supreme Court—and is a lovely tribute to the woman who would become the Notorious RBG." She also used the word *refreshing* when she noted, "It's refreshing to see a biopic where the wife is the main agent of toil, change and struggle, where the husband is supportive, loving, confident—and cooks dinner, too. It's reflective of the Ginsburgs' real-life egalitarian marriage, almost never seen in Hollywood films" (Walsh 2018).

Likewise, Nell Minnow, for Ebert Reviews, found "Stiepleman's affection for his aunt and license as an insider are palpable as he gently, perhaps too gently, teases her seriousness of purpose, her discipline, and her legendarily awful cooking" (Minnow 2018).

Finally, as films tend to be judged by their box office take, the film doubled its money, taking the $20-million budget and earning close to $40 million. But in a world full of blockbusters that earn $100 million, those numbers did not appear strong. Producers felt it didn't help that the documentary *RBG* opened in May 2018 and gained strong reviews, while *On the Basis of Sex* opened in December, causing a sense of RBG overload. Many creatives behind the scenes bemoaned the timing but had no control over things like actresses or directors entering and leaving the process, but each change caused the film to be the last in line to offer major coverage of what had become a legendary life.

HISTORICAL BACKGROUND

While some women served as local judges in western territories since the 1860s, the history of women in the judicial branch of the United States government began with Genevieve Rose Cline. In 1928, President Calvin Coolidge asked her to serve on the U.S. Customs Court (which later became the U.S. Court of International Trade). Judge Cline served on the court for twenty-five years.

Before women could be appointed to any judicial position, they had to obtain law degrees, and, before that, they had to be allowed to study the law. For this, Ada Kepley can be named the first woman to earn her bachelor of laws in 1870 in Illinois. While that state allowed women to study the law, it did not allow them to practice. Illinois banned women from taking the state bar exam. In a parallel to the Ginsburg's work on gender equality, Ada had married a fellow lawyer, Henry B. Kepley, who drafted a bill banning sex discrimination in professional occupations. It passed the legislature in 1872 (Mossman 2006).

In that same year, Charlotte E. Ray became the first African American female to graduate with a law degree in the United States. Ray attended the Howard University School of Law while also teaching there full time. She then gained admission as the first female (of any race) admitted to the District of Columbia Bar, thanks to Reconstruction-era policies that desegregated the nation's capital. Those policies also allowed Ray to become the first woman to practice in the District of Columbia Supreme Court, when she defended the wife in a divorce case titled *Gadley v. Gadley* (Smith 1993).

Just as the passage of the Nineteenth Amendment allowing women to vote meant to open up more opportunity for all women, the revocation of Reconstruction policies closed that same door on African American applicants. Still, most colleges continued to turn many women away from the study of law on the basis that they were taking up a seat a man could use. Men were culturally expected to be the salary earners of their future families, while societal expectations for middle- and upper-class women involved becoming wives and mothers.

More particular to Ginsburg's life, Harvard University's history with female students began in their Graduate School of Education, which admitted women in 1920. Fe del Mundo, a Filipino pediatrician, was the first woman to be admitted to Harvard Medical School in 1936, and Emily Gage became the school's first woman to complete a graduate degree when she earned her bachelor of divinity degree in 1957. Though the Harvard Law School was founded in 1817 and graduated its first African American male student in 1869, it did not begin to accept females until nearly one hundred years later, in 1950. Ginsburg earned her spot in Harvard Law School class of 1956 as one of nine women among nearly five hundred new students. At that time, she had already had her first child, a daughter named Jane.

When her husband gained a job in New York, Ginsburg had to leave Harvard and finish her degree at the Columbia School of Law, where she tied for first in her class at graduation. Having attended both universities also gave her the distinction of being the first woman to work on two major law reviews: the *Harvard Law Review* and *Columbia Law Review* (Hendricks 2020). Despite all these achievements, in that era, no law firm agreed to hire her. One Columbia professor finally suggested her (and only her) for a clerkship with a New York District judge. "I was Jewish, a woman, and a mother. The first raised one eyebrow; the second, two; the third made me indubitably inadmissible," Ginsburg said (Thulin 2018). In 1959, it was still legal to refuse to hire someone on the basis of their gender. After her clerkship, and with no other job offers, Ginsburg studied civil procedure for a year in Sweden, and then began her career teaching law at Rutgers University (Hendricks 2020).

Several laws had to come into effect before discrimination based on gender became an illegal practice, and none of them happened soon enough to help the young Ginsburg as she sought employment. The first piece of federal legislation to prohibit sex-based discrimination became the Equal Pay Act, passed in 1963. Then the Civil Rights Act of 1964 outlawed discrimination based on race, color, religion, sex, and national origin (in later years, this would be amended to include sexual orientation and gender identity). Signed into law by President Lyndon B. Johnson, it opened up opportunities for many underrepresented groups under the Title VII section, focused on the issue of equal employment. Still, women could be turned down if they were (or could become) pregnant during their employment. Some who had been hired were legally fired when they announced a pregnancy. It took another fourteen years to remedy that imbalance. The Pregnancy Discrimination Act of 1978 amended Title VII to "prohibit sex discrimination on the basis of pregnancy." It equated pregnancy with temporary disabilities and required employers to treat a pregnant employee in ways that would not violate disability standards. As with the way the IRS had to change their rules based on the case the Ginsburgs won, these pregnancy rights were argued in court and led to congressional action to clarify Civil Rights (Risen 2014). All these issues have been solved in court, a testament to the career that both Ginsburgs dedicated their lives to. Prejudices may still hold sway, but the act finally gave people the right to sue if they feel they have been denied equal treatment for any of those reasons.

To understand the widespread effect those laws had on other women entering the professional world, we can look at the other women in Ginsburg's class. One became a judge when she found she wasn't being made partner at the firms where she worked. One became an in-house counsel to a non-profit, which paid less than a private law firm but offered the satisfaction of helping others. One became a leader in legal advocacy for patients, and one went into academia (as Ginsburg had at the beginning of her own career). One authored legal textbooks, one focused on disability rights, and one worked in government departments focused on Civil Rights and helped desegregate hospitals and mental institutions. One worked in the lucrative world of New York real estate law, and one worked in banking law at Wells Fargo (Lithwick and Olmstead 2020).

Popular culture took a while to recognize the new order of things. The 1970 pilot episode of the iconic *Mary Tyler Moore Show* included an interview scene where the male boss, Lou Grant (Edward Asner), tells the female interviewee, Mary Richards (Mary Tyler Moore), "I figured I'd hire a man for it, but we can talk about it." He then asks her religion and her marital status, and she points out that those questions are illegal things to be asked. In her 2017 article about the continued relevance of that scene in that pilot forty-seven years after it first aired, Lisa Bonos writes that the deeper question comes when Lou asks Mary why she isn't married and she responds, "There's no simple answer to why a person isn't married" (Bonos 2017).

On the Basis of Sex presents the case of *Moritz v. Commissioner of Internal Revenue* fairly. The Ginsburgs argued this tax law case in front of the Tenth Circuit Court of Appeals over an up-to-$600 tax deduction for caregiver expenses that had not been offered to their client because he was a sixty-three-year-old bachelor. Only women could take the deduction, and the Ginsburgs recognized this as a discrimination based on gender—but unlike other cases brought by women, this case was arguing for rights for a man. They rationalized that if they won this, it would set the precedent for many, many cases of discrimination against women. They won. The court ruled for Moritz and, more importantly, determined that the code discriminated based solely on sex, which opposed the Fifth Amendment's guarantee of due process. It was the first time a provision of the Internal Revenue Code had been declared unconstitutional.

Being a film focused on the Moritz case rather than a full biopic, it never intended to give full coverage to Ginsburg's lengthy legal career, but it should be noted that, as an attorney, she argued six cases before the Supreme Court she would one day join. Most of those cases also involved sex-discrimination issues. In 1976, in *Califano v. Goldfarb*, she argued that the Social Security Act, which allowed women to receive full benefits from deceased husbands but only gave men the right to benefits if they had been receiving half their support from their wives at the time of death. In 1975, in *Weinberger v. Wiesenfeld*, she again argued against a provision of the Social Security Act. This one allowed both the children and the widow of a deceased man to receive benefits, but the benefits for a deceased wife and mother only went to the children. Ginsburg claimed that the Social Security Act unfairly discriminated on the basis of sex. Finally, in 1973, in *Frontiero v. Richardson*, Ginsburg supported a female lieutenant in the United States Air Force who had asked for a dependent's allowance for her husband. At that time, federal law stated that military wives were dependents, but husbands of female members of the military had to prove they needed over one-half of their wives' salaries to be financially stable. These cases raised her profile in the legal community, and she was appointed to the D.C. Circuit Court of Appeals in 1980.

Similarly, the film only infers her future on the Supreme Court when it shows actress Felicity Jones as the young attorney version of Ginsburg walking up the steps of One First Street, the Supreme Court Building. She blends into footage of the real Ginsburg, aged eighty-five, walking up those same stairs. Ginsburg would be only the second female with her appointment in 1993. The Supreme Court, established in 1789 by inclusion in the Constitution of the United States, gained its first female associate justice in 1981 with the appointment of Sandra Day O'Connor.

By 2021, three more women have joined the court. Before the others arrived and after O'Connor retired early to care for her elderly husband in 2006, Ginsburg served as the lone female justice. Multiple studies testing the influence of women on the courts, performed by associate professor of political science at the University of Georgia, Dr. Christina Boyd, prove how much they influence male fellow judges in panel decisions. Boyd wrote, "Group decision-making is better when you have diverse voices and perspectives involved, and women bring a unique set of experiences, backgrounds and worldviews to deliberation." Secondarily, studies show that "having a judiciary that represents society is essential for people to trust and believe in the courts" (Melton 2020).

Female presence on the court has made a difference in several cases. With both O'Connor and Ginsburg on the court in 1996, they helped create a 9–3 win in the case of *United States v. Virginia* (1996), which struck down the exclusion of women students from the Virginia Military Institute. With O'Connor retired and amid new justices considered more conservative, Ginsburg found herself in the minority but used her abilities to write strong dissents on cases she lost. In 2014, in *Burwell v. Hobby Lobby*, Ginsburg wrote that it eroded the separation of church and state, and, in 2013, in *Shelby County v. Holder*, she wrote that the ruling undermined the Voting Rights Act (Cohen and Dull n.d.).

DEPICTION AND CULTURAL CONTEXT

As noted in a personal interview with associate producer Karen Loop, the writing of the film began before Ginsburg had become a cultural icon, but as it took several years to reach the screen, it premiered long after the justice had become "the Notorious RBG." The nickname came in 2013 courtesy of a New York University law student, Shana Knizhnik, who was shocked by how she felt the Supreme Court's majority (by 5-4) ruling in *Shelby County v. Holder* had damaged voting rights. Justice Ginsburg read her dissent in the court for the record. In response, Knizhnik created the "Notorious RBG" tag and posted it to the internet's Tumblr site. The nickname is a play on her initials "RBG" and the "Notorious B.I.G." stage name of rapper Christopher George Latore Wallace, known professionally as Biggie Smalls as well as the Notorious B.I.G. Both the blog and the nickname went viral, not only on the internet but also out on the street with mugs, tote bags, and T-shirts bearing the Notorious RBG image. In 2015, Knizhnik partnered with journalist Irin Carmon to publish the book *Notorious RBG: The Life and Times of Ruth Bader Ginsburg*, which became a best-seller. Justice Ginsburg was said not to mind the "Notorious" nickname and admitted keeping a supply of Notorious RBG T-shirts on hand, some of which she gave as gifts (Hendricks 2020).

Combining the newsworthiness of her many dissents in favor of those considered underdogs and the new nickname brought Ginsburg into the public eye more than most associate justices of the Supreme Court. In 2015, comedian Kate McKinnon, a cast member of *Saturday Night Live*, added an impression of Ginsburg (originally misspelled Ginsberg in her first skit) to a repertoire that would grow to include Hillary Clinton and Elizabeth Warren. While on screen in that persona, McKinnon wrote a series of what she called "Gins-burns"—quick, pithy phrases that often put down those with whom she disagreed (Alter 2020).

In 2018 the documentary *RBG*, produced by Betsy West and Julie Cohen, premiered at the prestigious Sundance Film Festival. Reviewers raved, calling it "fierce and unexpectedly romantic," since so few knew much about the equal partnership she shared with her husband, or "Vital. A Fist-pumping, crowd pleasing doc" (Erbland 2018). Chosen by the National Board of Review as the Best Documentary Film of 2018, it also earned Academy Award nominations for Best Documentary Feature and Best Original Song. Hollywood Reporter reviewer Leslie Felperin wrote, "There is something deeply soothing about RBG, a documentary that, like its subject, Supreme Court Justice Ruth Bader Ginsburg, is eminently sober, well-mannered, highly intelligent, scrupulous and just a teeny-weeny bit reassuringly dull" (Felperin 2018).

As happens often in adaptations of real life, supporting characters are sometimes composites, since not everyone agrees to sell their life rights to filmmakers. This was not the case with the character of dean Erwin Griswold. Not only was he the dean of Harvard Law School from 1946–1967 (which coincided with Ginsburg's time as a student), he also then moved on to become the U.S. solicitor general under Presidents Lyndon Johnson and Richard Nixon from 1967 to 1973. One of the more famous cases Griswold handled came in 1967, when he defended the United States Government against Muhammad Ali in *Clay v. United States*. The famous boxer had refused to be drafted into the Vietnam War on the basis that his beliefs as a follower of the Muslim religion required him to file as a conscientious objector. Griswold lost that case. A few years later, when the Ginsburgs won the Moritz case in the Tenth Circuit, he petitioned the Supreme Court to take the case in hopes it would fail there. As is shown in the film, Griswold created a computer-generated list of all the laws that the Moritz ruling put on unsteady legal footing because they denied services based on sex. It is fair to note that that was not solely his personal opinion, evidenced by the realization that "personal computers wouldn't become available until the late 1970s, so Griswold's staff would had to have visited the Department of Defense to make it" (Thulin 2018). That list is the one shown in the film Ruth Bader Ginsburg then used to support this—and other—cases.

Daughter Jane Ginsburg is a supporting character who did allow herself to be portrayed, and, according to the producers, she also allowed them a free hand. Because of Ginsburg's requirement that her husband not be used as the antagonist in either the work or home spaces of the story, the dean served that purpose at work. The character of the daughter then filled that hole at home as the radicalized feminist who challenged her mother (who, in truth, needed no lessons on feminism). In truth, Jane Carol Ginsburg performed well in high school and college; received her J.D. degree from Harvard Law School; and earned a further degree, a doctor of law degree, from a university in Paris. She became the Morton L. Janklow professor of literary and artistic property law at the Columbia Law School and director of the Kernochan Center for Law, Media and the Arts at Columbia. She and her mother are the first mother-daughter pair to serve on the same law faculty in the United States (Littleton 2020).

FURTHER READING

Alter, Rebecca. 2020. "An Ode to Kate McKinnon's Ruth Bader Ginsburg Impression on SNL." Vulture. https://www.vulture.com/2020/10/snl-kate-mckinnon-ruth-bader-ginsburg-impression.html.

Assorted writers. Harvard Magazine. 2020. "At Home with Harvard: The Real History of Women at Harvard." https://www.harvardmagazine.com/2020/04/the-real-history-of-women-at-harvard#:~:text=In%201957%2C%20bachelor%20of%20divinity,the%20school's%20first%20woman%20graduate.

Bonos, Lisa. 2017. "3 Ways 'The Mary Tyler Moore Show' Pilot Is Still Relevant Today." *The Washington Post.* https://www.washingtonpost.com/news/soloish/wp/2017/01/26/3-ways-the-mary-tyler-moore-show-pilot-is-still-relevant-today/.

Cohen, Robert, and Laura J. Dull. n.d. "Teaching about the Feminist Rights Revolution: Ruth Bader Ginsburg as 'The Thurgood Marshall of Women's Rights.'" *The American Historian.* Accessed April 12, 2021. https://www.oah.org/tah/issues/2017/november/teaching-about-the-feminist-rights-revolution-ruth-bader-ginsburg-as-the-thurgood-marshall-of-womens-rights/.

Cushman, Clare. 2010. *Supreme Court Decisions and Women's Rights.* Washington, DC: Sage CQ Press.

Erbland, Kate. 2018. "'RBG' Review: Ruth Bader Ginsburg Gets an Energetic Documentary Befitting the Supreme Court Justice—Sundance 2018." IndieWire. https://www.indiewire.com/2018/01/rbg-review-ruth-bader-ginsburg-documentary-sundance-1201918946/.

Felperin, Leslie. 2018. "RBG: Film Review | Sundance 2018." *The Hollywood Reporter.* https://www.hollywoodreporter.com/movies/movie-reviews/rbg-review-1076848/.

Hendricks, Nancy. 2020. *Ruth Bader Ginsburg: A Life in American History.* Santa Barbara: ABC-CLIO.

Library at Washington and Lee University School of Law. Ruth Bader Ginsburg Reading List. https://libguides.wlu.edu/law/RBG/arguments.

Lithwick, Dahlia, and Molly Olmstead. 2020. "The Class of RBG." Slate. https://slate.com/news-and-politics/2020/07/the-women-of-harvard-law-rbg-1959.html.

Littleton, Cynthia. 2020. "In the Presence of Greatness: My Afternoon with Ruth Bader Ginsburg." *Variety.* https://variety.com/2020/tv/news/ruth-bader-ginsburg-interview-daughter-supreme-court-women-1234775461/.

Loop, Karen. Personal Interview conducted by author. January 14, 2020.

Melton, Marissa. 2020. "Female Supreme Court Justices Can Change the Conversation." *Voice of America.* https://www.voanews.com/usa/female-supreme-court-justices-can-change-conversation.

Minnow, Nell. 2018. "On the Basis of Sex." Ebert Reviews. https://www.rogerebert.com/reviews/on-the-basis-of-sex-2018.

Mossman, Mary Jane. 2006. *The First Women Lawyers: A Comparative Study of Gender, Law and the Legal Professions*. New York: Bloomsbury Publishing.

Risen, Clay. 2014. *The Bill of the Century: The Epic Battle for the Civil Rights Act*. London: Bloomsbury Press.

Smith, J. Clay. 1993. *Emancipation: The Making of the Black Lawyer, 1844–1944*. Philadelphia: University of Pennsylvania Press.

Strebeigh, Fred. 2009. *Equal: Women Reshape American Law*. New York: W. W. Norton & Company.

Thulin, Lila. 2018. "The True Story of the Case Ruth Bader Ginsburg Argues in 'On the Basis of Sex.'" *Smithsonian Magazine*. https://www.smithsonianmag.com/history/true-story-case-center-basis-sex-180971110/.

Walsh, Katie. 2018. "'On the Basis of Sex' Review: Biopic Beautifully Argues the Importance of Ruth Bader Ginsburg's Work." *Tribune News Services*.

Bibliography

Adams, Katherine, and Michael Keene. 2008. *Alice Paul and the American Suffrage Campaign*. Urbana: University of Illinois Press.

Assorted writers. 2020. "At Home with Harvard: The Real History of Women at Harvard." *Harvard Magazine*. https://www.harvardmagazine.com/2020/04/the-real-history-of-women-at-harvard#:~:text=In%201957%2C%20bachelor%20of%20divinity,the%20school's%20first%20woman%20graduate.

Baker, Ellen R. 2007. *On Strike and on Film: Mexican American Families and Blacklisted Filmmakers in Cold War America*. Chapel Hill: University of North Carolina Press.

Basinger, Jeanine. 1995. *A Woman's View: How Hollywood Spoke to Women, 1930–1960*. Middletown, CT: Wesleyan University Press.

Beauchamp, Cari. 1998. *Without Lying Down: Frances Marion and the Powerful Women of Early Hollywood*. Los Angeles: University of California Press.

Biberman, Howard. 1965. *Salt of the Earth: The Story of a Film*. Boston: Beacon Press.

Blanton, Deane, and Lauren M. Cook. 2002. *They Fought Like Demons: Women Soldiers in the Civil War*. New York: Random House.

Bonos, Lisa. 2017. "3 Ways 'The Mary Tyler Moore Show' Pilot Is Still Relevant Today." *The Washington Post*. https://www.washingtonpost.com/news/soloish/wp/2017/01/26/3-ways-the-mary-tyler-moore-show-pilot-is-still-relevant-today/.

Borda, Jennifer L. 2011. *Women Labor Activists in the Movies: Nine Depictions of Workplace Organizers, 1954–2005*. Jefferson City, NC: McFarland.

Brock, David. 2002. *Blinded by the Right: The Conscience of an Ex-Conservative*. New York: Crown Publishing.

Burkett, Abra. 2014. "Beyond GI Jane: Representation and Portrayal of Women Armed Services Members in Modern Military Movies." (Thesis, American University).

Cavell, Stanley. 1996. *Contesting Tears: The Hollywood Melodrama of the Unknown Woman*. Chicago: The University of Chicago Press.

Cohen, Robert, and Laura J. Dull. 2017. "Teaching about the Feminist Rights Revolution: Ruth Bader Ginsburg as 'The Thurgood Marshall of Women's Rights.'" *The American Historian*. https://www.oah.org/tah/issues/2017/november/teaching-about-the-feminist-rights-revolution-ruth-bader-ginsburg-as-the-thurgood-marshall-of-womens-rights/.

Cooney, Robert P.J., Jr., ed. 2015. *Remembering Inez: The Last Campaign of Inez Milholland, Suffrage Martyr—Selections from The Suffragist, 1916*. Half Moon Bay, CA: American Graphic Press.

Crist, Judith. 1967. *The Private Eye, the Cowboy and the Very Naked Girl: Movies from Cleo to Clyde*. New York: Holt, Rinehart and Winston.

Cushman, Clare. 2010. *Supreme Court Decisions and Women's Rights*. Washington, DC: Sage CQ Press.

Dodd, Lynda G. Fall. 2008. "Parades, Pickets and Prisons: Alice Paul and the Virtues of Unruly Constitutional Citizenship." *Journal of Law & Politics* 39: 340–432.

Donald, Ralph, and Karen MacDonald. 2014. *Women in War Films: From Helpless Heroine to GI Jane*. Lanham, MD: Rowman and Littlefield.

Dubois, Ellen Carol. 1978. *Feminism and Suffrage: The Emergence of an Independent Women's Movement in America, 1848–1869*. Ithaca, NY: Cornell University Press.

Farrell, Amanda, Robert Keppel, and Victoria Titterington. 2011. "Lethal Ladies: Revisiting What We Know about Female Serial Killers." *Homicide Studies* 15 (3): 228–252.

Fine, Richard. 1993. *West of Eden: Writers in Hollywood, 1928–1940*. Washington, DC: Smithsonian Institution Press.

Frank, Michael R. 1988. *Hud, Norma Rae, The Long, Hot Summer: Three Screenplays by Irving Ravetch and Harriet Frank, Jr*. New York: Penguin.

Frayling, Christopher. 2014. *The Yellow Peril: Dr. Fu Man Chu and the Rise of Chinophobia*. London: Thames and Hudson.

Fry, Naomi. 2020. "The Ongoing Relevance of 'Norma Rae.'" *The New Yorker*. https://www.newyorker.com/recommends/watch/the-ongoing-relevance-of-norma-rae.

Gottlieb, Daphne, and Lisa Kester. 2011. *Dear Dawn: Aileen Wuornos in Her Own Words*. New York: Soft Skull Press.

Graham, Sally Hunter. 1993–1994. "Woodrow Wilson, Alice Paul and the Woman Suffrage Movement." *Political Science Quarterly* 98, no. 4 (Winter): 665–679.

Hagelin, Sarah. 2013. *Reel Vulnerability: Power, Pain, and Gender in Contemporary Films and Television*. New Brunswick, NJ: Rutgers University Press.

Hamilton, Ian. 1990. *Writers in Hollywood: 1915–1951*. New York: Harper and Row.

Hendricks, Nancy. 2020. *Ruth Bader Ginsburg: A Life in American History*. Santa Barbara, CA: ABC-CLIO.

Heung, Marina. 1993. "Daughter-Text/Mother-Text: Matrilineage in Amy Tan's *The Joy Luck Club*." *Feminist Studies* 19, no. 3 (Autumn): 596–616.

Hill, Anita. 1998. *Speaking Truth to Power*. New York: Anchor Books.

Hodges, Graham Russell Gao. 2004. *Anna May Wong: From Laundryman's Daughter to Hollywood Legend*. New York: Palgrave Macmillan.

Holmlund, Christine. 1994. "A Decade of Deadly Dolls." In *Moving Targets: Women, Murder, and Representation*, edited by Helen Birch. Berkeley: University of California.

Holt, Nathalia. 2017. *Rise of the Rocket Girls: The Women Who Propelled Us, from Missiles to the Moon to Mars*. New York: Back Bay Books.

Horton, Andrew, and Julian Hoxter. 2014. *Screenwriting*. New Brunswick, NJ: Rutgers University Press.

Hull, N. E. H. 2012. *The Woman Who Dared to Vote: The Trial of Susan B. Anthony*. Lawrence: University of Kansas Press.

Jarrico, Paul, and Herbert Biberman. 1992. "Breaking Ground: The Making of *Salt of the Earth*." In *Celluloid Power: Social Film Criticism from Birth of a Nation to Judgement at Nuremberg*, edited by David Platt. Metuchen, NJ: The Scarecrow Press.

Johannsen, Robert. 1988. *To the Halls of Montezuma: The Mexican American War in the American Imagination*. New York: Oxford University Press.

Kamir, Orit. 2006. *Framed: Women in Law and Film*. Durham, NC: Duke University Press.

Kaufman, Amy. 2017. "Meet Allison Schroeder, the NASA-Loving Writer of 'Hidden Figures' Who Was Just Nominated for an Oscar." *The Los Angeles Times*.

Kessler-Harris, Alice. 2007. *Gendering Labor History*. Champaign: University of Illinois Press.

Lee, Joey. 2018. "East Asian 'China Doll' or 'Dragon Lady'?" *Bridges: A Journal of Contemporary Connections* 3 (1): 1–6.

Leonard, Elizabeth D. 1999. *All the Daring of a Soldier: Women of the Civil War Armies*. New York: W. W. Norton & Company.

Leong, Karen J. 2005. *The China Mystique: Pearl S. Buck, Anna May Wong, and Mayling Soong and the Transformation of American Orientalism*. Berkeley: University of California Press.

Leupp, Constance. 1909 (1998). "The Shirtwaist Makers' Strike." The Survey. Included in *How Did the Perceived Threat of Socialism Shape the Relationship between Workers and Their Allies in the New York City Shirtwaist Strike, 1909–1910?* by Thomas Dublin, Kathryn Kish Sklar, and Deirdre Doherty. Binghamton: State University of New York at Binghamton.

Lorence, James J. 1999. *The Suppression of "Salt of the Earth": How Hollywood, Big Labor, and Politicians Blacklisted a Movie in Cold War America*. Albuquerque: University of New Mexico Press.

Lumsden, Linda. 2019. "Historiography: Women Suffrage and the Media." *American Journalism* 36 (1): 4–31.

Maddux, Kristy. 2004. "When Patriots Protest: The Anti-Suffrage Discursive Transformation of 1917." *Rhetoric and Public Affairs* 7, no. 2 (Fall): 283–310.

Mayer, Jane, and Jill Abramson. 1994. *Strange Justice: The Selling of Clarence Thomas*. Boston: Houghton Mifflin Harcourt.

McCaughey, Martha, and Neal King, eds. 2001. *Reel Knockouts: Violent Women in the Movies*. Austin: University of Texas Press.

Monahan, Evelyn M., and Rosemary Neidel-Greenlee. 2000. *All This Hell: U.S. Nurses Imprisoned by the Japanese*. Lexington: University of Kentucky Press.

Morrison, Toni, ed. 1992. *Race-ing Justice, En-gendering Power: Essays on Anita Hill, Clarence Thomas and the Construction of Social Reality*. New York: Pantheon.

Mossman, Mary Jane. 2006. *The First Women Lawyers: A Comparative Study of Gender, Law and the Legal Professions*. New York: Bloomsbury Publishing.

Murdock, Maureen. 1990. *The Heroine's Journey*. Boulder, CO: Shambhala.

Norman, Elizabeth M. 1999. *We Band of Angels: The Untold Story of American Nurses Trapped on Bataan by the Japanese*. New York: Pocket Books.

Rajgopal, Shoba Sharad. 2010. "The Daughter of Fu Manchu: The Pedagogy of Deconstructing Representation of Asian American Women in Film and Fiction." *Feminism, Race, and Transnationalism* 10, no. 2 (April): 141–162.

Rashke, Richard. 2000. *The Killing of Karen Silkwood: The Story Behind the Kerr-McGee Plutonium Case*. 2nd ed. Ithaca, NY: ILR Press.

Risen, Clay. 2014. *The Bill of the Century: The Epic Battle for the Civil Rights Act*. London: Bloomsbury Press.

Russell, Sue. 2002. *Lethal Intent: The Shocking Story of One of America's Most Notorious Female Serial Killers*. New York: Pinnacle Books (Kensington Publishing Corp).

Schechter, Harold. 2003. *Fatal: The Poisonous Life of a Female Serial Killer*. New York: Gallery Books.

Shetterly, Margot Lee. 2016. *Hidden Figures*. New York: William Morrow.

Sklar, Robert. 1994. *Movie-Made America: A Cultural History of American Movies*. New York: Knopf Doubleday/Vintage.

Skrapec, Candice. 1994. "The Female Serial Killer: An Evolving Criminality." In *Moving Targets: Women, Murder, and Representation*, edited by Helen Birch, 241–268. Berkeley: University of California.

Smith, J. Clay. 1993. *Emancipation: The Making of the Black Lawyer, 1844–1944*. Philadelphia: University of Pennsylvania Press.

Smith, Jeff. 1999. "'A Good Business Proposition': Dalton Trumbo, Spartacus, and the End of the Blacklist." In *Controlling Hollywood: Censorship/Regulation in the Studio Era*, edited by Matthew Bernstein. New Brunswick, NJ: Rutgers University Press.

Starfield, Peggy. 2016. "Striking Women: *Salt of the Earth*, *Norma Rae* and *Bread and Roses*." In *Social Class on British and American Screens: Essays on Cinema and Television*, edited by Nicole Cloarec, David Haigron, and Delphine Letort. Jefferson City, NC: McFarland.

Stempel, Tom. 1988. *Framework: A History of Screenwriting in the American Film*. New York: The Continuum Publishing Company.

Strebeigh, Fred. 2009. *Equal: Women Reshape American Law*. New York: W. W. Norton & Company.

Vlessing, Etan. 2020. "Anita Hill Led Hollywood Commission Details Sexual Harassment Claims in Industry Workplaces." *Hollywood Reporter*, October 27, 2020.

Watson, Bruce. 2006. *Bread and Roses: Mills, Migrants, and the Struggle for the American Dream*. Westminster, UK: Penguin Books.

Watters, Jessica. 2017–2018. "Pink Hats and Black Fists: The Role of Women in the Black Lives Matter Movement." *William & Mary Journal of Women and the Law* 24: 199.

Weiss, Elaine. 2019. *The Woman's Hour: The Great Fight to Win the Vote*. New York: Penguin Books.

Welch, Rosanne, ed. 2018. *When Women Wrote Hollywood: Essays on Female Screenwriters in the Early Film Industry*. Jefferson, NC: McFarland.
Wuornos, Aileen, and Christopher Berry-Dee. 2004. *Monster: My Story*. London: John Blake Publishing.
Yarrow, Alison. 2019. *90s Bitch: Media, Culture, and the Failed Promise of Gender Equality*. New York: Harper Perennial.
Zahniser, J. D., and Amelia R. Fry. 2014. *Alice Paul: Claiming Power*. Oxford: Oxford University Press.
Zeitz, Christian David. 2016. "Dreaming of Electric Femme Fatales: Ridley Scott's Blade Runner, Final Cut and Images of Women in Film Noir." *Gender Forum* 60: 11–22.

Index

ABC Motion Pictures, 27
Academy of Motion Picture Arts and
    Sciences Awards (Oscars), 11, 15,
    16, 28, 31, 74, 80, 133, 139
Adams, Abigail, 96
Alexandra, Daniel, 59
Ali, Mahershala, 131
Alien, 60, 72
Alpha Suffrage Club, 99
American Arab Anti-Discrimination
    Committee, 68–69
American Civil Liberties Union,
    123, 145
American Federation of Labor, 19, 46
American Film Institute (AFI), 60, 80
American Revolution, 63–64
American Women's Suffrage Association
    (AWSA), 97–100
Angels of Bataan, 65–66
Anthony, Susan B., 97–98, 106
Anti-Asian xenophobia, 42, 46, 48–49.
    See also Racism
Anti-suffrage, 95, 99–100
Arlen, Alice, x, xvi, 27–28, 31, 35
Armstrong, Russell, 77
Asian American Journalists
    Association, 44
Asseyeu, Tamara, 15

Bancroft, Anne, 60–61
Barnes, Adalah, 95
Barret, Elizabeth, 66
Bass, Ronald, 41–42
Bates, Kathy, 145
Bathory, Elizabeth, 86
Beard, Mary Ritter, 102
Bechdel, Alison, xvi, 55
Bechdel Test, xvi, 55
Belazquez, Loreta, 65
Bergman, Andrew, 73
Biberman, Herbert, 1, 4, 10, 12
Biden, Joe, 112–113, 115, 119
    apologies to Anita Hill, 120
    refusal to call witnesses, 116, 119
    Senate Judiciary Committee Hill-
        Thomas hearings, 115–120
Black Lives Matter, 139–140
Bladerunner, 73
Blasey Ford, Christine, 124
Booth, John Wilkes, 90–91
Borginnes, Sarah, 64
Bostwick-Singer, Eugenia, 93
Botkins, Dawn, 83
Bridges, Beau, 17
Brock, David, 117
Brockovich, Erin, 31, 111
Broomfield, Nick, 83, 90

Brown, Jerry, 11
Brown v. Board of Education (1954), 135
Buck, Pearl, 51
Bunker, Chang and Ang, 44–45
Burleson, Jane, 102
Burlingame Treaty, 45–46
Burn, Harry T., xiv
Burning Bed, The, xx
Burns, Lucy, 94–95, 98, 103

Califano v. Goldfarb (1976), 150
Camp followers, 63–64
Campbell, Joseph, xvii–xviii, 24
Cannes Film Festival, 11, 19
Canright, Barbara, 134
Cashier, Albert (Jenny), 64–65
Cassidy, Joanna, 73
Catt, Carrie Chapman, xiv, 94–95, 98, 103
Chacon, Juan, 2
Chan, Charlie, 51
Chao, Rosalynd, 44
Charles E. Moritz v. Commissioner of Internal Revenue (1972), 149–152
Chavez, Cesar, 11
Cher, 28, 38, 74
Chin, Tsai, 43
Chinatowns, 45–46
Chinese Exclusionary Act, 46–47
Chinese immigration, 44–48, 54–55
Chinese Massacre of 1870, 46
Chinh, Kieu, 43
Civil Rights Act, 1964, 135, 148
  Title VII, 149
Civil Rights Movement, xv, 6, 20, 25, 108, 112, 115–116, 134, 135, 138–139, 145, 148–149
Civil War (American), xiv, 64, 97–98
Clarence Thomas Senate Hearing. *See* Hill-Thomas hearings
Clinton, William Jefferson, 60, 146
Cobb, Jerrie, 140
Cochran, Jacqueline, 140
Coffin, Martha Wright, xiii
Confirmation, xi, xix, 111–128
Corbin, Margaret, 63–64
Corley, Annie, 78
Costner, Kevin, 130, 137

Courage Under Fire, 69
COVID-19 virus, 48–49
Crazy Rich Asians, x, 48–49, 54, 56
Cushman, Pauline, 64–65

Danforth, Jack, 113, 119, 120–121
Davis, Geena, 72
Davison, Maude, 65–66
Declaration of Sentiments, xiii, 97
Dempsey, Patrick, 94
Department of Education, 113–115
Department of Labor, Women's Bureau, 9
Dern, Bruce, 78–79
Desert Storm, 66
Doggett, John, 117, 122–123
Douglas, Frederick, xiii
Dragon Lady Stereotype, 49–51, 53–54
Duerk, Alene, Admiral, 66
Dunst, Kirsten, 130, 137
Dyer, Amelia, 86

Eastman, Crystal, 102
Ebert, Roger, 35, 62–63, 80, 114, 147
Edmonds, Sarah, 64–65
EEOC (Equal Employment Opportunity Commission), 113–114, 116, 118–119, 121
Ehyophsta, 65
Emmy Awards, xvii, xx, 16, 54, 96
Empire Zinc Company, 2–3, 5, 8, 11
Ephron, Nora, x, xv–xvi, 27–28, 31, 35
Equal Pay Act (1963), 148
Equal Rights Amendment (ERA), xx
Executive Order 8802, 21, 134

Famuyiwa, Rick, 111–112, 123
Farmiga, Vera, 94
Farrow, Ronan, 125–126
Fell, Lewis, 81–82
Female Gaze, xv
Feminism, 20, 71, 105, 145, 152. *See also* Women's Suffrage
  First Wave, 45
  Lipstick, 106
  Second Wave, 9, 34
  Third Wave, 106
Field, Sally, ix, 15, 21
Fifteenth Amendment, 97

Index

Fisher, Lavinia, 86
Fonda, Jane, 15
Ford, Harrison, 73
Frank Harriet, Jr., xv–xvi, 15–16, 22
Fraser, Laura, 94
Friedes, Jennifer, 93
Friendly Fire, xx
Frontiero v. Richardson (1973), 150

Gage, Emily, 148
Garland, Merrick, 111
Garner, Jennifer, 69
Geer, Will, 1, 3
Gender gap, 101–102
Gigliotti, Donna, 129
G.I. Jane, x, 59–76
Ginsberg, Jane, 152
Ginsberg, Martin, 143–146
Ginsberg, Ruth Bader, xi–xii, xix, 143–148
   background, 148
   "Notorious RBG" appellation, 144, 151
   on women's civil rights, 149–150
Giroux, Jacqueline, 77
Glazer, Steven, 78, 83–84, 89
Glenn, John, 131, 136–137
Glory, xv
Goldberg, Whoopi, 93, 102
Golden Globes, 80, 96
Good Earth, The, 50
Good Girls Revolt, xx
Grant, Susannah, xv, 111, 114
Great Depression, 20
Greenberg, Robbie, 96
Grimke, Sarah and Angelina, 97
Grissom, Gus, 132

Hannah, Daryl, 73
Hardnett, Sukari, 116–117, 121
Harrison, Pat, xiv
Hatch, Orrin, 113, 116, 120
Hawn, Goldie, 74
Hays, Anna Mae, Gen., 66
HBO Films. *See* Home Box Office
Hells Canyon Massacre, 46
Henson, Taraji P., 130, 133
Heroine's Journey, xi, xviii, 24
Hidden Figures, xi–xx, 129–142

Hill, Anita, xi, 70, 111–114
   autobiography, 118
   background, 114–115
   Biden apologies, 120
   harassment by Clarence Thomas, 112, 115
   on Kavanaugh Hearings, 125
   polygraph, 116
   post-hearing harassment, 117–118
   Senate Judiciary Committee testimony, 111–117
Hill-Thomas hearings, 70, 73–74, 111–112
Hoerchner, Susan, 116–117
Hogan, Cynthia, 120
Hollywood Blacklist, 1, 9–10, 11–12
Hollywood Reporter, 31, 152
Home Box Office (HBO), xi, 93–94, 100, 102, 112, 119
Home of the Brave, 69
House Un-American Activities Committee (HUAC), 10, 12, 21, 37
Huerta, Dolores, 11
Hunger strikes, 103–104. *See also* Non-violent resistance
Hunt, Jane, xiii, 13
Huston, Angelica, 94

International Alliance of Theatrical Stage Employees (IATSE), 4, 37
International Union of Mine, Mill and Smelter Workers, ix, 1–2, 6
International Workers of the World (IWW), 20
Invisible War, The, 69
Iraq War, 69
Iron Jawed Angels, 104
Iron Jawed Angels, xi, xiv, xix, 93–109

Jackson, Mary, xi, 129, 133, 135–136, 137–138
Jarrico, Paul, 1–2, 4–5
Jemison, Mae, 133
Jencks, Clinton, 6–7
Jencks, Virginia Derr, 6–7
Jenkins, Patty, xv, 77, 78, 88
Jet Propulsion Laboratory (JPL), 134
Johnson, Katherine, xi, xx, 129, 133, 136–139

Johnson, Lyndon, 148, 152
Jones, Felicity, 144, 150
Jordan, Crystal Lee, ix, 15–16, 21–22, 24
Joy Luck Club, The, book, 41
Joy Luck Club, The, film, x, 41–57

Kaling, Mindy, 54
Kanin, Faye, xx
Kavanaugh Hearings, 120, 124
Keil, Lillian, 66
Keitel, Harvey, 72
Kennedy, Edward (Ted), 112, 117, 120
Kennedy, John F., 67
Kennedy, Robert, 11
Kenyon, Dorothy, 145
Kepley, Ava, 147
Kerr-McGee Nuclear Fuel Rod Producing Facility, 27, 29, 31–37
Khouri, Callie, 72
King, Coretta Scott, 11
King, Rev. Dr. Martin Luther, Jr., xv, 25
Kingston, Maxine Hong, 41, 52
Klain, Ron, 120
Korean War, 66–67
Kulix, 64

Lange, Dorothea, xv
Langley Air Base, xi, 131, 134, 135
Leavy, Megan, 69
Lehman, John, 70
Leibovitz, Annie, 73
Lever, Mimi, 143
Lewis, Dora, 102
Library of Congress, 5, 16
Ling, Helen, 134
Lipsitz, Raina, 72–73
Liu, Lucy, 51, 53–54
Loop, Karen, 143, 151
Loos, Anita, xv
Loving v. Virginia (1967), 146
Lu, Lisa, 43

MacKaye, Hazel, 99
Madsen, Michael, 72
Mako Mori Test, xvii
Mallory, Richard, 82–84, 88–89
Manic Pixie Dream Girl, xvii

Mann Act, 46
Marion, Frances, xv
Marshall, Thurgood, 146
Martindale, Margo, 94
McCarthy, Andrew, 44
McClintock Mary, xiii
McDaniel, Hattie, 50
McKinnon, Kate, 151
Me Too Movement, ix, 89, 118–119, 122
Medal of Honor, 64, 69
Mei-ling, Soon, 47
Melfi, Theodore, 129–130, 133
Mercury, 13, 140–141
Metzenbaum, Howard, 119–120
Mexican-American War, 64
Milano, Alyssa, 118
Milholland, Inez, 94, 102–103
Misogyny, stealth, 101
Molly Pitcher, 63–64
Monae, Janelle, 130, 133
Monster, x, xvii, 77–92
Moore, Demi, x, 59–63, 73–74
Moore, Tyra, 77–78, 82–83, 85
Morrison, Toni, xv
Mortensen, Viggo, 60–61, 63
Mott, Lucretia, xiii, 97
Moy, Afong, 44–45
Muck, Freida Lee, 119
Mulan, 42
Mulvey, Laura, xv
Murdock, Maureen, xviii
Murray, Patty, 118
Mystery of Dr. Fu Man Chu (1923), 49, 50

Nanjing massacre (Rape of Nanjing), 46–47
National Aeronautics and Space Administration (NASA), 131, 134, 136, 140
  Cape Canaveral, 132
  Space Race, 131
National American Women's Suffrage Association (NAWSA), xi, xiv, 94–95, 97–100, 103
National Association of Colored People (NAACP), 115, 135–136

National Association of Colored Women's Clubs (NACWC), 134–135
National Association of Women, 135
National Organization of Women (NOW), 34, 115
National Women's Party (NWP), 99–100, 103–105
Navy SEALs, x, 62, 67–68, 71
New York Times, 5, 27, 30–33, 35, 52, 125
Newcom, Elizabeth, 64
Nichols, Mike, xvi, 27–28, 35
Nineteenth Amendment, xiv, 96–100, 103, 105. *See also* Women's Suffrage
Non-violent resistance, 103–105
Norma Rae, ix–x, xvii–xviii, 15–26, 27, 29, 34–35
Nurses, military, 64–66
Nuyen, Frances, 43

Obama, Barack, xi, 111, 133
Occoquan Workhouse, 95–96, 100, 103–104
O'Connor, Frances, 94, 102
O'Connor, Sandra Day, 150
Office of Strategic Services (OSS), 67
Ogletree, Charles, 113
Oh, Sandra, 54
Oil, Chemical and Atomic Workers International Union, 31–33
On the Basis of Sex, xi, xix, 143–154
Orientalism, 48, 51
Ormond, Julia, 94
#OscarsSoWhite, 10, 139
Overkill, 78

Paltrow, Gwyneth, 93
Panetta, Leon, 66
Pankhurst, Emmeline and Cristabel, 94, 103
Parkhurst, Jane, 67–68
Parsons, Jim, 130, 137
Patriarchy, xix, 73
Paul, Alice, xiv, 94, 98, 100–106
Perkins, Frances, 19–20
Pittman, Leo, 80–81

Place, Martha, 90–91
Post-Traumatic Stress Disorder (PTSD), 85, 87
Pralle, Arlene, 78, 82–84, 89
Pregnancy Discrimination Act (1978), 149
Presidential Medal of Freedom, xi, xx, 20, 133
Private Benjamin, 74
Progressive Era, 106
Prostitution. *See* Sex work
Pussyhat Project, 107–108

Quintero, Esparanza, 2–4, 9, 11
Quintero, Ramon, 2–4

Racism, 42, 44–46
  Jim Crow South, 135
Ravich, Irving, x, xvi, 15–16, 22
Ray, Charlotte E., 147–148
Republic Pictures, 78
Revueltas, Rosaura, 2, 8, 10
Rex, 69
RBG (film), 152
Ricci, Christina, 78, 80, 85
Rich, Christopher, 43
Ride, Sally, 133, 140
Ritt, Martin, xvi, 15, 25
Roberts, Macie, 134
Robinson, Joanne, xv
Robinson, Sally, 93
Rock Springs Massacre, 46
Rock the Vote, 101
Rocky, x, 19
Roe v. Wade, 108
Rolling Stone, 63
Roosevelt, Eleanor, 20
Roosevelt, Franklin, 20, 21, 47, 134
Rose, Alex, 15
Russel, Kurt, xvi, 28
Ryan, Meg, 69

Said, Edward, 51
Salt of the Earth, ix, xviii–xix, 1–14, 23
Sampson, Deborah, 63–64
Sarandon, Susan, 72
Sargent, Aaron, xiv
Schroeder, Alison, xv, 129, 133

Schroeder, Pat, 113, 119, 137–138
Scott, Ridley, 59–61, 71, 73
Screen Actors Guild (SAG), 10, 37, 56, 82, 133
SEAL training. *See* SERE training
Senate Judiciary Committee, xi, 112–113, 116, 121, 125
Seneca Falls, xiii–xix, 97
SERE training (Survival, Evasion, Resistance, Escape), 68
Serial killers, 77, 79, 82–84, 86, 88
Sex discrimination, 101, 144, 147, 149–150
Sex work, 79, 81–82, 84–85, 88
Sexual abuse/harassment, xi, 60, 69–71, 79–81, 84–89, 115–116, 118–126. *See also* Tailhook Sexual Abuse Scandal
  Kavanaugh, Brett, 11, 111, 120, 123
  statistics, 118–119
  survivors, 87, 118
  Trump, Donald, and sexual misconduct, 89, 107
Sexy Lamp Test, xvii
Shaw, Anna Howard, 94, 98–99
Shephard, Alan, 132, 136
Shetterly, Margo Lee, xi, 129, 137, 139
Silent Sentinels, 95, 99–100, 103
Silkwood, x, xvi, 27–39
Silkwood, Karen, x, xvi, 27, 32–36
Silver, Ron, 29, 37
Simpson, Alan, 113, 116–117, 120
Sino-Japanese War, 46–47
Sisters of Charity, 64
Smith, Brooke, 94
Son of Sam Laws, 78
Sondergaard, Gale, 10–11, 12
Space Race, xi. *See also* National Aeronautics and Space Administration (NASA)
Spanish American War, 65
Specter, Arlen, 113, 115, 120, 139
Spencer, Octavia, 129–130, 133
Stanton, Elizabeth Cady, xiii, 97–98, 106
Steinem, Gloria, 144
Stereotypes, Asian, 49–50, 52–53, 68–69, 87. *See also* Dragon Lady Sterotype; Racism
of feminism, 71, 87, 105–106
Stevens, Doris, 99
Stiepleman, Daniel, 143, 147
Stone, Oliver, 42
Streep, Meryl, x, 16, 28, 31
Suffrage Parade, 98–99, 107–108
Suffragettes, 20, 96–100. *See also Iron Jawed Angels*; Women's Suffrage Movement
Sundance Film Festival, 96
Surratt, Mary, 90–91
Swank, Hilary, 94, 102
Sybil, xx

Taft Hartley Act, 7
Tailhook Sexual Abuse Scandal, 60, 70
Taiping Rebellion, 45
Tan, Amy, x, 41–42
Telluride Film Festival, 44
Temple Grandin, xx
Terrell, Mary Church, 135
Textile Workers Union of America (TWUA), 17, 21
Thelma and Louise, 60, 72–73, 94
Theron, Charlize, 78, 80
Thirteenth Amendment, 97
Thomas, Clarence, xi, 101
  background, 114–115
  pornography, 115, 117, 123
  Senate Judiciary Committee confirmation hearing, 112–114
  sexual harassment complaints, 115, 118, 121
Thomas, Virginia Lamp, 121–122
  January 6th insurrection, 122
Tom, Lauren, 43
Tomita, Tamlyn, 43
Toppan, Jane, 86
Toronto Film Festival, 44
Totenberg, Nina, 113, 115
Triangle Shirtwaist Factory fire, 19
Tubman, Harriet, xv, 64, 135
Turan, Kenneth, 63
Twentieth Century Fox, 15, 60
Twohy, David, 59–60

United States Congress, 8, 64
United States Sanitary Commission, 64

United States Supreme Court, 8, 108, 146–147, 150
  Brown v. Board of Education (1954), 135
  Califano v. Goldfarb (1976), 150
  Charles E. Moritz v. Commissioner of Internal Revenue (1972), 145
  United States v. Virginia (1996), 151
  women on the court, 150–151

Vanity Fair, 73–74
Vaughn, Dorothy, xi, 129, 133, 135–137
Vietnam War, 67
von Garnier, Katja, 93, 102, 105

Waithe, Lena, xvii
Walker, Mary, 64
Walt Disney Studios, 42, 68–69, 133
Wang, Wayne, 41
Ward, Fred, 37
Ward, Nancy (Nanyehi), 63
Warner Bros. Studios, 15
Warshovski, Reuben, x, 15, 24
Washington, Denzel, 69
Washington, Kerry, 111
Washington Post, 8, 94, 123
Waterston, Sam, 144
Weaver, Sigourney, 72
Weber, Lois, xiv
Weinstein Effect, 89, 118–119, 125–126. *See also* Sexual abuse/harassment
Wells, Ellen, 116
Wells-Barnet, Ida, 95, 99, 135
Wen, Ming-Na, 42
White Slave Act of 1910 (Mann Act), 46
Williams, Cathay, 65
Willis, Bruce, 73
Wilson, Michael, 1, 5, 9, 11–12

Wilson, Woodrow, xiv, 94–95, 100, 105, 134
Wineberger v. Wiesenfelt (1975), 150
Winfrey, Oprah, 41, 48–49
Winslow, Rose, 104
Wollstonecraft, Mary, 97
Women in the military, 63–67, 105
Women's Bible, 98
Women's Loyal National League, 97
Women's marches, 107–108
Women's Suffrage Movement, xiv, 13, 93–109. *See also Iron Jawed Angels*; National American Women's Suffrage Association (NAWSA); National Women's Party (NWP); Nineteenth Amendment; Suffrage Parade
Women's Suffrage Party, 98
Wong, Ali, 54
Wong, Anna May, 49–50, 53
World War I, 65, 95, 103, 105, 134
World War II, 6, 20, 37, 46–47, 52, 65–66, 134–135
Wright, Angela, 116–117, 121
Writer's Guild of America (WGA), 37, 114
Wuornos, Aileen, x–xi, 27, 30–33, 35, 77–78, 80–83
Wuornos, Britta, 81
Wuornos, Diane, 80–81
Wuornos, Keith, 81–82
Wuornos, Lauri, 80–82

Year of the Woman, The (1992), 118
Yellow Peril, 46. *See also* Anti-Asian xenophobia; Racism
Young, Sean, 73

Zedong, Mao, 47
Zero Dark Thirty, 69
Zivkovich, Eli, 16, 22

About the Authors

ROSANNE WELCH, PhD, serves as executive director of Stephens College MFA in TV and Screenwriting where she created a set of history of screenwriting courses (because history of film courses become history of directors courses and, thereby, history of great men) and teaches courses in one-hour drama. Her television writing credits include *Beverly Hills 90210*, *Picket Fences*, *ABCNEWS: Nightline*, and *Touched by an Angel*. Welch edited *When Women Wrote Hollywood* (2018), named runner up for the Susan Koppelman Award honoring the best anthology, multi-authored, or edited book in feminist studies by the Popular Culture Association. She coedited *Women in American History: A Social, Political, and Cultural Encyclopedia and Document Collection* (named to both the 2018 Outstanding References Sources List and to the list of Best Historical Materials by the American Library Association) and wrote *Why the Monkees Matter: Teenagers, Television and American Popular Culture*. Welch serves as book reviews editor for *Journal of Screenwriting* and on the editorial board for *Written By* magazine. In 2019, she was elected to the executive committee of the International Screenwriting Research Network for a two-year term. You can find her talk "The Importance of Having a Female Voice in the Room" from the TEDxCPP here: https://www.youtube.com/watch?v=8JFNsqKBRnA and other recorded lectures on her YouTube Channel here: https://www.youtube.com/user/DrRosanneWelch.

PEG A. LAMPHIER, PhD, teaches interdisciplinary humanities at California State Polytechnic University and American Women's History at Mount San Antonio College. Lamphier wrote *Kate Chase and William Sprague: Politics and Gender in a Civil Wary Marriage* (2003) and *Spur Up Your Pegasus: Family Letters of Salmon, Kate, and Nettie Chase, 1844–1873* (2009), and coedited with Rosanne Welch *Women in American History: A Social, Political, and Cultural Encyclopedia and Document Collection* (ABC-CLIO 2017) and *Technological Innovation in American History: An Encyclopedia of Science and Technology* (ABC-CLIO 2019). She writes Civil War mystery novels, including *The Lincoln Special* (2017), *The Great Show* (2017), *Rebel Belles* (2018), and *Iron Widow* (2019). Lamphier also writes historical biographies, *The Bold Life of Louis Palma di Cesnola* (2018), *Little by Little We Won: The Life of Angela Bambace* (2019), and *What a Woman Can Do: Artemesia Gentilseshi* (2021), as well as the gaslamp fantasy *Violent Delights and Vampires* (2018).

www.ingramcontent.com/pod-product-compliance
Lightning Source LLC
Chambersburg PA
CBHW060954230426
43665CB00015B/2193